Student Writing in Higher Education

New contexts

SRHE and Open University Press Imprint
General Editor: Heather Eggins

Current titles include:

Catherine Bargh *et al.*: *Governing Universities*
Ronald Barnett: *The Idea of Higher Education*
Ronald Barnett: *The Limits of Competence*
Ronald Barnett: *Higher Education*
Ronald Barnett: *Realizing the University in an age of supercomplexity*
Neville Bennett *et al.*: *Skills Development in Higher Education and Employment*
John Biggs: *Teaching for Quality Learning at University*
David Boud *et al.* (eds): *Using Experience for Learning*
Etienne Bourgeois *et al.*: *The Adult University*
Tom Bourner *et al.* (eds): *New Directions in Professional Higher Education*
John Brennan *et al.* (eds): *What Kind of University?*
Anne Brockbank and Ian McGill: *Facilitating Reflective Learning in Higher Education*
Stephen Brookfield and Stephen Preskill: *Discussion as a Way of Teaching*
Sally Brown and Angela Glasner (eds): *Assessment Matters in Higher Education*
John Cowan: *On Becoming an Innovative University Teacher*
Heather Eggins (ed.): *Women as Leaders and Managers in Higher Education*
Gillian Evans: *Calling Academia to Account*
David Farnham (ed.): *Managing Academic Staff in Changing University Systems*
Sinclair Goodlad: *The Quest for Quality*
Harry Gray (ed.): *Universities and the Creation of Wealth*
Norman Jackson and Helen Lund (eds): *Benchmarking for Higher Education*
Merle Jacob and Tomas Hellström (eds): *The Future of Knowledge Production in the Academy*
Mary Lea and Barry Stierer (eds): *Student Writing in Higher Education*
Elaine Martin: *Changing Academic Work*
David Palfreyman and David Warner (eds): *Higher Education and the Law*
Craig Prichard: *Making Managers in Universities and Colleges*
Michael Prosser and Keith Trigwell: *Understanding Learning and Teaching*
John Richardson: *Researching Student Learning*
Stephen Rowland: *The Enquiring University Teacher*
Yoni Ryan and Ortrun Zuber-Skerritt (eds): *Supervising Postgraduates from Non-English Speaking Backgrounds*
Maggi Savin-Baden: *Problem-based Learning in Higher Education*
Peter Scott (ed.): *The Globalization of Higher Education*
Peter Scott: *The Meanings of Mass Higher Education*
Anthony Smith and Frank Webster (eds): *The Postmodern University?*
Imogen Taylor: *Developing Learning in Professional Education*
Peter G. Taylor: *Making Sense of Academic Life*
Susan Toohey: *Designing Courses for Higher Education*
Paul R. Trowler: *Academics Responding to Change*
David Warner and Elaine Crosthwaite (eds): *Human Resource Management in Higher and Further Education*
David Warner and Charles Leonard: *The Income Generation Handbook* (Second Edition)
David Warner and David Palfreyman (eds): *Higher Education Management*
Diana Woodward and Karen Ross: *Managing Equal Opportunities in Higher Education*

Student Writing in Higher Education

New contexts

Edited by
Mary R. Lea and
Barry Stierer

The Society for Research into Higher Education
& Open University Press

Published by SRHE and
Open University Press
Celtic Court
22 Ballmoor
Buckingham
MK18 1XW

email: enquiries@openup.co.uk
world wide web: http://www.openup.co.uk

and
325 Chestnut Street
Philadelphia, PA 19106, USA

First Published 2000

A catalogue record of this book is available from the British Library

ISBN 0335 20407 4 (pb)   0335 20408 2 (hb)

Library of Congress Cataloging-in-Publication Data
Student writing in higher education: new contexts   /   edited by Mary R.
   Lea and Barry Stierer.
        p.   cm.
   Includes bibliographical references and index.
   ISBN 0-335-20408-2 (hb). – ISBN 0-335-20407-4 (pbk.)
   1. English language – Rhetoric – Study and teaching.
   2. Interdisciplinary approach in education. 3. Academic writing –
Study and teaching. I. Lea, Mary R. (Mary Rosalind), 1950–
II. Stierer, Barry.
PE1404.S84   2000
808'.042'0711–dc21   99–40895
                                                                      CIP

Typeset by Graphicraft Limited, Hong Kong
Printed in Great Britain by St Edmundsbury Press, Bury St Edmunds, Suffolk

Contents

Contributors   vii
Acknowledgements   x
Editors' Introduction   1
Mary R. Lea and Barry Stierer

Part 1: Student Writing: Practices and Contexts   15
 1 Academic Writing in New and Emergent Discipline Areas   17
   Mike Baynham
 2 Student Writing and Staff Feedback in Higher Education:
   An Academic Literacies Approach   32
   Mary R. Lea and Brian V. Street
 3 What Am I Supposed to Make of This? The Messages
   Conveyed to Students by Tutors' Written Comments   47
   Roz Ivanič, Romy Clark and Rachel Rimmershaw

Part 2: New Forms of Writing in Specific Course Contexts   67
 4 Computer Conferencing: New Possibilities for Writing and
   Learning in Higher Education   69
   Mary R. Lea
 5 Making Dances, Making Essays: Academic Writing in the
   Study of Dance   86
   Sally Mitchell, Victoria Marks-Fisher, Lynne Hale and Judith Harding
 6 The 'Personal' in University Writing: Uses of Reflective
   Learning Journals   97
   Phyllis Creme
 7 Writing in Postgraduate Teacher Training: A Question of
   Identity   112
   Mary Scott
 8 A Question of Attribution: The Indeterminacy of
   'Learning from Experience'   125
   Simon Pardoe

Part 3: Contexts of Writing and Professional Learning   147
 9 Writing for Success in Higher Education   149
    Janice McMillan
10 From Personal Experience to Reflective Practitioner:
    Academic Literacies and Professional Education   165
    Elizabeth Hoadley-Maidment
11 Schoolteachers as Students: Academic Literacy and the
    Construction of Professional Knowledge within
    Master's Courses in Education   179
    Barry Stierer

References   196
Index   203
The Society for Research into Higher Education   207

Contributors

Mike Baynham is a Senior Lecturer in the Faculty of Education, University of Technology, Sydney. His research interests lie in the application of insights from sociolinguistics to a range of educational and social issues. His book *Literacy Practices* (Longman, 1995) was shortlisted for the British Association of Applied Linguistics Book Prize.

Romy Clark worked as a teacher and teacher-trainer in English language teaching for many years, overseas and in the UK. She now coordinates Lancaster University's Academic Support Programme, providing workshops and tutorials in academic discourse practices. She has recently written (with Roz Ivanič) *The Politics Of Writing*, published by Routledge.

Phyllis Creme's background is in film studies and educational development with academic staff and students in higher education. Currently she is researching on student learning and writing at the University of Sussex. She is co-author (with Mary Lea) of *Writing at University: A guide for students* (Open University Press, 1997).

Lynne Hale is Head of English Language and Learning Support at Middlesex University. The service, which supports both international and home students, includes a dyslexia unit and offers a forum where questions and doubts about the study process can be explored.

Judith Harding is Associate Director of Learning Development in the Centre for Learning Development at Middlesex University. She works across the institution to develop contexts for dialogue about issues in learning and teaching, and is part of the team developing the Postgraduate Certificate in Higher Education course for new lecturers.

Elizabeth Hoadley-Maidment was formerly Senior Lecturer in the School of Health and Social Welfare at the Open University during which time she contributed to several university initiatives in the areas of academic literacies and English language support. She is now Deputy Education Board Secretary at the Royal College of Surgeons of England.

Roz Ivanič is a Senior Lecturer in the Department of Linguistics and Modern English Language at Lancaster University. Her interests include social approaches to literacy, educational linguistics, academic writing as a social practice, and alternative forms of knowledge and learning. Her publications include *Writing and Identity* (Benjamins) and, with Romy Clark, *The Politics of Writing* (Routledge).

Mary R. Lea is a Research Fellow in the Institution for Educational Technology at the Open University. She has extensive experience as both practitioner and researcher in the area of student writing. Her present work is concerned with the relationship between academic literacies and the use of new computer-mediated technologies for teaching and learning.

Janice McMillan is a Lecturer in the School of Education, University of Cape Town. She teaches in the field of adult education and training, working specifically with adults with non-traditional entrance requirements. Her research interests include access and curriculum development, the relationship between workplace and classroom learning, and project-based learning.

Victoria Marks-Fisher has worked as a dance practitioner, teacher and researcher in community and educational contexts (including further and higher education) for the past ten years. She is currently Lecturer in Dance at Oxford College of Further Education and a freelance animateur working primarily with Oxford Youth Dance.

Sally Mitchell is the Research Fellow on the Leverhulme Trust-funded project 'Improving the Quality of Argument in Higher Education' based in the School of Lifelong Learning and Education at Middlesex University. She is co-editor (with Richard Andrews) of a forthcoming book, *Learning to Argue in Higher Education* (Heinemann Boynton/Cook).

Simon Pardoe is an Honorary Research Fellow at Lancaster University, and also working freelance. He was previously a Teaching Fellow in the Department of Linguistics at Lancaster University, a tutor on the university's Academic Support Programme and at Lancaster Farms Young Offenders Institution, and earlier a further education lecturer in inner London.

Rachel Rimmershaw has worked in the Department of Educational Research at Lancaster University for 14 years. Her research in the area of academic literacy has included reading comprehension and learning from text, explanation for intelligent tutoring systems, collaborative writing, students' study practices and computer-supported collaborative study.

Mary Scott is a Lecturer at the University of London Institute of Education where her teaching responsibilities include an MA module 'Academic Literacies' and a course on thesis writing for research students. She has published a number of papers on academic writing and on the teaching of English.

Barry Stierer is a Senior Lecturer in the Centre for Language and Communications in the School of Education at the Open University. His interests are in the areas of teaching, learning and assessment in higher education – especially teacher education – having worked previously in the field of literacy teaching in schools.

Brian V. Street is Professor of Language in Education at King's College, London University and Visiting Professor of Education in the Graduate School of Education, University of Pennsylvania. He is best known for *Literacy in Theory and Practice* (Cambridge University Press, 1984) and a recent collection of essays, *Social Literacies* (Longman, 1995).

Acknowledgements

A longer version of Chapter 2 was originally published in *Studies in Higher Education*, Vol. 23, No. 2, 1998. We are grateful to the editors and publishers for their permission to reproduce it in an abridged form here.

Our thanks to Pam Burns at the Open University for her expert help in collating and editing the References section.

Editors' Introduction

Mary R. Lea and Barry Stierer

In this collection we have brought together 11 articles written by practitioner-researchers working in a range of international university settings. Our broad aim has been to bring to the attention of fellow university teachers some of the exciting work currently being done in the areas of student learning and academic literacy, within what we are calling *new contexts* for student writing in higher education. We use the term 'new contexts' to refer to two phenomena in today's higher education. First, we have in mind the writing practices emerging in settings other than traditional ones (for example, professional training, dance, English for academic purposes, computer conferencing). We also have in mind non-traditional writing practices emerging within traditional academic disciplines (for example, 'writing journals' in anthropology, and 'reflexive writing' and 'empathetic writing' in a number of subjects). We feel that the work emanating from these new contexts can contribute positively and significantly to our theoretical understanding of student writing in 'new' and 'old' contexts alike, as well as to the practical effectiveness of our everyday work with university students.

In assembling the book, we have been motivated by two objectives. First, in our role as university teachers and staff developers, we wish to bring the work reported in this collection to the attention of a wide audience of fellow practitioners. We believe that there are many practical implications arising from the contributions in the book which will enhance the quality of our colleagues' everyday work with students. For this reason, each chapter features work with students that will be immediately recognizable to fellow university teachers. Moreover, we have asked each contributor to draw out from their analyses the practical implications for teaching and learning activities.

Second, we have a strong interest, as educational researchers, in what we will refer to as *social practice perspectives* for understanding student writing in higher education. By identifying, and bringing together, work that has been informed by these perspectives, we are seeking to show how they are yielding new insights in this field, and at the same time to show how this work serves to validate and further refine social practice perspectives. It is possible that current teaching and research activities located in new contexts are especially amenable to these social practice perspectives. However, we believe that the conceptual issues raised by those activities have a relevance in more traditional settings as well.

Background

The developing research area of student writing in higher education is a highly topical one for two major reasons. Increasingly, in many countries, universities are becoming subjected to 'teaching quality audits' by national funding bodies. As a result, institutions are devoting more attention to the processes of teaching and learning, and more resources to the continuing professional development of their teaching staff. As an example, in the UK the implementation of the recommendations of the Dearing Committee has resulted in a national framework for the training of university lecturers in aspects of teaching and learning, leading to formal accreditation. We anticipate that issues of student writing and assessment will feature prominently in these training programmes.

At the same time, student intake and curriculum provision in universities are changing rapidly. As a result, students are coming from an increasingly wide range of educational, cultural and linguistic backgrounds to study in a number of diverse learning contexts which often no longer reflect traditional academic subject boundaries with their attendant values and norms. Additionally, there is an increasing recognition of the importance of lifelong learning and the necessity for universities to adapt their provision to make it possible for learners to enter higher education for training and retraining at a number of different points in their lives. As a consequence of these changes in the student body, universities are increasingly offering not only 'study skills' and 'learning support' courses in order to help non-traditional students to cope with the demands of university study, but also new-style courses featuring new writing and assessment practices. In parallel with these developments is a growing recognition of the importance of embedding support for student writing within the mainstream curriculum.

The contributors to this collection approach writing in higher education as a *social practice* (see, for example, Street 1984; 1993; Gee 1996; Lankshear 1997) which is embedded in the values, relationships and institutional discourses constituting the culture of academic disciplines in higher education. The social practice perspective adopted by all the contributors reflects an important conceptual shift in the study of student writing in higher education. Much of the existing work in this area approaches student writing from an essentially 'skills-based' perspective. That is, writing in higher education is assumed to be a competence which, once acquired, enables students to communicate their knowledge and understanding in virtually any context. The qualities of 'good writing' are assumed to be self-evident, and largely a matter of learning and mastering universal rules of, for example, grammar, usage and text organization. Explanations for students who experience problems with writing tend to locate the problem as a deficit in the student rather than question the way in which the 'ground rules' of academic writing become established and negotiated in particular academic contexts. This traditional 'skills-based' approach is manifest most clearly in the growing tendency to consign the teaching of writing to marginal 'study skills' and 'learning support' units, catering largely for students deemed to be non-traditional. The papers in this collection consider what it means to take a contrasting approach and to address the relationship between learning and writing in mainstream curriculum delivery.

The particular perspective adopted by this volume, which sees writing as a contextualized social practice, is a powerful tool for understanding the experience of students and teaching staff, and for locating that experience in the wider context of higher education at the present time. For example, it enables researchers to take into account a number of important changes in the policy and practice of higher education institutions in recent years, such as:

- the expansion of student numbers in higher education institutions;
- the opening up of new routes into university study;
- the increasing linguistic and cultural heterogeneity of students, in part due to the above two factors;
- the move away from curriculum delivery within clearly defined academic disciplines to interdisciplinary courses;
- the growth of vocationally oriented programmes, including courses for professional training, retraining and in-service training;
- the move away from fixed progression through degree programmes;
- increasing use of modular programmes;
- the diversification of assessment methods, incorporating a wider range of written genres (such as accreditation of prior learning, use of portfolios for assessment).

The social practice perspective underpinning the studies in this volume enables researchers to place these fundamental contextual factors at the heart of research into student writing, whereas the 'skills-based' perspective would view them as background (at best) and as irrelevant (at worst).

By adopting a social practice and contextual perspective the contributors are able to approach their research in this area from a starting position characterized by a number of theoretically driven premises. For example:

- The changing context in higher education forms an integral feature of writing and assessment practices, rather than mere background.
- To understand what 'counts' as 'good writing' in higher education requires an understanding of the culture of individual academic disciplines – their

histories, their positions relative to other disciplines, and the intellectual traditions which have led to certain genres of academic writing being perceived as self-evidently effective means for representing knowledge.

- What 'counts' as 'good writing' within any academic discipline is only partly an issue of how best to represent knowledge within that discipline. That is, it is also determined by the practices that have grown up around the discipline as it has gained the status of an academic 'subject'. In this sense, the privileged genres of academic writing in a subject area constitute language forms and usages which encode the ideological positions of participants within powerful institutions. The inverse of this process also pertains – that is, it is also the case that the practices of writing within academic disciplines constitute and perpetuate privileged forms of knowledge within those disciplines.

- The 'ground rules' of academic writing in a subject area are often not made explicit to students. They are often mediated by individual members of teaching staff – through, for example, their general advice on writing and their feedback to students on specific pieces of written work. What 'counts' as 'good writing' is therefore partly a matter of the individual preferences of teaching staff, or the individual interpretation by teaching staff of the ostensibly 'given' rules of good writing. This often leads to considerable variation in the way students are advised to write, despite the persistence of a model of writing based upon universal rules and upon the traditional essay form.

- The past few years have seen a rapid growth of new technologies in many aspects of teaching and learning in higher education – including a range of electronic media for the presentation of courses in both distance-education contexts and more conventional contexts, and computer-mediated communications between students and staff as well as among students. However, in spite of this apparent transformation in teaching and learning, and modes of course delivery, the issues surrounding student writing for assessment purposes appear to be remarkably stable.

The aim of this volume is to document the texture of everyday practices of academic literacy and assessment in the university – including the meanings and understandings of these practices held by participants – in a wide range of contexts, in order to build up a picture of the social processes through which 'writing' becomes constructed. In doing so, the volume aims to contribute to the collective enterprise of creating an 'ethnography of the disciplines', called for by Clifford Geertz (1976, cited in Beecher 1989). This approach is in sharp contrast with one that aims to develop teaching strategies helping students who are 'poor at writing' to acquire the skills necessary for success. Using methods drawn from social anthropology, social linguistics, life history studies and cultural studies, the research featured in this collection makes an important contribution to this new thinking about teaching and learning which aims to document the diversity of writing practices in higher education.

An overview of the chapters in this collection

The chapters we have commissioned for this volume represent the result of careful research on our part into current trends and developments in the field of student writing. Through our own familiarity with the literature, and through our participation in practitioner and researcher networks in the UK and abroad, we became aware of a growing body of work within what we are calling 'new contexts' for student writing in higher education. We felt that this work was extremely interesting in its own right, and also that it raised theoretical and practical issues which were timely and challenging. We therefore identified and approached key practitioner-researchers in this fledgling field with the intention of bringing their work to the attention of a wider audience.

The result of this background research and co-ordination is a volume which is highly diverse. The chapters in the collection vary considerably – in the styles of writing they adopt, in the kinds of issues they emphasize, and in the academic and professional backgrounds upon which they draw to support their accounts. Although many of the authors write in what might broadly be described as a 'social science research' style, this is by no means true of them all. The concern of some authors is primarily to gain a greater understanding of some aspect of the student experience, while for others the overriding aim has been to analyse and critique a set of teaching practices. Some authors frame their chapters using concepts and models drawn from research and scholarship, while others adopt a mainly pragmatic frame with the intention of drawing out the implications of their work for everyday teaching practice. And, as can be seen from the autobiographical sketches of the authors, a wide range of disciplinary and teaching backgrounds is represented here. We feel that this diversity strengthens the collection as a whole, in that it demonstrates the wide range of approaches currently being used effectively by practitioner-researchers in this field.

Before moving on to discuss the themes and issues addressed by our contributors, we feel an obligation to offer one point of clarification. Some readers of this book may be troubled by the tone used by some authors. To be specific, it may appear that one or other of us has indulged in a spot of gratuitous 'teacher-bashing' – that is, holding up the attitudes, or opinions, or practices, of specific university teachers for mockery or even contempt. This has certainly not been our intention. This issue bedevils educational research at all levels: it is not always easy to reconcile the objective of affirming one's respect for the work of fellow teachers with that of subjecting current practices to careful analysis. We can, however, sincerely state that none of the contributors to this book wished to single out and criticize individual teachers. We see their work as *examples* of widespread practice in higher education. That practice is an integral part of the professional culture of university teaching. All of the authors represented here are members of that culture, and have themselves engaged in practices not at all unlike those featured in the chapters. In this sense, any critiques offered in the book should be seen both as self-critique, and as a critique of our collective culture and activities, and not as an exercise in individual censure.

In the sections that follow, we have drawn out what we feel are the main ideas addressed by the collection as a whole. We have organized this over-view by means of the three broad themes which recur throughout the volume:

• Writing in the disciplines: the challenge of new contexts.
• Writing and vocationally oriented study in universities: are the 'old' genres up to the job?
• Writing and students' identities: whose agenda, whose knowledge, whose written forms?

Writing in the disciplines: the challenge of new contexts

Until fairly recently the pervading view of academic staff, and possibly also of students, appeared to be that writing was both homogeneous and trans-ferable and that it was not unreasonable to expect students to be able to write before entering the academy. This view reflects a historical under-standing of higher education in which a small number of privileged 18-year-olds followed single-subject or possibly joint honours degree courses in traditional academic subjects. However, as we illustrate above, higher edu-cation has changed rapidly, particularly in the last decade, and our social practice approach to writing would lead us to expect that institutional change would have direct implications for the student writer. The chapters in this volume provide evidence for this and the need to take account of the different writing requirements which exist at all levels: disciplines, subjects, courses, units or individual tutors.

There is now an increasing recognition of fundamental differences be-tween academic disciplines in terms of the written genres students are expected to master at university. For example, writing in history is not the same as writing in psychology; and writing in fields such as business studies or environmental studies requires engagement with a number of disciplin-ary genres. Much of the exploratory work into the nature of disciplinary genres has been undertaken at school level in Australia (Halliday and Martin 1993). In terms of higher education, this focus on disciplinary difference takes little account of the nature of writing in interdisciplinary environments or in emergent disciplinary areas. Many of the chapters in this volume challenge the value of teaching fixed disciplinary genres, as a strategy for supporting student writers, through an exploration of what is involved in writing in both old and emergent disciplinary areas. Mike Baynham, in Chapter 1, emphasizes that research now indicates that even in what may be regarded as traditional academic disciplines there is increas-ing evidence that these disciplines do not constitute the homogeneous

.discourse communities one might assume. He suggests, therefore, that disciplinary difference has implications for student writers writing themselves into a 'disciplinary politics'. This is so especially overtly in the new and emergent disciplines, such as in his own example – nursing – where the practices and politics of the 'new' discipline are crucial to our understanding of student writing.

Mary Lea and Brian Street, in Chapter 2, also focus on disciplinary diversity and the implications of this for student writers. They explore the possible consequences of modularity and the need for students to become adept at course switching as they move not merely between the implicit writing requirements of broader disciplinary genres but between different courses and units, in addition to understanding the requirements of individual tutors. In exploring what is involved in writing within and across the university they promote an 'academic literacies' model of student writing which, they believe, represents an advance on both a generic 'study skills' model and a discipline-based 'academic socialization' model of student writing. The 'academic literacies' model proposed by Lea and Street recognizes that issues in student writing are about much more than becoming familiar with static disciplinary genres, and are concerned with issues of epistemology, identities, discourses and institutional power relations.

Interestingly, Baynham identifies three similar perspectives, which he labels skills-based, text-based and practice-based. He does, however, focus a little more upon the discipline itself in suggesting that his practice-based perspective emphasizes the ongoing social and discursive practices through which any discipline is constituted.

Some of the authors look in detail at specific disciplinary contexts: environmental sciences (Simon Pardoe), philosophy (Mary Lea) and dance (Sally Mitchell, Victoria Marks-Fisher, Lynne Hale and Judith Harding). In her chapter, Phyllis Creme explores writing within social anthropology and the use of learning journals. She examines two contexts: the discipline-specific context of the second-year political anthropology course, and the first-year interdisciplinary course on 'death'. She suggests that the discipline-specific context permitted less freedom to write 'personally', since the emphasis was upon consolidating the students' academic competence within the discipline. In contrast, the interdisciplinary 'death' course allowed a great deal more personal reflection and making of links between course content and personal experience, beliefs and attitudes.

One question raised by a reading of Creme's chapter is how far 'the personal' can be deemed to play a part in university writing. Whereas Creme looks at what is arguably a traditional academic discipline, other authors are more concerned with newer disciplinary contexts; joining Baynham in exploring courses which merge professional reflective practice with theoretical knowledge are Elizabeth Hoadley-Maidment and Janice McMillan. Such courses, frequently designed as part of an ongoing professional development programme, use reflective writing as a way of encouraging students to consider the connections between concepts and issues in their courses and their own personal experience. Arising from these chapters are questions about the relationship between these new forms of writing and more traditional forms of written assessment. The authors explore some of the tensions that exist for student writers in these new contexts as they engage with forms of writing which may not fit a familiar essayist genre. McMillan sees her students as using their writing as a route to success in their studies, enabling them to cross the boundaries between their own professional expertise and the demands of the institution. Hoadley-Maidment considers this relationship as rather more problematic and asks how it is possible for students to bridge the gaps in their writing between theoretical academic knowledge and reflection-in-action. Lea, in her research on computer conferencing, questions how easy it is for students to make obvious connections between the more reflective written texts of the conference and the written work that students have to hand in for assessment which still requires a traditional 'essay' genre. Moving more specifically to the wording of assignment questions in a master's programme in education, Barry Stierer provides evidence for a number of contrasting disciplinary genres having been imported into the programme. He goes on to examine what the implications of these contradictory genres might be for student writers in terms of understanding assessment requirements. Moving into an area which one would not normally associate with writing at all, Mitchell and her co-authors are concerned with writing in the study of dance. They explore how students can be helped to engage with the formal writing requirements on their courses by examining the correspondences between writing and choreography – with an implication that other practical and/or creative activities can be used as a 'way in' to the writing process for some students.

Writing and vocationally oriented study in universities: are the 'old' genres up to the job?

Universities have been involved in the training and updating of professionals for a very long time. Indeed it has sometimes been said, only partly ironically, that universities have successfully positioned themselves as providers of training for virtually every professional group except (until recently) that of university teachers. There are nevertheless important changes taking place in the contexts within which such training is carried out. The growing emphasis upon 'lifelong learning' has resulted in a wider range of groups entering universities for work-related study at different career points. Courses have therefore become shorter and more free-standing, with less progression and continuity built into them. At the same time universities have come under increased pressure to open such courses up to people with appropriate work experience but not necessarily standard academic qualifications, and to configure their courses in order to ensure that enhanced professional competence is a demonstrable outcome of study. Set against this trend have been the moves within universities to consolidate their position as the apparently 'natural' providers of professional training. One way that universities have historically consolidated such positions is by endeavouring to elevate the academic status of the activities involved. It is consequently possible to observe university departments, that offer education and training in an area such as nursing, attempting to enhance the academic 'respectability' of their work by imbuing it with the paraphernalia of a 'discipline' ('Vice-Chancellors defend nurse training', *Times Higher Educational Supplement*, 15 January 1999), at the same time that pressure is brought to bear by policy-makers and some elements of the profession to enhance the practical relevance of the courses on offer ('Nurse teachers "not up to speed" on ward life', *Times Higher Educational Supplement*, 22 January 1999).

These trends carry with them significant implications for student writing and learning. For example, students engaged in pre-vocational training might be expected to acquaint themselves with the specialized professional discourses of the workplace they are preparing to enter, and at the same time be expected to demonstrate such knowledge and understanding by means of unfamiliar written genres, thus doubling the language-learning demands. And for professionals entering (or returning to) universities for post-experience or in-service education and training, there may well be profound tensions between their existing professional expertise and fluency with professional discourses, and the more academically oriented discourses and written genres they are expected to control in order to complete their studies successfully. Neither the literature on professional discourses (see for example Gunnarsson *et al.* 1997), nor that on professional knowledge and competence (see, for example, Eraut 1994) has given adequate attention to the role played by the genres of academic writing, privileged by universities in their courses for professional groups, in shaping such discourses and knowledge.

With these issues in mind, it is clear that vocationally oriented study in universities constitutes one of the most significant new contexts for student writing considered by this volume, since it is here that it is possible to examine the interrelationships between:

- rapid change in the higher education sector;
- tensions between 'real-world' and 'academic' learning;
- new forms of university work vying for academic status and respectability;
- tensions between professional/workplace discourses and academic discourses;
- tensions between traditional 'essayist' genres of academic writing and new styles of writing developed to support the acquisition and consolidation of professional knowledge.

Several of the chapters in this collection address issues surrounding writing and vocationally oriented study in universities. In Chapter 1, Mike Baynham examines the way in which the process of 'disciplinization' takes place in 'practice-based' university work, using nursing as the main case study. His analysis draws upon interviews with nursing students and teaching staff, and upon examples of students' written assignments. He argues that '[a] concept like "writing position" cannot be fully or richly understood without a discipline-internal awareness of what counts as knowledge and what counts as an authoritative disciplinary position, and this includes the awareness of internal diversity and conflict, as realized in the politics of the discipline'.

The study of dance is not, strictly speaking, professional training as such. Nevertheless, Sally Mitchell and her colleagues offer some interesting discussions in Chapter 5 of the tensions between practical/creative work in the university and the relentless downward pressure to conform to conventional models of academic writing. In this sense, their analysis helps to illuminate the broader question at stake in many of these new contexts – that is, of how best to match the knowledge, understanding and competence students expect, and are expected, to develop through their studies, and the forms and styles of academic writing available to them for displaying that knowledge, understanding and competence. They also describe some innovative classroom practice, which attempted to help students identify the parallels between their competence as choreographers and the process of academic writing, about which they often feel less confident.

In Chapter 7, Mary Scott examines these issues in the specific context of the postgraduate initial training of schoolteachers. She compares the writing styles of students' assignments within two sets of assessment arrangements – before 1992, when a considerable amount of postgraduate teacher training was based in the university; and after 1992, when postgraduate teacher training became located almost exclusively in schools. She concludes that, although the specification for teacher trainees' written assignments in the pre-1992 arrangements appeared to give considerable flexibility to the way students structured their writing, and addressed the relationship between theory and practice, the most successful of these actually organized their writing using the traditional academic essay as the model. On the other hand, the assignment specifications within the post-1992 arrangements formally required trainees to discuss the linkages between theory and practice, but their assignments tended to evaluate the relevance of theory tokenistically, and generally through the practical perspectives of the staff in their placement institutions.

In Chapter 8, Simon Pardoe examines a writing task that represents an attempt to simulate a form of professional writing regularly produced in the workplace students are preparing to enter – in this case an environmental impact assessment. His analysis focuses on the concept of 'attribution', by which he means the kinds of significances students may attribute to a particular activity in relation to their learning and professional acculturation. He shows how students' apparent errors in their execution of the writing task are due, at least in part, to their tendency to attribute their confusion to the educational context in which the assignment was constructed, rather than to problems that are in fact inherent in the professional context which the task is intended to simulate. In other words, their familiarity with the position of 'student' took precedence, in their interpretation of the writing task, over their position as 'trainee professional'. He concludes by offering useful suggestions for ways in which students on vocationally oriented studies can be helped to understand how 'learning from experience' is constructed within specific tasks.

In Chapter 10, Elizabeth Hoadley-Maidment discusses a number of issues surrounding the relationship between academic writing and the concept of the 'reflective practitioner'. She questions the wisdom of importing writing forms and assessment approaches from traditional academic disciplines when devising assignments on professionally oriented courses, and invites fellow practitioners to consider how the vocational discourses of the professions relate to the academic discourses they expect students to use in their writing. She also provides a useful review of critiques of the concept of the 'reflective practitioner', which has virtually acquired the status of orthodoxy in many quarters.

These concerns are echoed by Barry Stierer in Chapter 11. He examines the tension between academic and professional 'orders of discourse' within the writing requirements on master's courses in education. In his analysis of specifications for written assignments within one modular MA programme in education for schoolteachers, he shows how students need to negotiate their way through a wide range of written genres and academic cultures – often without explicit acknowledgement that such diversity exists. Like Hoadley-Maidment, he questions the pertinence within professionally oriented modules of genres of writing imported from traditional academic disciplines such as sociology and psychology.

Writing and students' identities: whose agenda, whose knowledge, whose written forms?

We return here to a suggestion made earlier that student writing at university has tended to be regarded as both homogenous and transferable from context to context both from outside and within the university. Implicit in this perspective is the assumption that writing is concerned with a set of decontextualized skills which bear little relationship to issues of personhood and identity. Many of the authors in this volume see issues of identity as playing a large part in student writing. They conceptualize the academy as making demands on student writers which frequently result in conflicts between academic ways of knowing and writing, and other ways of knowing and writing from other more familiar contexts. Charles Bazerman (1981) explores ways in which academic knowledge is constructed in different subject areas. He examines four contexts which are identifiable in the writings of established academics: the object under study, the literature of the field, the anticipated audience, and the author's own self. His analysis recognizes the crucial importance of the writer's self in the academic writing process. Why, then, should we conceptualize the work of student writers as being any different? In her study of mature adult students, Ivanič (1998) further explores the importance of the self by making distinctions between the 'autobiographical self', 'the discoursal self' and the 'self as author'.

In Chapter 6, Phyllis Creme examines the nature of 'the personal' in student writing, and suggests that in their journal writing students were able to present a strong authorial voice in ways they did not feel able to do in more conventional essay-type assignments. She explores the conflicts inherent for students in writing in a subject area – social anthropology – which encourages reflexivity on the one hand and yet recognizes the 'problematic' status of personal knowledge in student writing on the other.

Mary Scott's chapter (7) is concerned with the sense of agency of student writers following a postgraduate certificate in education course. She suggests that there is an inherent problematic in the close correspondence which is often assumed by examiners between students' writing and their own identities as creative and active practitioners. She suggests that it is more valuable to see students' written texts as examples of discourses shaped by social conventions – as displays of 'performance' rather than as 'competence'. As she puts it, steering between the Scylla and Charybdis of 'performance' and 'competence' is no easy task. Whereas 'competence' may be associated with a student teacher's in-built creativity and therefore implies writing cannot be taught, 'performance' may suggest that writing can be reduced to 'rules of realization' or 'transferable skills'. For Scott, neither encapsulates the real tensions that are present for students in their negotiations of the writer's sense of self in the contrasting worlds of the university and the school.

In Chapter 3, Roz Ivanič, Romy Clark and Rachel Rimmershaw concentrate upon the possible messages that are conveyed to students by the different kinds of tutor feedback that they receive on their work. From the students' perspective, these are concerned with: messages about themselves; about the function of academic writing; about the values and beliefs underpinning institutions. All these messages may create contradictions for students in terms of their own identity. Students inevitably read feedback from their tutors in terms of evaluation of themselves; if they receive feedback indicating that their work is inadequate this easily becomes translated into feelings of personal inadequacy. Discouraging feedback, therefore, affects students' self-esteem.

Mary Lea takes a rather different approach to the nature of identity when she explores in Chapter 4 the positions that students and tutors take up in their contributions to computer conferences. She uses the linguistic concept of modality to examine the ways in which students and tutors implicitly make commitments to their views of academic knowledge and how they use the written texts of the conference to position themselves in relation to the academic content of the course. She suggests that in an undergraduate philosophy course, tutors and students take up more traditional roles, whereas in the new environment of the MA course in the 'applications of information technology in open and distance education' tutors act more in the role of facilitators, with students assuming more control over their interpretation of what counts as valid academic knowledge.

Lea and Street see issues of identity and personhood as central to their model of academic literacy which recognizes the value of the beliefs and assumptions about writing and knowledge that students bring to the academy. As both Stierer and McMillan illustrate in their chapters, this is of particular importance in relation to adult learners and no more so than for established professionals. Stierer considers the kinds of problems posed for professional teachers who can find themselves positioned as novices by the university. This positioning conflicts with both the professional experience that they bring with them to their studies and with their professional purposes for studying. Stierer explores how the writing requirements of their course position them not as developing professionals but as novice academics.

Dance students may feel comfortable with their own creative practices. However, as Mitchell and her colleagues explore in Chapter 5, tensions and conflicts arise when students are required to write within the context of their course. The authors draw here on Harré's model of personal identity formation in offering a socially oriented explanation for the choreography and the writing tasks. One of the ideas that they explore is how in choreography the student has to 'make a case for her dance as a successful realization of a dance idea', with clear connections with the writing process.

On reading the chapters in this volume we are left with a strong impression that student academic writing is concerned with much more than the reproduction, or even the representation, of ideas. The whole process of writing involves making meaning in a very specific academic context, both the new and the old. The authors point to instances where knowledge, and therefore inevitably meaning, is contested by both staff and students. They explore what such contestation can mean for student writers and the different ways in which issues of identity are played out in the writing process. The contributors to this volume illustrate repeatedly that in their writing academic knowledge is not merely taken up by students and transmitted back to their tutors through the process of assessment. Instead, students in both new and old disciplinary areas are finding ways in which they can use their writing as a vehicle for the exploration of what counts as knowledge in the new contexts of today's higher education.

Part 1

Student Writing:
Practices and Contexts

1

Academic Writing in New and Emergent Discipline Areas

Mike Baynham

Introduction

> The student who is asked to write like a sociologist must find a way to insert himself into a discourse defined by this complex and diffuse conjunction of objects, methods, rules definitions, techniques and tools . . . In addition he must be in control of specific field conventions, a set of rules and methods which marks the discourse as belonging to a certain discipline. These vary even within disciplines: a reader response critic will emphasize one set of textual elements, a literary historian another, and the essays produced will contain these differences.
>
> (Ball *et al.* 1990: 357)

So pity the poor nursing student, who is required to write at times like a sociologist, at others like a philosopher, yet again like a scientist and finally as a reflective practitioner! Much of the literature on disciplinarity assumes, even when it is discussing phenomena of heterogeneity, blurring and crossing (see Klein 1993), the lineaments of traditional disciplines. In a set of interrelated studies conducted at the University of Technology, Sydney (Baynham *et al.* 1995; Lee *et al.* 1995; Gordon *et al.* 1996; Lee 1997) we were particularly interested in discipline areas where complex combinations of disciplinary influences intersect, in the 'new' discipline areas of the 'new' university.

A basic assumption is that, in order to understand the problematic of the novice writer, we need to understand the disciplinary contexts within which they are required to write, or more specifically the disciplines they are writing themselves into. But I would also like you to keep in your mind's eye the image of the harassed first-year nursing student, hurrying from lecture to tutorial, backpack full of photocopied journal articles, notes and guidelines for an essay on the sociology of nursing, a clinical report, a case study, a reflective journal. They are certainly living disciplinary and textual heterogeneity.

Recent advances in the understanding of disciplines and disciplinarity (see Messer-Davidow *et al.* 1993) emphasize that, rather than being neat homogeneous discourse communities, academic disciplines are radically heterogeneous and constituted in difference. Nowhere is this more apparent than in the emergent 'practice-based' disciplines of the new university. Disciplinary heterogeneity and difference have significant implications for student academic writers who can be understood as writing themselves into a 'disciplinary politics', by which I mean the internal tensions and conflicts over such issues as what counts as knowledge, what should be where in the curriculum and how it should be valued, where boundaries within and between disciplines should be drawn. Students are learning to take up writing positions in the context of this diversity and its accompanying tensions. In this chapter I will explore the implications of this approach in the areas of nurse education and adult education, drawing out implications for both research and pedagogy in academic literacies.

I will begin by identifying three perspectives on the theorization of academic writing. The first, a 'skills-based' approach to the teaching of academic writing, assumes that there is a generic set of skills and strategies that could be taught and then applied in particular disciplinary contexts. The second, 'text-based', linguistic approach assumes a relatively homogeneous discipline, with text types to be discovered, analysed and taught. The third, 'practice-based', approach proposed here investigates student writing as both text and practice, arguing that, most crucially, the student writer is learning to take up disciplinary positions in a discourse 'community'. Where the disciplinary positions are conflictual, overlapping or indeed blurred, the student academic writer will be working within the disciplinary politics that is produced. Lea and Street (Chapter 2) also explore a tripartite approach to student writing drawn from their research on academic literacies in UK university settings.

This chapter will be illustrated with data from a series of related studies which investigated the discipline-specific aspects of student writing in new and emergent disciplines, focusing in particular on the ways in which the disciplinary practices and politics are crucial to an understanding of student writing (understood as both product and process) and the ways in which students learn to construct powerful writing positions in text.

A concept like 'writing position' cannot be fully or richly understood without a discipline-internal awareness of what counts as knowledge and what counts as an authoritative disciplinary position, and this includes the awareness of internal diversity and conflict, as realized in the politics of the discipline.

So where does this leave the student writer? In the concluding section of this chapter I will argue that academic writing pedagogy must make the concerns of disciplinarity, disciplinarization and consequent writing positions central – in other words, as Graff (quoted in Klein 1993) suggests, we must 'teach the conflicts'.

Three perspectives on academic writing

The *skills-based approach* to the teaching of academic writing underpins the traditional 'study skills' approach to teaching academic writing and assumes that there is a generic set of skills and strategies, such as 'essay-writing' or 'referencing', that can be taught and then applied in particular disciplinary contexts. Using a skills-based approach, students are typically provided with pre-sessional courses or ongoing support sessions in study preparation, often in mixed disciplinary groups, with the implication that they can take the skills they learn and apply them in their particular disciplinary context. A major criticism of this approach is that it tends to ignore the discipline-specificity of writing requirements.

The *text-based approach* draws on the resources of linguistic analysis, in particular register (see Halliday and Martin 1993) and genre analysis (Swales, 1990; Freeman and Medway 1994), to understand the discipline-specific nature of writing tasks. Register analysis can characterize the language of history or science, while genre analysis focuses on the text types that are required – for example, the history essay, the laboratory report, the case report. There is now plenty of evidence of the language demands of particular discipline areas which can be used to design discipline-specific curricula to support academic writing. One problem with the text-based approach, however, is that it often assumes a relatively homogeneous discipline, with text types to be discovered, analysed and taught. To talk glibly about 'the language of science or history' can gloss over significant differences within disciplines which, as we shall see, are increasingly identified by studies of disciplines and disciplinarity themselves.

The *practice-based approach* emphasizes the social and discursive practices through which a discipline constitutes itself. A lot of the pioneer work in this regard has been carried out in the study of scientific communities (Latour 1987; Bazerman 1988; Myers 1990). Such studies look at how fields are constituted and maintained, how novices are socialized into the practices which are constitutive of the field. Messer-Davidow *et al.* (1993) present a collection of such studies across a broad range of discipline areas, including accounting, social sciences, economics, art history and medicine. From a practice perspective, we are interested in how students as novices are brought into the typical discursive practices of the discipline, whether it be literary criticism, ethnographic fieldwork or participating in laboratory experiments.

In shifting the emphasis on to the ways in which disciplines are constituted it is, however, important not to lose touch with the sharply focused specificity which text-based studies provide. Language is, after all, a major means (if not necessarily the only means) by which disciplinary knowledge is constituted, reproduced, contested and added to, and learned. We need precise linguistic accounts of the linguistic means that are deployed in specific disciplinary contexts, but we also need to recognize the complexity and specificity of these contexts. So combining both the text and the practice perspective (texts and practices) has a powerful potential.

Academic writing, disciplinarity and difference

So far I have suggested the need to move away from a generic, skills-based approach to understanding academic writing in two directions, first in making use of the resources of linguistic analysis to capture the specific features of the language used in different disciplines, and second in problematizing the social practices of the discipline itself.

Ball *et al.* (1990: 342), quoted at the beginning of this chapter, focus on the diversity within disciplines as well as across them, a point that is picked up and expanded by Goggin (1995: 12):

> What complicates research and pedagogy on writing in the disciplines is that epistemological and discursive diversity exist not only across disciplines, but also within disciplines. As Kenneth Ruscio (1987: 333) has argued, 'though institutional boundaries conveniently demarcate clusters of academics, the situation is actually more complicated. There is diversity within diversity as different types of professionals exist side by side in the same setting.' Ruscio's argument is supported by Reiff and Kirscht's (1992) study of the inquiry processes of members from social sciences, natural sciences, and the humanities. Their study shows that the process of academic inquiry is dynamic, shifting along personal and disciplinary lines, with individual scholars and researchers often crossing disciplinary boundaries to pursue their research questions (cf. Klein 1993). These kinds of hybrid moves across fields account in part for the growing diversity within fields.

So student writers are writing themselves into this diversity, not into the convenient fiction of a homogeneous history, geography or sociology.

New and emerging discipline areas

The authors reviewed so far have been concentrating on the disciplinary shape of traditional university disciplines. In this chapter, however, I will be presenting case studies of student writing practices in new and emerging areas, where the focus is not on the traditional discipline, but rather on the formation of professions, nurses, adult educators, engineers, what might be called 'practice-based' disciplines.

These new and emerging areas will typically draw on a range of disciplines. Let us take adult education as an example. The adult education theorist Griff Foley (1995: 15) identifies a range of disciplines, including sociology, psychology, geography, philosophy and economics, which impact on adult education as a field of study. Knowledge from these disciplines is, of course, not imported raw but is 'recontextualized', in Bernstein's (1990) sense. Within adult education as a field of study there are different schools of thought, with different versions of what counts as knowledge, or even the boundaries of the field (Foley 1995: 14). These involve major epistemological cleavages, for example, around positivist, interpretative and post-positivist accounts of knowledge and action. All of this adds up to the disciplinary terrain on to which the student adult educator is introduced. To paraphrase Ball *et al.*, when the adult education student is asked to 'write like an adult educator' this will be the terrain he/she will learn to inhabit. By mapping out the major dimensions of this terrain, we can develop an account of the 'disciplinary politics' which the student is writing him/herself into. To illustrate this, I would like to consider nursing education as a case study.

The data I will present below were taken from a study of student academic writing practices in three discipline areas – nursing, information studies and women's studies – at the University of Technology, Sydney, a new Australian university (in the sense that it was formed in the 1989 restructuring of higher education in Australia) whose mission statement identifies it as providing education for the professions. The data collected included interviews with students and lecturers/markers, support materials for the courses and examples of student writing. Below, first-year nursing students and their lecturers talk about writing and the disciplinary issues of nursing. I will also discuss issues arising in a first-year essay-writing task for a subject 'Professional Responsibilities in Nursing' which focuses on the changing social roles of the nursing profession.

Nursing education: a case study

One of the significant issues in nursing education has been the shift, over the last decade or so, from a 'practice-oriented' to a professionalized' conception of nursing (see Gray and Pratt 1989; 1995). This has coincided with the shift of nursing training/education out of the hospitals and into the universities. So one aspect of the disciplinary politics of nursing is precisely this shift from practice-oriented to professionalized concepts of nursing. Another tension which is central to nursing education is that between practical knowledge and theorized knowledge. Like adult education, nursing draws on a heterogeneous disciplinary base, most strikingly in the contrast between the science-based, clinical subjects and the ethical subjects. Underlying these subjects are very different conceptualizations of what counts as knowledge, the clinical subjects being underpinned by the positivist scientific paradigm, the ethical subjects by an interpretative or post-positivist perspective on what counts as knowledge. The shift into academia of nursing training/education produces in turn processes of disciplinization, where nursing is pressured to constitute itself as a 'proper' discipline. (Again there are interesting parallels with adult education as a field of study.) As Webb (1992: 747) suggests:

Table 1.1   The disciplinary politics of nursing

Practice-based	vs	Professionalized
Practical knowledge	vs	Theorized knowledge
Homogeneous disciplinary base	vs	Heterogeneous disciplinary base
Clinical subjects (positivist)	vs	Ethical subjects (interpretative/critical)

Processes of disciplinization: nursing as a 'proper' discipline; nurse educators as 'proper' academics

Gender politics of the nursing profession: 'doctors and nurses'

Nursing is a relatively young academic discipline. Like other disciplines which have attempted to establish respect and credibility, such as psychology and sociology, nursing has sought to do this by imitating longer-established disciplines and in particular the traditional or physical sciences.

Underpinning all of this is what might be termed the 'gender politics' of nursing, the construction of nursing as a handmaiden profession in relation to its other, the medical profession. This disciplinary politics of nursing (see Table 1.1) constitutes the context into which nursing students are writing themselves.

In the following extracts, nursing lecturers and a nursing student discuss some of these tensions:

There is a big gap between those working in theoretical areas and those in practical areas which is nowhere near being breached and it will be a long time before it's breached. This puts students in an interesting position. It is probably less problematic now but 4–5 years ago when our students went out to practise after graduation they were treated very badly because they were seen to be trained in an institution that was inappropriate for training nurses, by people who were too distant from nursing and in areas that were irrelevant to nursing. Now because there is an increasing number of university-trained nurses practising, that has started to dissipate but the tension underneath this has not been resolved. This is largely to do with the political climate in the hospitals; there is a dominant natural sciences medical approach to health care and there is an issue of how nurses fit into that. It's very complicated. If there is so much to be sorted out it would be hard to envisage any sort of discipline unity or clarification as to what is appropriate in the discipline for a long time.

(Lecturer interview)

I think those tensions reflect the tension for nursing because the universities seem to be teaching people about all these airy-fairy things and out in the real world they're saying they can't even fill a catheter but that's not true. What we do teach them is about real nursing but it's more than that, and I think that the faculty has to understand that people in the practice area have legitimate concerns which must be addressed by us, and I think the practice must address the fact that nursing has got to develop a profession. The only way you can develop a profession is developing thinking people. That's the tension for nursing.

(Lecturer interview)

The same lecturer identifies the disciplinary cleavages between the positivist scientific perspective and the interpretative or post-positivist approach, while arguing for their interrelatedness in the nurse education curriculum:

I'm not so sure that nursing is so well established as an academic discipline that it in fact has traditions. Apart from – I suppose there is a clear division between those that approach it from a scientific point of view and those who approach it from humanities. I don't know that they are in any way competitive, or at least theoretically they are not competitive.

Interviewer: They deal with different aspects.

Yes, exactly. Some people might want to argue that they are distinct and self-contained approaches to understanding nursing and that they can stand alone. I don't think that's the case, I think that's a mistaken view. My academic work has been in that area of nursing where it's seen to be primarily a human science discipline rather than a physical science discipline.

Within that, I suppose I would say the divisions are not so clear, though I would certainly have some sympathy with those views that derive from the non-positivist epistemologies, post-structuralist thinking. Although I'm not always in agreement with them as they are applied to nursing, but my background would be more akin to those approaches.

Another lecturer speaks more explicitly about the tensions between the scientific and humanities-based components of the curriculum:

The major tension I would have to face is that I started in the K. programme which was very much a humanities programme and we did things like important skills to develop a student's thinking, their critical writing skills, there is much less emphasis on how to nurse. When I came over to this campus there was very much a focus on the nursing things, the science and the nursing, and there was less emphasis about ethics and law and critical thinking and the humanities, the meaning of caring, the meaning of being a person. So the assignments that I had to mark were really bad. I thought, I can't believe that these people are in the third year of their programme and they cannot write, they cannot think, they cannot critique other people's work. So that was a real dilemma for me and I think that was the tension for the faculty, we had this terrible battleground between one group of people feeling that one campus wasn't teaching how to nurse and the other wasn't teaching how to think. Over several years we've got a common understanding but there's still tension there.

(Lecturer interview)

So how do students experience the disciplinary tensions between nursing as a science-based curriculum and its ethical, humanistic dimensions? The following student expresses her surprise about the range of what counted as an appropriate topic in nursing journals:

When I started to look for articles, I found there were more than I thought. I thought that, being in the nursing field, journals would focus on hypertension, neck problems, new drugs, etc., but I was surprised they have a lot of articles based on hazards happening in the workforce, nurses' perception of hazards, nurses' fears about dealings with AIDS patients, things like autonomy, authority, where does your responsibility stop and what are the boundaries. It was good.

(Student interview)

The same student identifies confusing differences between the kinds of writing that are expected of her in different parts of the programme:

But for medical, surgical, if you have to write about care for a person with AIDS, you either know or you don't know. This semester we had a case on cardiac failure and that was another one where you have to go and read how the heart works, how it pumps, where does it go wrong and why does the patient present with such and such and you have to learn. I did learn from that assignment. But for this assignment, I felt that for me it was good because I spent time thinking about it, I didn't do much reading, I didn't learn very much but certain things did catch my attention, especially the need for nurses to prove that we are people with nurses, we're not just handmaidens, which I always felt. I felt that it was never being argued enough about but I know now that's not true, but it hasn't really made me a better nurse.

(Student interview)

In the following extract, the student articulates something of the underlying politics of the nursing and medical professions:

So for university back home in Singapore we were taught what were your responsibilities, what are you accountable for, what are you accountable to, but we were never taught why nurses need autonomy, why you should feel you have a decision to make about your patients' well-being. We always were with the doctors, of course you have your differences with the doctors and you get doctors who work with you and you get doctors who think they are doctors and you're just a nurse. But it [autonomy] has never been a main issue.

(Student interview)

In this section I have tried to sketch some of the broad parameters and tensions within which nursing students are writing. My argument is that the tension between positivist and critical hermeneutic versions of what counts as knowledge, the shift towards professionalization of nursing, the emphasis on nursing as a 'proper' academic discipline are constitutive of the contexts within which the students are writing. I will illustrate this in the next section with an example from a first-year undergraduate writing task.

'Professional responsibilities in nursing' essay topic

The 'professional responsibilities in nursing' subject comes from the first year of the undergraduate nursing course. As suggested above, it focuses on the changing social roles of the nursing profession and encapsulates in many ways the tensions we have been exploring in the nursing education curriculum, particularly in relation to the professionalization of nursing. The writing task demanded of the students is an expository essay which explicitly invites the students to address the professionalism issue:

> Nurses will not be able to properly fulfil their professional responsibilities until they have greater autonomy and authority – discuss.

Students taking up writing positions: voicing in the nursing essay

Drawing on notions of 'authoring', 'authority' and 'authorization' of truth statements (see Lindstrom 1993), I will examine a range of ways in which student writers authorize statements, including through the incorporation of the voices of others into their essays. Unsurprisingly, the most common-place strongly authorized statements in the essays tend to be supported by appeals to the literature (theorized knowledge). Others – still highly valued, as it turns out – produce appeals to experience (practical knowledge), 'what nurses think and do', rather than 'what the literature tells us that nurses think' in support of their developing argument. Both strategies interpolate the voices of others into the text – on the one hand the voices of established academic sources, on the other the voice of experience.

Yet, as we shall see, it is a mistake to set up a simplistic opposition between weakly authorized statements invoking experience and strongly authorized statements invoking theorized knowledge. From other highly valued essays we will examine data showing how the student writers can produce strongly authorized statements by appealing to experience, apparently flouting the 'academic' requirement of appealing to theorized knowledge. I would suggest that an explanation for this apparent anomaly lies in the disciplinary politics of nursing itself, in its emergence as a discipline, in the pull of different constructions of nursing, specifically between nursing as a field of practice and nursing as a professionalized and thus theorized discipline.

Here are some examples of the two contrasting ways in which the student writers authorized statements in their essays. The first is an authorization based on experience of what nurses typically do:

Lack of sufficient autonomy and authority is seen when a nurse has to have a physician authorize a pathology test when the nurse suspects the patient has a urinary tract infection. Some physicians who trust experienced staff will leave blank signed forms for nurses to fill out if they see the need arising (S. White, Regisered Nurse, personal communication, 6 October 1994). In this instance the nurse needs more autonomy and authority so they can fill in a form and send a sample to the laboratory thereby saving precious time and also initiating treatment quicker which will eventually benefit the patient. When nurses see that a patient is being sufficiently hydrated and has no further need of an intravenous drip, they have to inform the doctor who will then authorize the removal of the cannula. Nurses are sufficiently educated to make these judgements but due to lack of autonomy and authority are unable to do so.

(Kirsten)

Kirsten's statements about nurses' need for autonomy and authority, in which greater autonomy and decision-making on the part of nurses are shown to be improving care for the patient, are authorized by examples from experience, not from the research literature. Interestingly, this effect is significantly reinforced when the writer uses the 'personal communication' referencing convention to authorize a particular statement, based on experience from the field rather than from an academic source. Immediately following this, Kirsten authorizes a statement by sourcing it to an academic reference:

According to Kiereini (1980) nurses have been making independent decisions regarding management of their patients without wanting to accept accountability for their decisions.

So Kirsten's essay uses a mix of these two strategies, which seems to be successful, as her essay is well received. The marker's comments are interesting, however. While giving the essay a better than average B grade, the comment is:

The weakness in your argument lies in a lack of support for claims . . .

In contrast to Kirsten's essay, which draws on both the authorization-from-experience and the academic sourcing strategy, other essays, such as Sue's (graded A) and Lorraine's (graded B), rely almost entirely on the academic sourcing strategy. Virtually every statement they make can be traced back to an academic source:

Ironically, Beaumont (1987) states that *some* nurses themselves are reluctant to receive responsibility and accountability for their actions, as they are 'low risk takers' and fear mistakes. However, a study done by Kramer and Scmalenberg (1988, cited in Collins and Henderson 1991: 25), [claims] that nurses preferred to work in an environment which encouraged autonomous practice. Furthermore, Schoen (1992) confirmed their claims and concluded that a number of research including her own, have discovered a positive link between autonomy and job satisfaction.

(Sue)

In Sue and Lorraine's essays, what nurses say/think/feel/do is constructed purely through the filter of the research literature. Nurses are present in the text only as reconstituted or recontextualized into a body of research.

So how do these authorization strategies operate in the less successful essays? We will look at Deirdre's essay, (graded E) and Karen's essay (graded C–).

In the health care system the doctors have the most autonomy and authority this 'male dominated profession used the path to professionalism to ensure themselves of financial security and autonomy' (Short and Sharman 1987: 199). Nurses believe that if they follow this same path to professionalism they too will have an increase in financial rewards, status, autonomy and authority as seen by those who have already benefited from their standing as a profession. This push for nurses to become professionals puts a great strain on the so called doctor nurse relationship, the college of surgeons 'asserted that the medical practitioner was the natural leader of the health care team and that there should be a revival of trust and loyalty on the part of nurses' (Palmer and Short 1993: 155). The doctor still dominates the health care system and see that through nurses pushing for professionalism that they are no longer seen as a loyal part of the health care team. Nurses believe that this is not true and that doctors should be educated to have a greater appreciation of nursing theory and practice, that decision making processes should be reviewed and that changes in hospital administration could ease tension between nurses and doctors.

(Karen)

In Karen's essay we find examples both of the academic sourcing strategy, with quoted statements attributed to sourced authors, and the unattributed appeal to experience:

Nurses believe that this is not true and that doctors should be educated to have a greater appreciation of nursing theory and practice, that decision making processes should be reviewed and that changes in hospital administration could ease tension between nurses and doctors.

The arguments are voiced, not from the research literature, but through the mouths of generalized doctors and nurses. Take the following statement, from a later stage of Karen's essay:

Nurses have very little authority in their profession even though they have a close relationship with the patient they have very little authority over them. It is the doctor who always has the final say on patient treatment.

Karen's essay seems to dramatize an argument between real life doctors and nurses about who does what, what are the boundaries and divisions of responsibility for health care.

Deirdre's E grade, according to the subject outline, 'represents a performance which reflects little understanding, or gives little evidence of a serious attempt to meet the expectations of the assigned task'. Her essay starts with the following:

Many nurses have seen the achievement of a professional standing as an important goal in advancing the interests of nurses and health care consumers. In particular, it has been said that it will increase nurses' autonomy and status, and therefore their capacity to achieve the aims of nursing and fulfil their professional responsibilities.

The marker's comments are as follows:

You have quoted this word for word from the subject outline without acknowledgement. This is plagiarism.

Deirdre's apparent adoption of the impersonalized unattributed academic voice is destabilized because the reader/marker can in fact trace it back to an attributable source that is rather close at hand, the subject outline.

Later on in the essay, Deirdre shifts further into the personalized experiential voice by switching to the pronoun 'we':

So even though nurses must still take orders from doctors, we display professionalism through choosing appropriate care, professionalism, using our knowledge to choose what care will give them the best benefits, while providing emotional care.

. . .

On the other hand, if every professional in the organization exercised complete autonomy, the organization would eventually collapse. If we had too much autonomy, the profession would experience problems such as lack of agreement between nurses, administrators and patients.

Ivanič and others (Ivanič and Simpson 1992) have raised the issue of such pronoun choices as resistances to the impersonalizing academic conventions. It is beyond the scope of this paper to explore why this writer made these choices, but it is clear that the shift into 'we' is a significant shift into an experiential voice. The issue, surely, is one of informed choice. As writers we can consciously take risks, use strategies which flout dominant conventions based on informed choice. We can also produce docile, conventional texts. But this is based on awareness of the options. A writer who has not been made aware of the options is not in a position to make an informed choice.

Deirdre's appropriation of wordings which are bound to spring to the attention of the reader/marker who probably wrote them is perhaps indication enough of her unfamiliarity with key underlying conventions of academic writing. That plagiarism is a complex issue and that what counts as plagiarism is itself a social construct is well documented (Scollon 1995) but again is beyond the scope of this chapter. I will conclude this case study by looking at an essay that raises the question of docility and risk in writing.

Mark's essay: thematizing the argument

Mark's essay is one of the most highly rated by the marker (A–) yet it does not rely heavily on the docile academic sourcing strategy which we saw in Sue and Lorraine's essay:

> Due to the fact that the nursing profession is so diverse and becoming even more so, until nurses unite, establish their practice at different levels and situations, their levels of autonomy and authority will be undermined. 'Increasingly, nurses are taking responsibility for their practice and gaining a new autonomy in their work' Reid (1993: 30) and Flint (1993: 66) agree 'everyone in a professional role, whether lawyer, doctor, teacher, or midwife, must be able to practise autonomously and use his or her professional judgement'. This brings in the argument that some nurses want to take greater control of their workload and duties, and to be accountable for them, whilst some want to take minimum control. However, in direct conflict to these ideas, is the dominance that doctors have over nurses. Leach (1993) discusses that, with few exceptions, nurses work under medical control. The medical profession controls admissions, discharges and what goes on in between, even if the patient had been admitted for purely nursing care. There is going to be conflict between the nurse and the doctor, and if, according to the definitions of autonomy stated earlier, the right of self government to determine the course of one's life by oneself is accepted, then these nurses are not fully autonomous, and therefore unable to have full responsibilities for nursing decisions.
>
> This, one could argue, is possibly one of the reasons many nurses have sought to become nurse practitioners. The latter want to be given full responsibility for nursing management decisions, to be able to implement those decisions using authority and to be held accountable for those decisions.

Instead, what Mark seems to do is thematize the argument, concentrating not on what the research literature tells us nurses think/feel/do or on what experience tells us, but on the implications of the argument (between autonomy and subordination, between different sections of the nursing profession, between doctors and nurses). Mark seems to take up a confident summative voice. Where Deirdre appears to take up this voice, in the first paragraph of her essay, the effect is destabilized because the reader/marker recognizes a verbatim appropriation from the subject outline. Where Mark quotes it is to back up or elaborate an argumentative position that he has already introduced. The strategy is therefore quite different from that of Sue or Lorraine in which the text is constructed almost entirely from sourced material.

'Teach the conflicts'

In this chapter I have somewhat complicated the picture of student academic writing practices within new and emergent discipline areas along the lines suggested by Goggin (1995). The skills-based approach to the teaching of academic writing assumes that there was a generic set of skills and strategies that can be taught and then applied in particular disciplinary contexts. The text-based approach assumes a relatively homogeneous discipline, with text types to be discovered, analysed and taught. I am suggesting, in line with writers such as Ball *et al.* (1990) that, most crucially, the student writer is learning to take up disciplinary positions in discourse and that this needs to be taught explicitly:

> If students are to see themselves as something other than 'inspired' or 'shooting the bull' or 'guessing' – representations of disciplinary activity which posit them as essentially passive in relation to the work in hand – we must begin to make visible and available the machinery which produces the university's disciplines and its multiple discourses.
> (Ball *et al.* 1990: 357)

Where the disciplinary positions are conflictual, overlapping or indeed blurred (see Geertz 1975, cited in Klein 1993) the student academic writer will be working within the disciplinary politics that is produced. So where does this leave the student writer? In this section I argue that academic writing pedagogy must make the concerns of disciplinarity, disciplinarization and consequent writing positions central – in other words, as Graff (quoted in Klein 1993) suggests, we must 'teach the conflicts'.

As I suggested earlier in the nurse education case study, a major conflict is between, on the one hand, the practice-oriented account of nursing and the experiential ways of knowing that it makes authoritative and, on the other hand, the professionalized, disciplinary account of nursing, with its consequent impersonalization and generalization of the nursing subject. We have seen how these conflicts work within the texts examined earlier, producing at one moment highly valued, if docile, texts in the impersonalized disciplinary voice (Sue and Lorraine's). Other similarly valued essays (Kirsten and Mark's) draw on the strategy of authorization from experience, though running the risk of the critical marker's comment. The less successful essays (Karen and Deirdre's) appear to fail both in making authoritative statements in the impersonalized disciplinary voice and in the generalized experiential voice of 'what nurses think'. Mark's essay seems to thematize the conflict itself between the experiential/practice-based account and the impersonalized disciplined account of nursing. While appearing somewhat unconventional, i.e. not docile, in terms of the conventions of academic writing, it is highly valued by the marker.

It is worth noting that the tensions and conflicts between the experiential/practice-based voice and the impersonalized disciplinary voice and the consequent availability of writing positions are a major theme of the work of Ivanič and others (see Ivanič and Simpson 1992) on critical language awareness approaches to the teaching and learning of academic writing, as they are in Ball *et al.* (1990) and, indeed, are taken up by other writers in this volume (see Stierer, Chapter 11). Here they map very specifically on to the shift of nursing into the academy with its consequent professionalization and disciplinization. This would suggest that the disciplinary politics of nursing is not in itself limited to nursing alone, in that it draws on issues that are clearly broader than nursing such as the positivist/critical hermeneutic discourses as well as theory–practice divides.

'What every student needs to know' about academic writing is precisely the ways in which taking up or rejecting writing positions involves taking up or rejecting disciplinary positions. This is not a pedagogy to be offered *instead* of a focus on the technical aspects of academic writing (of course someone needs to talk Deirdre through the social meanings of plagiarism, to give her the skills to quote and reference effectively). It provides a complementary layer in which the student academic writer can explore the writing/disciplinary/subject positions that are available along with the areas of blurring, overlap and conflict that create difficulties and choices in taking up an authoritative position in writing.

Conclusion: intrinsic and embodied readings

An underlying theme of this chapter has been, in a sense, how lecturers/markers read student writing and how students read the circumstances within which they are required to write. Here I take 'reading' in a broader pedagogical sense: how we read these texts as people concerned with the teaching of academic writing. I want to suggest that there are two broad ways of characterizing this: first, the idea of intrinsic reading or an intrinsic reading; second, the idea of embodied reading and embodied readings. What do I mean by this?

An intrinsic reading is one which reads the pedagogical issues of student texts in terms of skills or technologies. Learner writers in this version will have greater and lesser degrees of skill in, for example, incorporating wordings and meanings into text. They will to a greater or lesser extent have available to them the linguistic technologies to do so. An embodied reading is one that reads the text as an embodiment of the disciplinary politics within which it is produced, and as an embodiment of the processes of subject production at work as learner writers engage with the writing demands of the discipline. In this chapter I argue that such embodied readings are an essential basis for academic writing pedagogy.

2

Student Writing and Staff Feedback in Higher Education: An Academic Literacies Approach

Mary R. Lea and Brian V. Street

Introduction

The opinion is often expressed that standards of student 'literacy' are falling, whether at school or in higher education; many academic staff claim that students can no longer write. 'Back to basics' ideas are now fast taking hold in today's higher education. Recently, we received an award from the UK's Economic and Social Research Council to conduct a research project entitled 'Perspectives on Academic Literacies: an Institutional Approach' that attempted to look at these issues in more depth. The research looked at perceptions and practices of student writing in higher education, taking as case studies one new and one traditional university in south-east England. Set against the background of numerous changes in higher education in the UK and increasing numbers of non-traditional entrants, this research has been concerned with a wider institutional approach to student writing, rather than merely locating 'problems' with individual students. One of the main purposes of the research has been to move away from a skills-based, deficit model of student writing and to consider the complexity of writing practices that are taking place at degree level in universities. As a starting point, the research adopts the concept of academic literacies as a framework for understanding university writing practices.

Academic literacies

Learning in higher education involves adapting to new ways of knowing: new ways of understanding, interpreting and organizing knowledge. Academic literacy practices – reading and writing within disciplines – constitute central processes through which students learn new subjects and develop their knowledge about new areas of study. A practices approach to literacy takes account of the cultural and contextual component of writing and reading practices, and this in turn has important implications for our understanding of issues of student learning. Educational research into student learning in higher education has tended to concentrate on ways in which students can be helped to adapt their practices to those of the university (Gibbs 1994): from this perspective, the codes and conventions of academia can be taken as given. In contrast, our research is founded on the premise that in order to understand the nature of academic learning, it is important to investigate the understandings of both academic staff and students about their own literacy practices without making prior assumptions as to which practices are either appropriate or effective. This is particularly important in trying to develop a more complex analysis of what it means to become academically literate. We believe that it is important to realize that meanings are contested among the different parties involved: institutions, staff and students. Viewing literacy from a cultural and social practice approach, rather than in terms of educational judgements about good and bad writing, and approaching meanings as contested can give us insights into the nature of academic literacy in particular and academic learning in general; through researching these differing expectations and interpretations of university writing we hope to throw light on failure or non-completion, as well as success and progression.

The notion of academic literacies has been developed from the area of 'new literacy studies' (Barton 1994; Baynham 1995a; Street 1984), as an attempt to draw out the implications of this approach for our understanding of issues of student learning. We have argued elsewhere (Lea and Street 1997a) that educational research into student writing in higher education has fallen into three main perspectives or models: study skills; academic socialization; and academic literacies (see Figure 2.1). The models are not mutually exclusive, and we would not want to view them in a simple linear time dimension, whereby one model supersedes or replaces the insights provided by another. Rather, we would like to think that each model successively encapsulates those above it, so that the academic socialization perspective takes account of study skills but includes them in the broader context of the acculturation processes we describe below, and likewise the academic literacies approach encapsulates the academic socialization model, building on the insights developed there as well as the study skills view. The academic literacies model, then, incorporates both of the other models into a more encompassing understanding of the nature of student writing within institutional practices, power relations and identities, as we explain below. We take a hierarchical view of the relationship between the three models, privileging the 'academic literacies' approach. We believe that in teaching as well as in research, addressing specific skills issues around student writing, such as how to open or close an essay or whether to use the first person, takes on an entirely different meaning if the context is solely that of study skills, if the process is seen as part of academic socialization, or if it is viewed more broadly as an aspect of the whole institutional and epistemological context. We explicate each model

Figure 2.1   Models of student writing in higher education

Study skills
Student deficit
• 'fix it': atomized skills; surface language, grammar, spelling
• sources: behavioural and experimental psychology; programmed learning
Student writing as technical and instrumental skill

Academic socialization
Acculturation of students into academic discourse
• inculcating students into new 'culture'; focus on student orientation to learning and interpretation of learning task, e.g. 'deep', 'surface', 'strategic' learning; homogeneous 'culture'; lack of focus on institutional practices, change and power
• sources: social psychology; anthropology; constructivism
Student writing as transparent medium of representation

Academic literacies
Students' negotiation of conflicting literacy practices
• literacies as social practices; at level of epistemology and identities; institutions as sites of/constituted in discourses and power; variety of communicative repertoire, e.g. genres, fields, disciplines; switching with respect to linguistic practices, social meanings and identities
• sources: 'new literacy studies'; critical discourse analysis; systemic functional linguistics; cultural anthropology
Student writing as meaning making and contested

---

in turn as both a summary of our major findings in the research project and as a set of lenses through which to view the account we give of the research.

The study skills approach has assumed that literacy is a set of atomized skills which students have to learn and which are then transferable to other contexts. The focus is on attempts to 'fix' problems with student learning, which are treated as a kind of pathology. The theory of language on which it is based emphasizes surface features, grammar and spelling. Its sources lie in behavioural psychology and training programmes and it conceptualizes student writing as technical and instrumental. In recent years the crudity and insensitivity of this approach have led to refinement of the meaning of 'skills' involved and attention to broader issues of learning and social context, what we (Lea and Street 1997a) have termed the 'academic socialization' approach.

From the academic socialization perspective, the task of the tutor/adviser is to inculcate students into a new 'culture', that of the academy. The focus is on student orientation to learning and interpretation of learning tasks, through conceptualization for instance of a distinction between 'deep', 'surface' and 'strategic' approaches to learning (Marton *et al.* 1997). The sources of this perspective lie in social psychology, in anthropology and in constructivist education. Although more sensitive both to the student as learner and to the cultural context, the approach could nevertheless be criticized on a number of grounds. It appears to assume that the academy is a relatively homogeneous culture, whose norms and practices have simply to be learnt to provide access to the whole institution. Even though at some level disciplinary and departmental difference may be acknowledged, institutional practices, including processes of change and the exercise of power, do not seem to be sufficiently theorized. Similarly, despite the fact that contextual factors in student writing are recognized as important (Hounsell 1988; Taylor *et al.* 1988), this approach tends to treat writing as a transparent medium of representation and so fails to address the deep language, literacy and discourse issues involved in the institutional production and representation of meaning.

The third approach, the one most closely allied to the 'new literacy studies', we refer to as academic literacies. This approach sees literacies as social practices, in the way we have suggested above. It views student writing and learning as issues at the level of epistemology and identities rather than skill or socialization. An academic literacies approach views the institutions in which academic practices take place as constituted in, and as sites of, discourse and power. It sees the literacy demands of the curriculum as involving a variety of communicative practices, including genres, fields and disciplines. From the student point of view a dominant feature of academic literacy practices is the requirement to switch practices between one setting and another, to deploy a repertoire of linguistic practices appropriate to each setting, and to handle the social meanings and identities that each evokes. This emphasis on identities and social meanings draws attention to deep affective and ideological conflicts in such switching and use of the linguistic repertoire. A student's personal identity – who am 'I'? – may be challenged by the forms of writing required in different disciplines, notably prescriptions about the use of impersonal and passive forms as opposed to first person and active forms, and students may feel threatened and resistant – 'this isn't me' (Lea 1994; Ivanič 1998). The recognition of this level of engagement with student writing, as opposed to the more straightforward study skills and academic socialization approaches, comes from the social and ideological orientation of the new literacy studies. Allied to this is work in critical discourse analysis, systemic functional linguistics and cultural anthropology which has come to see student writing as being concerned with the processes of meaning-making and contestation around this meaning rather than as skills or deficits. There is a growing body of literature based upon this approach, which suggests that one explanation for student writing problems might be the gaps between academic staff expectations and student interpretations of what is involved in student writing (Cohen 1993; Lea 1994; Street 1995; Lea and Street 1997b; Stierer 1997; Jones *et al.* forthcoming).

The research

During 1995–96 we carried out research at two universities, one new and one traditional, in south-east England. Ten interviews were conducted with staff in the older university and 21 students were interviewed, either individually or in small groups. At the new university, 13 members of academic staff and 26 students were interviewed in the same way. The interviews at both institutions included the directors of quality assurance units and 'learning support' staff.

One of our initial research objectives was to explore the contribution of ethnographic-based research to educational development in higher education. The short length of the project limited the full in-depth ethnographic approach which such research could warrant. However, we did adopt an 'ethnographic style' approach (Green and Bloome 1997) to the research which included conducting in-depth, semi-structured interviews with staff and students, participant observation of group sessions and attention to samples of students' writing, written feedback on students' work and handouts on 'essay' writing. A major part of the research has included a linguistically based analysis of this textual material. As the research progressed we realized that this was an equally important source of data which we needed to consider in relation to the interview data. As researchers we were able to benefit from our own situated knowledge of the institutional settings within which we were researching. Adopting an ethnographic style approach to the research, within settings of which we already had prior knowledge, enabled us to move away from the focus on transcribed interview material to a more eclectic approach, merging the importance of understanding both texts and practices in the light of staff and student interpretations of university writing.

Our research, then, was not based on a representative sample from which generalizations could be drawn but rather was conceived as providing case studies that enabled us to explore theoretical issues and generate questions for further systematic study. Our approach, therefore, was in the ethnographic tradition described by Mitchell (1984). Rather than applying 'enumerative induction' (as in much scientific and statistical research) as a means to generalizing, and for establishing the 'representativeness' of social data, Mitchell advocates what he terms 'analytical induction':

> What the anthropologist using a case study to support an argument does is to show how general principles deriving from some theoretical orientation manifest themselves in some given set of particular circumstances. A good case study, therefore, enables the analyst to establish theoretically valid connections between events and phenomena which previously were ineluctable.
>
> (Mitchell 1984: 239)

In the present context, the tutors and students whom we interviewed and the documents we collected can be taken as case studies of different perspectives on academic literacies. While not representing a sample from which generalizations can be drawn regarding the whole of English higher education, these case studies can point to important theoretical questions and connections that might not otherwise be raised. The data, for instance, enable us to explore the hypothesis that, viewed as 'academic literacies', the beliefs and practices of tutors and students constitute a different kind of evidence than if the same data were viewed in terms of skills or academic socialization. These accounts can, for instance, provide evidence for differences between staff and students' understanding of the writing process at levels of epistemology, authority and contestation over knowledge rather than at the level of technical skill, surface linguistic competence or cultural assimilation. We have therefore approached our research data in order to acquire insights and conceptual elaboration on our three models of student writing and to generate from them analytic induction rather than 'enumerative induction'.

The unstructured, in-depth interviews examined how students understand the different literacy practices which they experience in their studies and in what ways academic staff understand the literacy requirements of their own subject area and make these explicit to their students. We gave participants the opportunity to reflect upon the writing practices of the university, at different levels and in different courses, subject areas and disciplines, and to consider what influences were being brought to bear upon them not only from within the university but also from other writing contexts. We asked staff to outline, as they saw them, the writing requirements of their own disciplines and subject areas and to describe the kinds and quantities of writing that were involved for their students. We also asked them to talk about their perceptions of student writing problems and the ways in which these were addressed at both an individual and departmental level. Students explained the problems that they experienced with writing at the university and their perceptions of the writing requirements of different courses and subject areas. We also collected copious amounts of documentation from both staff and students: handouts on essay writing; examples of students' written work; course handbooks; assignment guidelines.

A further objective of our research was to contribute towards an institutional understanding of academic literacy practices in higher education, and we therefore began the project with a focus upon three traditional categories: humanities; social sciences; and natural sciences. In both universities we began by carrying out interviews with academic staff within each category and then went on to interview students. Early in the research it became clear from the interview data we were collecting that the traditional boundaries that we had identified to frame the research were in many senses irrelevant, particularly for students. Our interviews with students alerted us to the fact that old disciplinary divides were often not appropriate as research categories.

The diverse nature of the degree programmes at preliminary level resulted in students engaging in what we term 'course switching' which, we suggest, can be paralleled with linguistic code switching (Gumperz 1982). Such switching may occur within traditional academic disciplines in a traditional sense (physics, anthropology) or within 'fields of study', such as modular programmes or interdisciplinary courses that incorporate elements of different disciplines and of interdisciplinary courses (Asian studies, business studies), or to specific modules or course units within programmes (twentieth-century women's literature, operations management). In so doing, they are having to interpret the writing requirements of different levels of academic activity. Such switching may also encompass the different demands of individual subject tutors and their personal interpretations of writing requirements. As students switch between such disciplines, course units, modules and tutors, different assumptions about the nature of writing, related to different epistemological presuppositions about the nature of academic knowledge and learning, are being brought to bear, often implicitly, on the specific writing requirements of their assignments. Evidence from interviews with tutors and students and from handouts prepared for students on aspects of 'good' writing suggests that it is frequently very difficult for students to 'read off' from any such context what might be the specific academic writing requirements of that context. Nor, as we shall see below, did the provision of general statements about the nature of academic writing help students with the specificity of demands in each context.

We also interviewed learning support staff in both institutions. The data collected from these interviews reinforced the views expressed by students that many of the difficulties they experienced with writing arose from the conflicting and contrasting requirements for writing on different courses and from the fact that these requirements were frequently left implicit. Learning support staff also questioned whether academic staff were aware that they were asking for specific ways of writing knowledge from their students.

Requirements of student writing: staff interpretations

The interviews with staff would suggest that academic staff have their own fairly well-defined views regarding what constitute the elements of a good piece of student writing in the areas in which they teach. These tend to refer to form in a more generic sense, including attention to syntax, punctuation and layout and to such apparently evident components of rational essay writing as 'structure', 'argument' and 'clarity'. Their own disciplinary history had a clear influence on staff conceptualizations and representations of what were the most important elements to look for in students' writing at both levels, although the epistemological and methodological issues that underlay them were often expressed through the surface features and components of 'writing' in itself – as we detail below. It was this confusion, we argue, that led to difficulties for students not yet acquainted with the disciplinary underpinnings of faculty feedback. This confusion was compounded by the move towards multi-disciplinary courses at degree level and the modular system that was fully in place at one of the universities. As a result, although faculty understanding of student writing was often described in disciplinary terms, for example, 'In history the use of evidence is particularly important', or 'In English we are looking for clarity of expression', in practice staff were often teaching within programmes which integrated a number of disciplinary approaches and where the writing requirements consequently varied.

Additionally, some academic staff were teaching in courses where even the traditional disciplines were looking at new ways of communicating that discipline outside the academic community, developing what we term 'empathy' writing: in physics, for instance, students were asked to write texts for non-specialist audiences, such as House of Commons select committees, or commercial groups, to 'empathize' with their readers' lack of disciplinary knowledge and at the same time take account of their desire or need to know. In management science, mathematical principles were used to address commercial problems, and writing reports for putative clients was an essential part of student writing for assessment. The writing requirements of these exercises differed from those of more standard 'essay text' kinds of writing, but the same students may encounter both in their progress through a degree programme.

Despite this variation in modes of writing across disciplines and fields of study, many staff we interviewed were still mainly influenced by specific conceptualizations of their own disciplines or subject areas in their assessments of students' writing. The twin concepts of 'structure' and 'argument' came to the fore in most interviews as being key elements in student writing, terms which we examine more closely below. Even though staff generally had a clear belief in these concepts as crucial to their understanding of what constituted a successful piece of writing, there was less certainty when it came to describing what underlay a well-argued or well-structured piece of student work. More commonly, they were able to identify when a student had been successful, but could not describe how a particular piece of writing 'lacked' structure. We suggest that, in practice, what makes a piece of student writing 'appropriate' has more to do with issues of epistemology than with the surface features of form to which staff often have recourse when describing their students' writing. That is to say, underlying, often disciplinary, assumptions about the nature of knowledge affected the meaning given to the terms 'structure' and 'argument'. Since these assumptions varied with context, it is not valid to suggest that such concepts are generic and transferable, or represent 'common sense ways of knowing' (Fairclough 1992b), as the reference to 'writing problems' frequently implied. We believe that this finding has considerable implications for current attempts to define generic skills.

The research data, then, suggest that, while academic staff can describe what constitutes successful writing, difficulties arose when they attempted to make explicit what a well-developed argument looks like in a written assignment. At the level of form, one tutor is able to explain clearly what he wants:

I need my students to have an introduction which sets the scene and a main body which covers a number of issues highlighted in the introduction and introduces economic theory, application and analysis. Students need to be critical, to evaluate, to try and reach some sort of synthesis and then to simply summarize and conclude. You need a good solid introduction leading into your main body, and each part of your main body will be crafted and it will link with the next. It will have a professional feel about it and will not describe but will critically analyse, and then it will lead into a summary and conclusion.

However, the descriptive tools he employs – 'critically analyse', 'evaluate', 'reach a synthesis' – could not be explicated further. As another lecturer put it:

I know a good essay when I see it but I cannot describe how to write it.

This lends credence to the idea that elements of successful student writing are in essence related to particular ways of constructing the world, and not to a set of generic writing skills as the study skills model would suggest. A successful university lecturer is likely to have spent many years developing acceptable ways of constructing her own knowledge through her own writing practices in a variety of disciplinary contexts. Other writers have explicated in some detail how writing practices construct rather than merely reflect academic knowledge (Bazerman 1988; Berkenkotter and Huckin 1995). These practices, then, are integrally related to the ways in which staff constitute their own academic world-view and their own academic knowledge. Faced with writing which does not appear to make sense within their own academic framework, they are most likely to have recourse to what feel like familiar descriptive categories such as 'structure and argument', 'clarity' and 'analysis', in order to give feedback on their students' writing. In reality their own understandings of these categories may be bound by their own individual disciplinary perspective, but they may be less meaningful outside this framework and therefore not readily understood by students unversed in that particular orientation of the discipline. Our later analysis of a student essay illustrates this in some detail.

Writing requirements: student interpretations

The research interviews with students revealed a number of different interpretations and understandings of what students thought that they were meant to be doing in their writing. Students described taking 'ways of knowing' (Baker *et al.* 1995) and of writing from one course into another only to find that their attempt to do this was unsuccessful and met with negative feedback. Students were consciously aware of switching between diverse writing requirements and knew that their task was to unpack what kind of writing any particular assignment might require. This was at a more complex level than genre, such as the 'essay' or 'report', lying more deeply at the level of writing particular knowledge in a specific academic setting.

Students knew that variations of form existed, but admitted that their real writing difficulties lay in trying to gauge the deeper levels of variation in knowledge and how to set about writing them. It was much more than using the correct terminology or just learning to do 'academic writing' – as what we term the 'academic socialization' model would suggest – and more about adapting previous knowledge of writing practices, academic and other, to varied university settings:

> The thing I'm finding most difficult in my first term here is moving from subject to subject and knowing how you're meant to write in each one. I'm really aware of writing for a particular tutor as well as for a particular subject. Everybody seems to want something different. It's very different to A levels, where we used dictated notes for essay writing.

Such common descriptions in interviews with students did not appear to support the notion of generic and transferable writing skills across the university.

Students themselves often internalized the language of feedback. They knew that it was important to present an argument and they knew that structure played an important part, but had difficulties in understanding when they had achieved this successfully in a piece of writing. Students would frequently describe how they had completed a piece of work that they believed was well constructed and appropriate to the subject area, only to receive a very low grade and fairly negative feedback. They often felt unsure and confused about what they had done wrong. What seemed to be an appropriate piece of writing in one field, or indeed for one individual tutor, was often found to be quite inappropriate for another. Although students frequently had guidelines, either from individual tutors or as departmental documents on essay writing, they found that these often did not help them very much with this level of writing. They felt that such guidelines dealt with matters that they knew from A level or access courses. These involved issues broadly defined as structure, such as those concerned with the formal organization of a piece of writing – introduction, main body, conclusion – or as argument, involving advice on the necessity of developing a position rather than providing 'just' a description or narrative. Students could assimilate this general advice on writing 'techniques' and 'skills' but found it difficult to move from the general to using this advice in a particular text in a particular disciplinary context. In both universities, the majority of the documents offering guidelines of this nature that we analysed took a rather technical approach to writing, concentrating on issues of surface form: grammar, punctuation and spelling. They also dealt fully with referencing, bibliographies and footnotes, and supplied warnings about plagiarism. They rarely dealt with the issues that students reported they had most difficulty grasping in terms of how to write specific, course-based knowledge for a particular tutor or field of study.

The conflicting advice received from academic teaching staff in different courses added to the confusion. For example, in some areas students were specifically directed to outline in detail what would follow in the main body of a traditional essay, while other tutors would comment 'I do not want to know what you are going to say'. Many different conventions were to be found around the use of the first person pronoun in student writing. Even within the same courses, individual tutors had different opinions about when or if it was appropriate to use this. Such conventions were often presented as self-evidently the correct way in which things should be done.

Students' perceptions were influenced by their own experiences of writing within and outside higher education. An example of this was the A level entrant who came unstuck when she wrote a history essay drawing on just one textual source as she regularly and successfully had done in English. Similarly, a BTEC entrant to the traditional university had worked in industry for five years and was used to extensive succinct report writing, but, when confronted with a traditional essay text in politics, as part of a course in public administration and management, he had no idea how to go about writing this piece of work.

Students took different approaches to the course switching that they experienced. Some saw it as a kind of game, trying to work out the rules, not only for a field of study, a particular course or particular assignment, but frequently for an individual tutor. They adopted writing strategies that masked their own opinions, in a sense mimicking some implicit or even explicit convention. There were, for instance, the first-year history students who had learnt to hide what they thought behind 'it can be said' rather than using the first person in their writing, and had also learnt how to balance one recognized author against another as a way to present their own personal viewpoint in their writing. On the other hand, a mature student writing social policy felt severely constrained by his inability to bring his years of trade union expertise into his essay on present-day poverty. He did not feel comfortable with the pragmatic approach of playing to the rules of the game, which seemed to require him simply to juxtapose data from different sources and to eschew personal knowledge.

Relations around student writing: interpreting feedback

So far, we have attempted to outline some of the indications in the research data for conceptualizing variety in the different interpretations and understandings of student writing we encountered. These variations exist within and across courses, subjects and disciplines – and between students and academic tutors in many different contexts. They are constituted both in the linguistic form of the texts – the written assignments and the accompanying feedback – and in the social relations that exist around them – the relationships of power and authority between tutor and student – and they are manifest in the divergent literacy practices integral to text construction. Central to our understanding of both the varieties of academic literacy practices which students engage in across the university and the relations which exist around text production is an examination of the ways in which written feedback is interpreted by staff and students.

As we have illustrated, the research has been concerned with a textual examination of tutor written feedback on student work – both on standard feedback sheets and in the margins of assignments – and with students' interpretations of the meanings that they attach to this feedback both in general and in relation to a specific piece of written work. This analysis has raised questions about the relationship between feedback and epistemological issues of knowledge construction. How is feedback being used to direct students to develop and write their academic knowledge in very specific ways within particular courses which are implicitly presented as 'common sense ways of knowing'? We have already illustrated a feedback genre within which the use of descriptive categories – such as 'structure' and 'argument' – may embed contrasting conceptual understandings. As we have suggested, such terms tend, therefore, to be rather elusive, particularly for students, and may be more usefully understood in their gatekeeping role or at a more complex ideological level within an institutional hierarchy than as the unproblematic generic requirements of student writing.

One useful way of examining the relationships around texts may, then, be to start by examining the feedback that staff give to students as a genre. By examining some of the genres of students' written work and the genre of staff feedback on it we may be able to make more sense of the complex ways in which staff and students construct appropriate ways of knowing and reproduce appropriate forms of disciplinary and subject knowledge. There is a dynamic within the feedback genre, for instance, which works to both construct academic knowledge and maintain relationships of power and authority between novice student and experienced academic. Assumptions about what constitutes valid knowledge may be inferred by analysing feedback, but frequently such assumptions remain implicit, as in the feedback on the essays analysed above.

The ways in which speakers or writers indicate their implicit commitment to the truth of what is being said – what linguists refer to as 'modality' – vary with types of text and social relations (see Lea, Chapter 4, for a further discussion of modality). Tutor comments frequently take the form of what we term 'categorical modality', using imperatives and assertions, with little mitigation or qualification. The first page of the student anthropology essay analysed above has the following comments: 'Explain'; 'A bit confused'; 'Linkage?'; 'Too many unlinked facts here. Can't see argument'. This categorical modality is also expressed here and frequently in the essays we have seen by means of orthographic marks such as '?', '!' or '(...)', indicating disagreement, doubt, criticism. The '?' frequently indicates not a genuine question which tutor and student are engaged in explicating, but rather is used as a kind of expletive, or as a categorical assertion that the point is not 'correct'. In the essay in question there are seven unattached question marks, many with this function, and six bracket signs '(...)' indicating links that should have been made, in the space of $3\frac{1}{2}$ pages. One has only to imagine other kinds of modality that could be expressed in this context to recognize the conventional and categorical nature of this usage: mitigated comments such as 'you might like to consider', 'have you thought about', 'in my opinion', 'perhaps', and open-ended questions such as 'could this be interpreted differently?', 'is there a link with other comments here?' etc. would evoke a different modality (more provisional or mitigated), create a different genre and evoke a different interpersonal relationship between student as writer and tutor as marker than that indicated by the comments we describe here. In these the tutor clearly and firmly takes authority, assuming the right to criticize directly and categorically on the basis of an assumed 'correct' view of what should have been written and how. Students, however, may have a different interpretation of feedback comments. The anthropology student in question could not make sense of the feedback comment 'Meaning?' on his text. For him both the meaning of what he was saying and the development of the argument in his own text were clear. Even where students indicate in interviews that they did not understand the comment, thought it unfair or even disagreed with it, few if any challenge the tutor's right to make such comments. It appears, then, that written feedback on students' work is not merely an attempt at communication or at learning a 'discipline' or at socialization into a community – although it clearly has elements of all of these – but is also embedded in relationships of authority as a marker of difference and a sustainer of boundaries.

Additionally, institutional procedures were implicated in the ways in which students were able to read, understand and make use of feedback on their work. In the new university, where a fully modular system was in operation, it was reported to us by both staff and students alike that in many instances students did not receive feedback on assessed written work until they had completed their studies for the module. Inevitably, students found that they were unable to benefit from receiving feedback in this manner since they generally found comments to be specific to a particular piece of work, or at the least to the module being studied, and they reported that such feedback frequently bore no relationship to their studies in the subsequent module. Academic staff reported that they were unable to make best use of standard feedback sheets because these were received by students after module completion.

> The problem with the modular system is that every piece of work they [the students] do is for assessment purposes. It is not until they are well into the second module that they get the results from the first. Effectively there is no feedback.

Evidence such as this led us to suggest that we consider the analysis of writing in the university as an 'institutional' issue, not just a matter for particular participants. The institution within which tutors and students write defines the conventions and boundaries of their writing practices, through its procedures and regulations (definitions of plagiarism, require-ments of modularity and assessment procedures etc.), whatever individual tutors and students may believe themselves to be as writers, and whatever autonomy and distinctiveness their disciplines may assert.

Future directions

Our research, then, indicates the variety in both the writing practices that students engage with as part of their university courses and the complex nature of the feedback they receive from tutors. These writing practices and genres are not simply concerned with technical matters in which 'appropriate' skills are acquired and novices become members of an expert community, as in the first two models described above (see Figure 2.1). The third model, that of academic literacies, from which we are viewing these data, suggests a more complex and contested interpretation, in which the processes of student writing and tutor feedback are defined through implicit assumptions about what constitutes valid knowledge within a particular context, and the relationships of authority that exist around the communication of these assumptions. The nature of this authority and the claims associated with it can be identified through both formal, linguistic features of the writing involved and in the social and institutional relationships associated with it.

During the course of the research we have identified three thematic categories originating from both students and staff as ways of looking at students' writing. The first is focused on the student and suggests that students lack a set of basic skills that can be dealt with primarily in a remedial study skills or learning support unit. This takes no account of the interaction of the student with institutional practices and is based on the underlying principle that knowledge is transferred rather than mediated or constructed through writing practices. The second, identified most clearly by students, is derived from the interaction of student and tutor and is concerned with issues such as student and tutor assumptions and understandings of assignment titles, tutor feedback on students' written work and, for the students themselves, the importance of their own 'identity' as writers rather than simply of skills in becoming an academic writer. The third theme is at a broadly institutional level and concerns the implications of modularity, assessment and university procedures on student writing.

These three themes, focused broadly on students, student–tutor interactions, and the institution, now need to be examined more fully against the changing 'fields of study' and student 'course switching' to which we have referred. All three, we argue, are located in relations of power and authority and are not simply reducible to the skills and competences required for entry to, and success within, the academic community. The current movement away from traditional academic disciplines and subject areas, within which academic staff have conceptualized their own and their students' writing practices, makes a broader perspective critical in understanding the 'problems' being identified in student writing. Without such a perspective, such problems tend to be explained mainly with respect to the students themselves or seen as a consequence of the mass introduction of 'non-traditional' students. From an academic literacies perspective such explanations are limited and will not provide the basis for reflection on learning and teaching in higher education that Dearing (1997) and others are calling for. Exploration of these themes within an academic literacies perspective may provide, we suggest, a fruitful area for research and for teacher training in higher education in the coming years.

3

What Am I Supposed to Make of This? The Messages Conveyed to Students by Tutors' Written Comments

Roz Ivanič, Romy Clark and Rachel Rimmershaw[1]

Introduction

Students receive an immense variety of types of response to their writing, all carrying different messages about university values and beliefs, about the role of writing in learning, about their identity as a student, and about their own competence and even character. It must be very difficult for them to know what they are supposed to make of some of these: how to respond to the responses. Our aim in this chapter is to identify some of the range of ways of responding to student writing, and to reveal some of the messages carried by these different types of response. We hope we will stimulate all tutors who have responsibility for responding to students' writing to evaluate their practices critically, and to recognize the sorts of effects their responses may have on the fledgling writers in their charge.

The data for this paper comprise a selection of responses by tutors to students' writing from those we have collected from two academic settings: our own university in the UK and the communication skills unit in an African university. However, the practices to which we are referring are not confined to the contexts from which these examples are taken, and raise issues of relevance to those concerned with academic literacies in higher education worldwide.

There are five subject tutors who teach a range of subjects within the social sciences at Lancaster University. All the subject tutors have to 'mark' in the sense of 'grade': to write a number to evaluate the work on a given scale. Of the four English for academic purposes (EAP) tutors whose work we refer to, some work in the UK university, others in the African university. The circumstances in which they work (rather than the differences between their institutions) are to some extent responsible for their ways of responding to students' writing. Two of the EAP tutors (A and B) teach compulsory communications skills classes in which the assessment counts towards the students' final degree. In this respect these two EAP tutors are rather like subject tutors, except that they must assess the writing in terms of its success as communication, rather than in terms of what it communicates. Tutor C's situation is similar, in that her course is compulsory and graded. The difference is that she uses the 'process approach' to the teaching of writing, which involves a lot of drafting, discussion and redrafting towards the production of final versions of writing. She sets students academic tasks such as argumentative essays, critical reviews and research papers on 'general domain' topics such as AIDS and pollution. Tutor D, by contrast, works in an academic support programme, running workshops and individual tutorials designed to support students in the writing they are required to do across the university. This provision is not compulsory, but available to any student choosing to take advantage of it. Work undertaken on the academic support programme is not part of the students' accreditation, and consequently is not graded.

The chapter discusses the following aspects of responses to student writing:

• different styles of response;
• the nature and purpose of responses;
• the possible messages students may receive from different types of response;
• implications for subject staff development and for EAP provision.

In each section we will draw attention to differences between subject tutors' and EAP tutors' responses.

Different styles of response

Table 3.1 compares the overall content and style of nine sample responses, selected to cover a wide variety of types of response. It shows that responses vary enormously in quantity. The quantity depends, of course, partly on how much time tutors have. However, we suggest that the amount of time and detail tutors put into their responses to students' work depends primarily on their values, their beliefs about the nature of university education, about the role of writing in learning, and about the role of their responses in all this. They will have developed particular working practices to support these beliefs. Those tutors who give minimal responses perhaps see the task of reading students' writing as largely administrative, and/or do not consider students to have the sort of role in the academic community which merits engaging in dialogue with them. Those who give a lot of feedback must believe that reading and responding to students' work serves more than just administrative purposes. We will develop this idea in the rest of this section and the next.

The tutors' circumstances, values, beliefs and working practices become particularly interesting when we consider the relationship between specific textual comments and general comments, and where the comments were written. Very few subject teachers organize their courses in such a way that they have time to see their students' writing in progress, enormously desirable

Table 3.1 Nine different styles of response to student writing

Tutor	Specific comments	General comments
Subject tutor A	None	A grade only
Subject tutor B	None	Three lines written in black biro at the end of the essay, plus a grade
Subject tutor C	An occasional tick in the margin in red biro	Six lines written in red biro at the end of essay, plus a grade
Subject tutor D	27 numbers on the text in pencil, with hand-written notes in pencil on a separate sheet	Note 27 is a general comment, plus a grade
Subject tutor E	28 numbers on the text in pencil, with word-processed notes on a separate sheet, to be discussed in a tutorial	More than 31 lines at the beginning of the word-processed notes, plus a grade
EAP tutor A: *Communication Skills Course*	None	'Fair' at end
EAP tutor B: *Communication Skills Course*	Several underlinings, wavy lines, arrows, short corrections and remarks, written directly on the student's text in red pen	None
EAP tutor C: *Communication Skills Course: Process Approach*	Exclusively positive comments and suggestions in green pen in the margin of the text and on the tops and bottoms of the pages	About half a page of positive comments and suggestions for development at the end of the text
EAP tutor D: *Academic Support Programme*	Up to 50 numbers on the text in pencil, with matching numbered notes, to be discussed in a tutorial	About four lines in pencil at the end of the numbered comments

though this would be. In all but the rarest of cases, subject tutors are looking at a final product of the writing process, and are reading with the primary aim of grading. This may explain the fact that, on the whole, subject tutors seem to focus more on general comments. All of them put a grade at the end, and all except subject tutor A wrote something to support that grade. Subject tutors vary enormously, however, in whether and how much they respond to the details of what the students have written. Subject tutors A and B appear not to see any purpose in reading and responding to their students' writing other than to contribute to the assessment process. Subject tutors D and E, by contrast, provide a large quantity of numbered responses to the text itself – so many, in fact, that they are written on a separate sheet. The sheer quantity of these specific comments on the text indicates that these tutors believe that they should be engaging with what the students have written, as well as assessing it. The fact that the comments are written on a separate sheet is significant, too. One reason for using a separate sheet is to ensure that the comments are as legible as possible – they are very obviously intended to be read. They have the status of a separate document: a message specifically from the tutor to the student about their work, rather than 'marking' in the sense of 'putting marks on' – defacing? – what the students have written. We suggest that the separate document is more respectful to the students' writing than comments written directly on it.

The four EAP tutors vary enormously in the balance between general and specific comments, and in the place of these comments. EAP tutor B's style is, perhaps, typical of the uncertainty or insecurity on the part of many tutors as to what, exactly, the status or function of their responses is. EAP tutors C and D, by contrast, are working with a very clear view of what they are doing and why. They share the 'during, not after' philosophy associated with the 'process approach' to the teaching of writing (see Freedman 1980 for this philosophy; and Clark and Ivanič 1997, Chapter 4, for discussion of issues associated with this approach). This means that the main purpose of responses is to help students improve their texts, which they will redraft after the tutor has seen them. For EAP tutor C, there is not even any need to 'respect the student's text', as we mentioned when discussing subject tutors D and E, because this text is a rough draft. The responses are part of an ongoing collaboration between tutor and student to produce a good end product: hence the comments and suggestions written in any available space on the text. Tutor C is also working with the philosophy of 'exclusively positive comments', advocated by some 'process approach' theorists and practitioners (see Zak 1990). Even though EAP tutor D is not herself a subject tutor, she makes an enormous number of responses to specific details of content in the text, rather than corrections of its form. This focus on meaning reflects EAP tutor D's belief that coherence is a crucial aspect of academic writing, and that this depends on meaning, not form.

Both subject tutor E and EAP tutor D write their responses with the express intention of discussing them in a one-to-one tutorial with the student writer. By inviting students to discuss their responses, these tutors are giving the message that they do not have the last word on what the student has written: their comments are not final, but part of a dialogue.

The choice of writing implement is interesting, too. In our sample, these include pencil, black biro, green pen, red pen and word processor. It may be over-interpreting to suggest that these choices make a difference, but some things students have said to us indicate that they do. Anything written in pencil suggests tentativeness: it can be discussed, rubbed out, altered. It also suggests trust, even collaboration between student and tutor: the pencil marks are there to help the students rather than to put them in their place. At the other extreme is the red pen. This is conventionally the

symbol of teachers' superior knowledge and their right to make unchallenge-
able judgements. The black biro represents, perhaps, the least difference
between the tutor and the student: they are using the same writing implements; they are on equal terms in a joint project. The word processor
is a new form of technology to use for responding to students' writing. By
using a word processor, subject tutor E shows both consideration for her
students and how important she thinks it is for them to read her detailed
comments. On the face of it the word processor seems to be a relatively
neutral tool for the task. However, some students have recently pointed out
to us that word-processed notes seem formal, fixed and unnegotiable:
they do not have the personal, provisional quality of the pencil-and-rubber
technology.

The nature and purpose of responses

In this section we show how responses can serve many different functions,
both intentionally and unintentionally. We analyse the actual nature and
wording of selected comments by subject tutors B, C, D and E, and by EAP
tutors B and D, reproduced on the following pages. You may like to read
these before moving on to our analysis. We are purposely focusing on
samples which include negative comments, as these allow us to discuss a
wider range of issues.

SUBJECT TUTOR B

General Comment
(1) You make a number of good points but don't really answer the
    question.
(2) You need to pay more attention to the structure of your essays.

SUBJECT TUTOR C

General Comment
(1) This is a very satisfactory essay.
(2) However, your arguments are undermined by the use of the per-
    sonal pronoun.
(3) K . . . M . . . is not an established authority – or not yet, anyway.
(4) Avoid the use of personal pronouns and expressions like 'In my
    view' in all academic work.

SUBJECT TUTOR D

Specific Comments
(1) Unnecessary words.
(2) This paragraph contains many points each of which you could discuss in more detail.
(3) 'and'? These are the same thing!
(4) Whatever 'poetic' means! This is culturally and historically determined.
(5) means the same: avoid unnecessary repetition.
(6) You already asked this qu. in the last para.
(7) This part in brackets needs explaining, Difficult for whom? which dialect(s)?
(8) Good point!
(9) Good to mention values. Here you only talk about the value people place on different types of language; wider social values affect language choice too, e.g. value assigned to woman, different types of work, education . . .
(10) Not quite 'needs'; more 'technology'.
   . . .
(21) No. There is no proof that 'the intelligence and language level' of any social group is higher or lower than any other. Some people just 'fit the system' better than others.
(22) Good point. Not necessarily 'simplifying' here, but moving with the times.
(23) So how can one say the older form had higher 'quality'?
(24) OK, but it's important to separate this argument from the one about language *use*.
   Teaching grammar does not necessarily improve language use.
(25) Important point.
(26) You should show *how* you have used your reading by making references in the text.
(27) There are some good points here, but a lot of confusion too.
   I hope my notes help you to write more clearly.

SUBJECT TUTOR E

General Comment

(1) It is clear that you have considered the topic seriously and you have identified and illustrated three very important ways in which learners encounter frustration.

(2) Moreover you suggest a number of measures that teachers could take to avoid such learner frustration.

(3) I wanted you on occasions to go into more detail about these measures and I feel that, although your analysis stems from your HTS, some of your proposals are more theoretical than they are practical.

(4) I wanted to know more about how you intend to operationalise your ideas.

(5) I think that you rather unfairly make the teacher to be the 'villain' and the 'transgressor' and the learner the aggrieved, innocent 'victim'.

(6) I am thus a bit worried about the balance of your assignment.

(7) I quite agree that it is right and proper that learners' rights and preferred learning strategies are respected but I wonder if you do not somewhat underestimate the onus that is put upon the teacher by the institution and society to build on what learners bring to the classroom in attempting to augment those skills and knowledge.

(8) There are one or two occasions when I find it difficult to follow your logic and sometimes I feel your argument overly relies on an emotional appeal rather than on reflective and considered thought.

(9) However, I suppose we all have such feelings and I feel rather churlish in putting this forward as criticism.

(10) The tricky bit is how to productively turn these feelings into plausible and acceptable action.

(11) A good starting point for more thought.

Specific Comments

(1) Yes, what you claim is true but there's something that makes me feel rather uncomfortable about your opening statement and it's taken me a long time to figure out what I think it is that worries me. I've finally come to the conclusion that it is the juxtaposition of the two issues that you mention. This seems to me to suggest a 'teachers versus learners' scenario. If your intended readership is ELT personnel in your own country then I wonder if they too might not feel somewhat alienated by what amounts to a criticism of teachers.

(2) I'm not sure what you mean by 'full learning'.

(3) Is this a conscious or unconscious action on the part of the learner? If the latter, to what degree should the learner be held

responsible? Similarly, if a teacher unconsciously affects learning adversely, to what degree should s/he be held responsible? Are the two situations comparable in adjudging culpability? An interesting question.

(4) What other things? A new paragraph would be helpful here.

. . .

(23) Yes, this seems unfair.

(24) True but inadequate control of grammar can equally easily lead to communicative breakdown. It doesn't seem productive to put the two in opposition. Maybe better seen as complementary.

(25) Good supporting quote.

(26) Correction of factual content is certainly more prominent in real-life interactions.

(27) I don't think I personally would include this as an 'oral activity'.

(28) Therefore maybe there ought to be a gap between the asking of a question and the response.

EAP TUTOR B

Specific Comments

(1) Puts ? in the margin.

(2) Writes 'Are you sure?' in the margin beside a factual comment.

(3) Crosses out and rewords.

(4) Writes 'incomplete sentence'.

(5) Puts a tick in the margin.

(6) Writes 'who?' above a pronoun.

(7) Puts 'sp' to indicate misspellings.

(8) Writes 'not clear' in the margin.

(9) Puts a wavy line in the margin.

EAP TUTOR D

Specific Comments

(1) Great contextualization!

(2) Good, you tell your reader your intentions but the last part is vague, I think. I'd like to know a bit about your line of argument.

(3) Not sure what you mean here.

(4) Interesting! I didn't know that.

(5) Any concrete examples?

(6) Not sure why you're telling me this here.

(7) Why not 'I'?

(8) By whom, when, where, and why?
(9) All your own thoughts?
(10) Do you want to avoid sexist language?
(11) Doesn't this contradict what you said on page 2?
(12) Yes, but you haven't said WHY.
(13) Why are you passivizing?
(14) Is this the best tense here?

General Comment
I found this very interesting and learned a lot!
With a bit more work – mainly *explaining* your arguments – this should be fine, as far as I (a non-expert) can tell.

We propose that responses fall into the following six categories:

- explain the grade in terms of strengths and weaknesses;
- correct or edit the student's work;
- evaluate the match between the student's essay and an 'ideal' answer;
- engage in dialogue with the student;
- give advice which will be useful in writing the next essay;
- give advice on rewriting the essay.

Of course, we cannot be sure that the tutors themselves would agree with our analysis, nor for that matter that the students who received these comments will have read them all in the way we do here. Ziv (1984) has suggested that students often interpret 'interested response' comments as evaluations.

Explain the grade in terms of strengths and weaknesses

This function appears in all the subject tutors' comments, for reasons we have already discussed. Table 3.2 summarizes the way in which the subject tutors' comments explain the grades.

All the tutors are making both positive and negative comments, although paying far more attention to the negative – perhaps to ensure the students know the weaknesses of their work so that they do not challenge a relatively low grade. The key difference between subject tutors B and C on the one hand, and D and E on the other, is that D and E indicate *precisely* what was strong or weak. For example, subject tutor D's student knows that what she wrote at point 8 is one of the good points mentioned in comment 27, whereas subject tutor B's student only knows that she 'made a number of good points', but does not know which they were.

It is particularly interesting to contrast subject tutor E with all the others in the way they worded their comments. Subject tutor E is the only one who

Table 3.2   Focus on justifying grades in subject tutors' comments

Subject tutor	Parts of response which have the function of justifying grades
B	The first sentence
C	The whole comment
D	Most of the comments carry this function: comments 1, 2, 3, 4, 5, 6, 7, 9, 10, 21, 23, 24, 26, 27 all function to justify a *low* grade
E	The whole of the general comment, and most of the detailed comments carry this function

phrased his comments explicitly as his personal view. He used the words 'I' and 'me' 21 times in this extract from his comments, particularly in the overall comment, and in detailed comment 1. He makes his evaluations subjective by using expressions such as:

> I find it difficult to follow your logic
> I wanted to know
> I'm not sure what you mean by
> I wonder
> I don't think I personally would
> I feel
> This seems to me to suggest

The EAP tutors in our sample do not put a grade on the work to which they are responding. EAP tutor B will, eventually, be required to recommend a grade on the basis of this draft, but at this point she does not want to give an indication of what that grade might be. In so far as they pass judgement at all, it is to give indications of what *might* affect their grade, and to encourage the writers by indicating the positive features of what they have written. EAP tutor D, particularly, makes sure that she includes very positive comments alongside any suggestions for improvement.

Evaluate the match between the student's essay and an 'ideal' answer

This function and the next are both based on the underlying belief that the tutor is the arbiter of what is right. Under this heading we focus on the sorts of thing which are particularly the prerogative of subject tutors to judge.

There is, we suggest, a continuum from the sort of academic assignment which clearly has an ideal answer to the sort of open-ended assignment in which a wide range of answers are possible. The majority of assignments in the social sciences are probably at the open-ended pole of the continuum: this is certainly the case for the assignments in our sample. However, even for open-ended assignments, tutors often indicate that what the student has written falls short in some way of what they would have judged as 'good' or 'ideal'. Subject tutor B gives a hint that there is an ideal way of answering, if not an ideal answer, by writing '[you] don't really answer the question'. There are some hints in subject tutor D's response: comments 21 and 24 are telling the student what she should have written on these specific topics, and comment 26 is telling her something about how she should have written the essay. Subject tutor E also indicates what would have pleased him more: notice the expressions in his general comments 'I wanted you . . . to go into more detail' (sentence 3) and 'I wanted to know more about' (sentence 4). In his detailed comment 28 he indicates what he would have judged as 'correct' or 'good' when he writes 'Therefore maybe there ought to be . . .'. These all show the student that there was something different she might have written which would have been better in the tutor's eyes.

The scare quotes around the word 'ideal' signal that there is no 'ideal' answer in social science and humanities writing assignments. But a given tutor might have strong views about what to expect in a good assignment, and in such cases students who want a good mark need to put some effort into sussing out how their tutor would answer their own question, what the tutor's ideas, preferences and 'obsessions' are (Rimmershaw 1993).

Correct or edit the student's work

Compared with the two previous categories, very few of the subject tutors' comments in our sample are aimed at correcting or editing the student's work: perhaps only subject tutor D's comment 3, and subject tutor E's comment 4. EAP tutor B, however, is clearly focusing on this function. All except, perhaps, the first comment are corrections. We do not want to suggest that this observation on our sample represents a clear distinction between the aims and purposes of subject tutors and of EAP tutors. It is, in fact, quite common to find subject tutors who see it as their business to edit and correct students' work as well as justifying grades, but we have not included any in our sample. Similarly, there are many EAP tutors who do *not* see this as their primary aim when responding to students' work: EAP tutor D is an example.

Engage in dialogue with the student

Although this sounds as if it should be the major function of tutors' responses, we have found it to be surprisingly rare. Subject tutor D shows an interest in engaging in debate over content with the student, but it is always couched in terms of a veiled or outright disagreement with what she has written. Her comments 4, 7, 9, 21, 22 and 23 all engage with the content of what the student has written, but they are full of indications that what she put in the first place was insufficient, controversial or wrong.

There is plenty of evidence in subject tutor E's comments that he sees engaging in debate with the student as one of his aims. In his general comments, the expressions 'I wanted you . . . to go into more detail' (sentence 3), 'I wanted to know more about, (sentence 4) and 'I wonder if you do not somewhat underestimate' (sentence 7) all invite further discussion. His detailed comments 1, 3 and 24 are long and thus contributions to dialogue, focusing on his reaction as a reader (comment 1) and on other possible ways of seeing the issues (comments 3 and 24). Comments 3 and 4 include questions: the hallmark of open-endedness.

EAP tutor D's comments also contain lots of questions (comments 5, 8, 9, 10, 11, 13, 14). She engages with the student in dialogue about content, but to a lesser extent than subject tutor E and in a rather different way. Her comments 2, 4, 8 and 11 are all asking for elaboration and elucidation of the content from the perspective of an interested reader rather than an informed subject specialist. However, she also engages in discussion with the writer about linguistic choices and matters of presentation and form: her comments 7, 9, 10, 13 and 14 are examples of this.

EAP tutor D's comment 3 is particularly interesting as an example of engaging in dialogue with the student. She comments 'Not sure what you mean here', asking the student what she meant, rather than making a correction based on what she assumed she meant. She is simply identifying a part which she did not understand and leaving the question of whether and how it needs to be improved open to discussion. This contrasts strongly with subject tutor D's comment 5, 'Means the same: avoid unnecessary repetition' and EAP tutor B's practice of crossing out and rewording the student's writing. It is all too common for tutors to correct or edit student's work on the basis of their assumptions; far more productive, and less dangerous, we suggest, to take the view that students usually *are* trying to mean something, that we do not necessarily know what that intended meaning is, that our job is to find out what it is and help them find a way of expressing it (see Zamel 1985).

Give advice which will be useful in writing the next essay

Some subject tutors' comments very explicitly have this aim. Subject tutor B's second sentence, 'You need to pay more attention to the structure of your essays', and subject tutor C's last sentence, 'Avoid the use of personal pronouns and expressions like "In my view" in all academic work', are typical cases of this. They are giving blanket statements of advice about what the student must do to improve next time. One of the problems with this is that advice such as subject tutor B's does not give any indication of *how* the student is to achieve what he is recommending. Another problem is that the advice that one tutor gives may not apply when writing for another tutor. Subject tutor C's advice contradicts what other tutors actually accept in the same department.

In addition, some comments can be used as advice for future essays, even if not phrased as such. For example, several of subject tutor D's negative comments could be interpreted in ways which are sufficiently general as to constitute advice for writing a future essay. Obvious examples are comments 1, 5 and 26 – criticisms of this essay which amount to guidelines to be followed for all essays. The EAP tutors do not make any overt mention of learning from this essay for the future. However, several of their comments can be associated with general advice; most of EAP tutor D's comments could be translated into a checklist of things for the learner to consider in many places in many essays, for example:

1. Be sure to contextualize.
2. Tell your reader your intentions, and your line of argument.
5. Give concrete examples to back up your arguments.
6. Ask yourself: why this now? – ensure it is clear to the reader why you have included a particular point in a particular place.
10. Decide your position on sexist language and stick to it.
12. Where you put forward an argument or point of view, say WHY you think this way.
13. If you use a passive, be sure there is a reason.

Give advice on rewriting this essay

All the EAP tutors in our sample are responding to drafts of essays, and the comments of EAP tutors B and D function explicitly as advice on rewriting the essay. By contrast, none of the subject tutors in our sample were responding to drafts of essays, so strictly speaking this category is irrelevant for them. However, subject tutors sometimes respond *as if* the student were going to rewrite the essay. Subject tutor D's comments 7 and 10, and subject tutor E's detailed comment 4 appear to be giving advice on improving this essay, but it was in fact the final version. This kind of advice – very specific, but too late – is very common. Specific advice on one essay can only be useful for writing the next (probably quite different) one if the student is able to generalize from it.

Conclusion

We suggest that tutors' overarching purpose in responding to student writing has a powerful shaping effect on the nature of their comments. Even though the comments by subject tutors D and E, and those by EAP tutor D, are similar in style (as we pointed out earlier), there is a striking contrast in the particular way they are worded. This can be explained, we suggest, by the fact that the subject tutors must, in the last resort, use their comments to justify their grades, whereas the EAP tutor has the more developmental aim of helping the student rewrite her essay.

An implication of our study is that tutors do not always give a great deal of thought to what they are attempting to achieve through their responses to students' writing. Some are neglecting the opportunity to fulfil some of the possible functions. Some are slipping from one function to another, without signalling as much to the student. Looking at this from the point of view of the students on the receiving end, we do indeed wonder what they are supposed to make of it. It is not surprising that they find such responses confusing, do not appreciate their purposes and are unable to benefit fully from them.

The possible messages students may receive from different types of response

Turner's (1993) study of students' reactions to feedback at Lancaster University suggests that most students do try to make sense of the responses they receive. He found that, while some students felt daunted by detailed comments, others were frustrated by brief ones. They often complained that they do not receive enough feedback, that what they get is not comprehensive enough, that it is not helpful, not legible, or not timely. Some students talked about feeling 'validated' by detailed responses, and saw that they allowed useful learning, even though it was specific to a particular piece of writing. So, while there will be strong individual differences, it is safest to assume that the majority of students value feedback, and that providing nothing more than grades deprives them of a valuable learning opportunity. Studies by Radecki and Swales (1988), Cohen and Cavalcanti (1990), and Leki (1990) provide further evidence and discussion of this.

If students are going to take their tutors' responses seriously, then it matters very much what they contain. We will consider here what messages might be conveyed to students by different types of response: messages about themselves; messages about the function of academic essay writing; and messages about the values and beliefs which underpin universities as institutions.

Messages about themselves

The ideology of educational institutions in most countries is that tutors are superior to students, and everything tutors write will inevitably be affected by this power differential. Unless they take positive action to challenge this belief (their own and their students') that they are superior, their comments, like everything else they do, will reproduce and reinforce it. Like all ideologies, this effect works insidiously, below the level of consciousness: not all tutors intend to reinforce their positions of power over students.

As a result of the power differential, whatever the tutors' intentions, students are likely to read their responses for possible evaluations of themselves.

Not only that, but they are also likely to expect negative evaluations, and to interpret many tutors' comments to mean 'What you wrote is inadequate' and, by extension 'You are inadequate'. All comments which can possibly lead to this interpretation therefore have the potential to undermine students, to sap their confidence, to increase their sense of inferiority. The students interviewed by Turner (1993) revealed how discouraging feed back affected their self-esteem, their confidence and their whole approach to a course.

Ideally, tutors' comments could help to build students' sense of membership of the academic community, rather than emphasizing their role on the margins of it or, worse, seeming to exclude them from it. Carefully worded responses can encourage students, and give them a sense that what they are writing is valued. Subject tutor E and EAP tutor D both seem to be attempting to do this.

Messages about academic writing

The very fact that tutors grade what students have written conveys messages about it: that student writing is an object to be measured, that writing is the only way, or at least an important way, of proving our knowledge, intelligence and effort, and that tutors have the sole right and responsibility for assessment. But these are not necessary characteristics of student writing. Writing can be used for purposes other than assessment, such as ungraded communication among students and tutors; and students can show their capabilities by other means and media. Forms of collaborative assessment can be introduced in which students have roles, rights and responsibilities in the feedback and evaluation process.

Even while writing is being used as a means of assessment, the way tutors respond to it can convey messages about its value and functions.

- By giving only a grade or evaluation, as subject tutor A and EAP tutor A did, tutors give the firm message that writing is no more than an object to be measured. This message can be counteracted by any form of response beyond a grade or evaluation.
- Focusing on form rather than content, as EAP tutor B did, conveys the message that grammatical accuracy and appropriateness are the qualities which matter most in writing. By contrast, focusing on what students have to say, as subject tutors D and E and EAP tutors C and D did, conveys the message that writing is about meaning-making.
- By giving mainly evaluative comments, tutors reinforce the view that students' academic writing is an imperfect version of professional academic writing. But they are not responding to it in the way they respond to the writing of their professional peers. In contrast, when they respond with questions and contributions to dialogue with the student, tutors construct student writing as part of ongoing communication between people interested in the same issues and questions.

- Evaluative comments also convey the message that tutors are arbiters of writing standards. This is just as true of positive evaluations, such as EAP tutor C's, as it is of negative evaluations. Even if tutors do have to take this role in relation to student writing, they may want also to be seen as assistants in writing development – and this does not only apply to EAP tutors.

Messages about university values and beliefs

Styles of response differ in the messages they convey about the values and beliefs which operate within the institution. Tutors' responses to students' writing can convey the message that values and beliefs are absolute, culturally specific, or functional. Some present conventions as absolute values of the academic community as a whole – comments such as 'Don't use "in my view" in academic work'. Others present conventions as determined by disciplinary or departmental culture – comments such as 'In history we don't . . .'. Yet others present conventions as determined by 'neutral' functional considerations – comments such as 'A new para would be helpful here'.

Tutors comments convey messages about students' and tutors' roles and relationships, about the nature of knowledge, and about academic conventions and orthodoxies. As we have shown, different types of response reveal different beliefs about the role of a student in the academic community, ranging from being a fully-fledged member with authority and knowledge-making rights, to being on the margins, scarcely a member of the community at all. There are also varying messages about the relations of power and status between students and tutors. Comments can foreground the inequality which results from tutors' roles as assessors, as subject tutors A–D do. Alternatively, they can foreground collaborative aspects of the tutor–student contract, as EAP tutor D's comments do.

Some responses give the impression that there are right and wrong answers, right and wrong perspectives, or right and wrong views – some of subject tutor D's comments are good examples of this. Such comments convey an objective view of knowledge. The alternative is for tutors to value and pay due consideration to students' views, and to phrase their own views in the first person, as subject tutor E and EAP tutor D do. These responding practices represent knowledge as subjective. Comments can reveal beliefs about the relative value of knowledge and wisdom: whether the work of academics is to create and reproduce a body of knowledge and information, or to analyse and discuss issues with wisdom and understanding. Most of the detailed responses in our sample value wisdom and understanding rather than knowledge, with the possible exception of subject tutor D's. More specifically, comments contain covert messages about such things as what counts as sufficient justification for a particular point, what counts as an acceptable argument, what counts as an adequate explanation. These micro-messages are more likely to be discipline-specific, but some may be framed as values of the academic community as a whole.

More generally, responses can also convey ideological messages about the extent to which the institution is monolithically authoritative or open to diversity and change. We suggest that responses which do not admit or encourage alternative content and/or forms have the covert effect of valuing orthodoxy. They suggest that the institution is omnipotent and unassailable. By contrast, responses which leave matters of content and/or form open to question support an ideology of pluralism and the possibility of change.

Some suggestions for improving the feedback process

The main implication of what we have been discussing is that success at university involves a great deal more than just 'skills'. Students need a great deal more than a 'tool kit' in order to find out the values and practices of universities, and to locate themselves within them (see Clark and Ivanič 1997, especially Chapter 4).

Implications for subject staff development

We are all reluctant to make changes in our work practices unless we can find 'meaning' in the changes (Fullan 1991). Any programme of staff development needs to be sensitive to tutors' concerns about what their role is in the institution, about their workload, about what students most need help with in writing. It needs to address their beliefs (for example, about their role as educators), their values (for example, about what is worth their while to spend time on), and their understandings (for example, about the nature of the writing process) and not just their practices: not just what they do, but why they believe that they do it in that way. So, for example, if tutors say that they believe students already know how to write essays, or they would not have gained a place in higher education, workshops could explore tutors' own experiences of learning to write, and the difficulties they faced on the road to academic community membership. If tutors say they feel under pressure to prioritize research and publication, and that giving detailed feedback on student writing would take more time than they could spare, workshops could encourage them to look at the functions of what they currently do, and/or at the use which students are able to make of the kinds of comments and markings put on their work. This could lead them to find things they will do less of, or even stop doing at all.

In our experience, staff could benefit from being made more aware of the issues raised in this paper. The following are some points which are particularly worth emphasizing on staff development courses:

- Give thought to the quality, quantity and timeliness of feedback – if necessary, change the way you run the course so as to be able to give more and better feedback at times when the students can use it. Possibly set fewer essays and respond to drafts as well as to final versions.

- Demystify criteria for assessment before students write their assignments.
- Treat student writing as communication by engaging in debate with students about what they write, not just correcting or evaluating it.
- Think about the effect of where you write the comments and the writing implements you use: consider changing your practices if necessary.
- Recognize the messages which feedback is giving to students about themselves, about writing, and about university values and beliefs, and think about alternative styles and wordings of your responses.
- Recognize the value of giving positive as well as negative comments wherever you can, and of including non-judgmental questions and statements in your responses.
- Notice the difference it makes if you phrase your comments in the first person, showing that they are personal views, not objective truths.
- Whenever possible, follow written feedback with oral discussion in tutorials.

Implications for EAP provision

All the points listed above are relevant to EAP tutors when they respond to student writing. In addition, EAP tutors might develop courses which help students to become 'ethnographers' of the new communities they are entering (see Clark 1992; 1993; Clark and Ivanič 1991; Clark *et al.* 1990). This would include helping them to develop strategies for finding out what criteria will be operating in the assessment of their writing, what styles of response their tutors use, and what they are supposed to make of them. One way of doing this is for students to look at past essays from particular courses, respond to and 'evaluate' them, and then look at and discuss the tutor's comments and evaluation.

The kinds of comments we have identified from both subject tutors and EAP tutors suggest that much useful feedback can be given on writing *as communication* by an interested reader without drawing on subject expertise, so EAP tutors could build on this by facilitating peer feedback on student writing. Not only could this approach reduce the time involved in one-to-one work, it would also send messages about community membership and ownership of conventions to students who participate.

EAP tutors need to do a great deal more than just judging students' writing as right or wrong by some mythical criteria of communicative competence. It is important to recognize variety in academic practices: those of us working in this area should be concerned with the actual tasks which students are currently engaged in, and should examine these practices critically, both for ourselves and with our students.

EAP tutors might also try to encourage students themselves to demand more, better and more timely feedback. Work with students focusing on how to obtain the kind of feedback they think they need might be an important way of handing some of the choices about feedback back to those who will use it. As one of the undergraduate students referred to earlier put it (in Rimmershaw 1993):

> After all, tutors often express what they expect from their students in terms of length, references, presentation of essays, so should we not be able to express our needs in terms of responding to our work?

Note

1. The ideas in this chapter originated in an activity conducted by Rachel at Lancaster University in which a group of undergraduate students analysed some tutors' comments as a class activity. Rachel then presented some of the issues and outcomes to the Teaching of Writing Group. Romy and Roz developed these into a workshop for a colloquium at the Communication Skills Unit, University of Dar es Salaam. We are grateful to the students involved, other members of the Teaching of Writing Group and colleagues in Dar for their contributions to the development of these ideas.

Part 2

New Forms of Writing in
Specific Course Contexts

4

Computer Conferencing: New Possibilities for Writing and Learning in Higher Education

Mary R. Lea

Introduction

Within today's higher education moves towards teaching on-line are becoming increasingly common. Computer conferencing is now being used in both distance learning and more traditional university settings. Although there is a substantial body of research which is concerned with computer conferencing and student learning (Mason and Kaye 1989; Mason 1993; O'Connell 1994) it appears that very little is known, as yet, about the nature of these written texts from a linguistic perspective and, more particularly, the relationship between students' use of computer conferencing and their assessed written work. In these new learning domains both students and tutors are having to become familiar with new ways of constructing knowledge through writing. In this chapter I hope to explore the part that this new form of written communication might play in student learning. I do this by examining a number of different conceptual frames to help gain a greater understanding of the relationship between knowledge, language form and the genre conventions involved in learning. I conclude with some implications of exploring these texts for practitioners who are interested in using computer conferencing in their own course design, delivery and assessment.

The research reported upon here is less concerned with the collaborative and social nature of learning than with the part that conference interactions can play in the construction and negotiation of academic knowledge. It draws on data from two different Open University courses and builds upon other work which has examined the complexity of academic literacy practices in higher education (Giesler 1994; Stierer 1997; Lea and Street 1998). Other authors in this volume explore the notion that academic literacy practices are central to the construction of academic knowledge (Baynham, Chapter 1; Pardoe, Chapter 8; McMillan, Chapter 9; Stierer, Chapter 11). I draw on a similar theoretical perspective in order to examine learning in these new environments and suggest that we need to understand more about the kinds of literacy practices that students engage with when they are using computer conferencing for learning. In other words, what kind of writing is this, what kinds of relationships between tutors and students are implicated in this writing, and what part is it playing in the process of learning and teaching?

Computer conferencing is being used by academic staff in higher education in a number of different ways. It can be an integral part of course design where the course is actually delivered on-line, either completely or partially: in this instance students have no choice about whether to contribute to the conference or not. Alternatively, tutors may set up a computer conference to provide a forum where students may discuss both academic and more general issues with other students on the course and with the tutor. In this case contributing to the conference may be an optional activity for students. Conferencing can also be used by tutors as the main way of discussing academic issues and giving feedback to students – for example, postgraduate research students studying at a distance. The way in which a conference is being used will depend in part upon the nature of the course and whether it is being delivered in a face-to-face or distance situation. I concentrate here upon two distance learning courses being delivered by the Open University, UK. These courses have been chosen as exemplars because they embed rather different and contrasting academic content and contexts.

A423: Philosophical Problems of Equality is a fourth-level (equivalent to final year) undergraduate philosophy course, in which students are required to use computer conferencing as part of their studies. Students access the conference via First Class, a closed intranet system. Some face-to-face tutorial support is also available. Students have access to their own tutor group conference, and this includes particular sub-conferences on each written assignment. Students are encouraged to make contributions concerning their course to their tutor's conference, in a sense mimicking a face-to-face seminar. As one tutor put it when interviewed:

> The idea is that the conference should be a substitution for the academic discussion that students would get in a traditional university. The idea of the discussion is to test students' understandings and to try out the construction of philosophical arguments.

Students also have access to a national conference for A423 and to a 'Philosophers' chat' area for all philosophy students in the Open University. The main body of the course is delivered through traditional print-based course materials, and it is quite possible for students to follow and complete the course without making any conference contributions.

H802: Applications of Information Technology in Open and Distance Education is a rather different course to A423. It is a module of the Open University's MA in open and distance learning and it is delivered primarily via the Web. This course uses a Web-based electronic bulletin board system for conferencing, and the conferencing is used as a major site of learning for participants on the course. Students are divided into four different tutor groups, with tutors acting as 'facilitators'. Unlike traditional print-based distance learning courses, students on this course have little in the way of ready-prepared printed material. Instead they have access to Web-based resources and links to other suggested Web sites. Students on this course are expected to make their own contributions in terms of other relevant Web-based course materials. Additionally, as an integral part of the course, students are required to show evidence of their use of conferencing when writing their assignments. The course guide suggests that:

> The amount of time you will spend reading set material is much reduced from normal OU courses, and the amount of time you will spend in practical activities, on-line interaction, collaborative work and Web searching is much increased.
>
> . . . working in this way is different from learning through studying traditional print materials.

New forms of text

Goodman and Graddol (1996) explore the increasing use and importance of multimodal texts which, unlike traditional written texts, 'use devices from more than one semiotic mode of communication simultaneously'. Writing and images, pictures and photographs for example, are brought together in one text, and making sense of the text involves the reader in making sense of, and creating meaning from, all the different parts of the complete text. Goodman and Graddol suggest that such texts are becoming increasingly important in global communications. In the two courses being reported upon here, in order to make the most appropriate use of these new learning environments, students have to learn how to negotiate what are usefully described as multimodal texts. They have to use a knowledge of both visual and written codes in order to become successful participants in these conference settings.

Figure 4.1 illustrates the relationship between these two codes. It shows the conference desktop which uses the Open University's First Class intranet conference system. Students enter the tutor conference for their tutor on A423 by clicking on the appropriate icon – for example, *A423 Ian's conference*. Additionally they can enter a number of other general conference areas where they can communicate with students and tutors from other tutor groups – for example, *A423 Equality*. *Philosophers' Chat* (the icon for which does not appear directly on this desktop) is designated for non-academic matters, not directly related to the substantive content of the course. Below these icons, representing different 'areas' of the course, students and tutors make their contributions. Clicking on the message icons to the left of the contributor's name enables participants to read or reply

Figure 4.1   A423 conference desktop

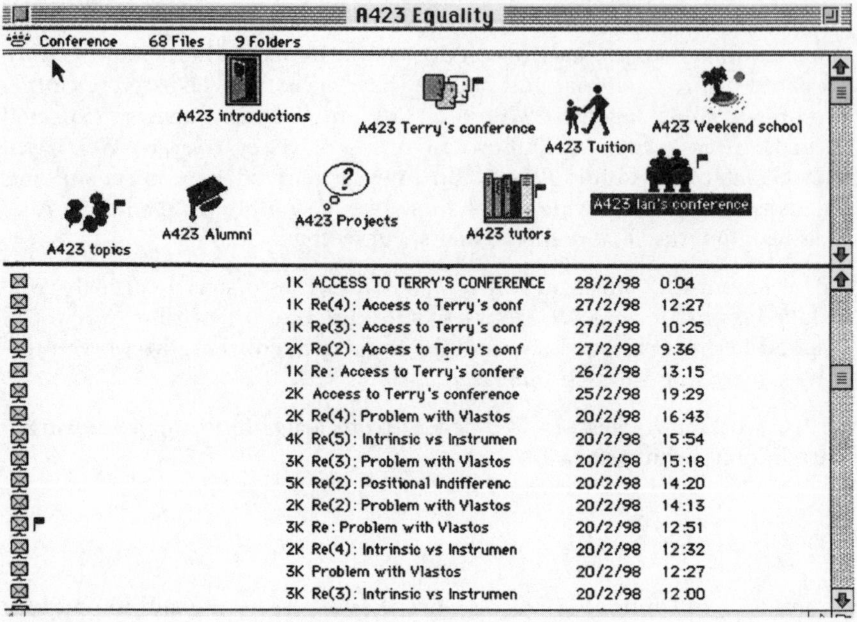

to messages (for the purposes of anonymity, the participants' names have been removed).

Figure 4.2 shows the plenary area for H802. It, too, has its own designated tutor group spaces and a plenary discussion area for general course issues; students can also contribute to the 'Café' on more social/chat issues. Notice the welcome message from one of the course tutors.

At first sight these created spaces may appear neutral and arbitrary, merely a place within which written communication can take place between students and students, or students and tutors. But the organization of the conference in terms of different virtual spaces and rooms has important implications, not just in terms of where knowledge is being constructed, but also what kind of knowledge it is. Participants have choices to make about where to post messages – in which space or room. Students and tutors can take on a number of different roles and identities depending upon the choices that they make around time and space: when to post, where, how and to whom. They may choose to compose a detailed message off-line or make an immediate response to a posting. The conference structure results in participants engaging in a variety of practices; these practices have implications for the kind of knowledge that is eventually recorded as a conference contribution, and, therefore, result in knowledge being codified within the conference setting. If students feel confident that their contribution is academically valid they will choose to 'post' in the tutor conference. They

Figure 4.2 H802 plenary area

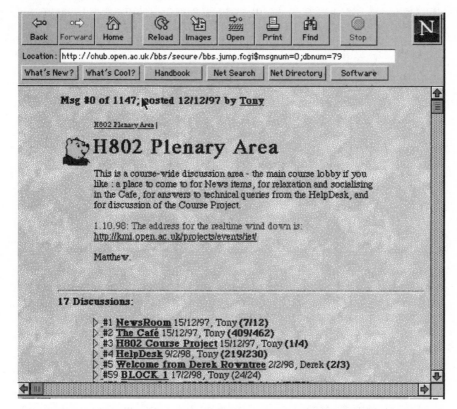

may then decide whether the contribution is more suitable for a 'space' reserved for messages around written assignments or the general tutor conference. Alternatively they may not feel confident about making postings to the tutor conference and post to the national *A423 Equality* conference which ensures that their contribution is not directed at their own individual tutor. The interface can, therefore, be used to recreate something akin to the contexts that speakers normally depend upon to make sense of everyday face-to-face conversation. The spaces constructed within the conferences reflect the different contexts that speakers naturally 'read off' in everyday conversation. They also reflect the different relationships of power and authority that are embedded in academic settings, particularly the relationships between tutors and students.

In a different context, that of spoken language, Dell Hymes's work focuses on the 'ethnography of communication'. His analysis is valuable, however, when exploring the written texts of computer conferences. Hymes (1994) illustrates the importance of the speech community, the speech situation, the speech event and the speech act. He suggests that we need to be concerned with speakers' shared contextualized knowledge of the different elements that go to make up a speech act, including: setting; scene; purposes; channels; norms of interaction and interpretation; genres. To get a more complete picture of the part that contributing to the conference might play in student learning and ultimately to assessed writing, it is useful to draw on Hymes's analysis and consider participation in the conference as 'a communicative event on-line'. Hymes is primarily concerned with the interactional and contextual features of communication. He suggests that an 'ethnography of communication' is essential in understanding language use and that we should not separate off different elements of language usage for research purposes. It is always important to focus upon the use of language in the complete context:

> One must take as context a community, or network of persons, investigating its communicative activities as a whole, so that any use of channel and code takes its place as a part of the resources upon which the members draw.
>
> (Hymes 1994: 11)

Following from Hymes, it is therefore important to explore all the different elements of the conference, including interactions not recorded by the conference transcript. If we do not do this, and concentrate upon the written conference transcript itself, we run the risk of mistaking this record for evidence of the whole learning process. Jones (1998) cautions against this and refers to the use of private email between students or from student to tutor, which is not recorded in the conference history. In this instance we can regard this use of one-to-one email as a literacy practice and could usefully explore the role that it might play in the learning process.

Once we start to regard participation in the conference as a 'communicative event on-line' – evidence of communication within a 'speech' or 'discourse' community – then we can begin to examine the ways in which students have to engage with a whole range of different practices – evidence of which is not always recorded – in order to become successful participants in the conference. Research carried out on the two courses outlined above included both in-depth telephone interviews at the end of the course and on-line 'interviews' with students throughout their course about their use of conferencing. This has given a level of interpretation beyond merely looking at conference postings and message histories and, therefore, has enabled a more complete understanding of the different practices that are involved in the construction of academic knowledge. For example, students on all courses report the need to print off conference contributions so that they can highlight and annotate these written texts in ways which feel more familiar to them. Additionally, most do not make immediate responses to conference postings but need time to reflect before preparing a contribution off-line, with all that entails in terms of redrafting and editing texts, before the final considered 'product' is put up on the conference.

Developing academic knowledge

I return now to the idea that computer conference postings reflect the different relationships of power and authority that are embedded in academic settings. Cooper and Selfe (1990) suggest that computer conferences, as new environments for learning, support the development of an 'internally persuasive discourse', and that this allows students to use writing in the conference as a way of 'thinking against' conventional academic discourses. In this way students can resist the normative function of academic discourse and therefore have the opportunity to challenge teacher-centred hegemony. Cooper and Selfe (1990) focus upon the importance of talking and writing as a way of coming to terms with theories and concepts raised in their course – a writing course for undergraduates. By introducing their own perspectives in conferencing, students are able to resist academic positioning. This idea of a move away from the traditional role of teacher as expert is evidenced in much of the broader literature on the use of computer conferencing; the new role of the tutor is as facilitator.

The evidence from the interviews with students on A423 would suggest that whether such a shift takes place depends very much upon the academic context of the course and the kind of model of teaching and learning that is being adopted in the course. Although computer conferencing tends to be presented both as a homogenous genre (Yates 1996) and as having a set of characteristics which enable the breaking down of traditional relationships in learning contexts (Mason and Kaye 1989), this research points to a more complex scenario. The philosophy students reported that they valued tutor contributions more highly than contributions from other students; they tended to ignore messages from other students in preference to the authoritative postings of their tutor. This may have been because the conference here was, in effect, designed to replicate face-to-face tutorial support. In H802 no such comments were made by students in their interviews: contributions from other students were rated as highly as those from tutors. A number of different factors may account for the contrast. The latter was a postgraduate course and students were encouraged to be authoritative in their contributions; tutors made a conscious attempt to act as facilitators rather than 'knowledge holders'. The academic content of this course – its theoretical knowledge base – is, arguably, still in its infancy, and the received body of wisdom is still being actively constructed; many references are made to Web-based resources which are regarded as equally valid as referenced printed texts. There is therefore a very real contrast between both the academic content and the context of these two courses and, arguably, the institutional relationships of power and authority between students and tutors which are embedded in both course design and course materials. In part, these relationships would seem to be a determining factor as to whether students are really able to challenge teacher-centred hegemony as Cooper and Selfe (1990) suggest. Even on H802, students expressed concern about the lack of contributions from their tutors, despite the fact that tutors were acting as facilitators. Not surprisingly, since tutors are responsible for marking written assignments, they are still regarded as 'knowledge holders' even if their contributions are, on the face of it, not valued more highly than those from other participants.

Work on written academic genres by Berkenkotter and Huckin (1995) suggests that such genres embed very complex relationships of power and authority between different members of academic communities; that these are far from static but remain shifting and dynamic. Cooper and Selfe (1990) argue that using conferencing provides students with opportunities to resist a particular interpretation of facts. They seem to be suggesting that it is the conference genre *per se* which results in the breaking down of more traditional relationships between students and tutors. Evidence from the conferences on the two courses studied here would suggest that such opportunities, if they exist, do not reside in one homogeneous conference genre. The different genre types are a result of the relationship between the academic content and context of the course and the ways in which the technology is being used in a particular setting. In other words, it is not the use of conferencing itself which enables students to develop the internally persuasive discourse that Cooper and Selfe value so highly. Equally import-ant are the actual and realized relationships between tutors and students that are embedded within the conference, and these may well depend upon more traditional institutional university roles and expectations being taken up by both tutors and students.

Whether we are doing more than replicating traditional ways of learning in conference settings depends upon the learning environments that are being created within any particular course. Inevitably, these new environ-ments replicate some aspects of traditional forms of learning since they are still reflecting institutional structures – and therefore practices – which have not been replaced just because students are now using conferencing as part of their learning. As I have indicated, the philosophy course appears to replicate what we might consider to be a more traditional model of tutor-led learning; the conference seems to provide students with a structure that has similarities with a face-to-face tutorial. The tutor often makes a definitive comment on a topic under discussion or 'sets the record straight' if students appear to have misunderstood a philosophical concept:

> I think what Janet is saying is that Rawl's principle of equal prospects for equal abilities contradicts his differing principle. The latter says we should do whatever makes things best for the worst off. But doing that might in some circumstances, involve not doing anything to equalise prospects at all. In other words, his equal opportunity principle might rule out what his difference principle requires. So either, in such a situation, he does what the difference principle requires, and breaks the equal opportunity principle (this is the sentence in the Study Guide beginning 'The arguments supporting . . .') or he ensures fair equality of opportunity but thus breaks the difference principle (this is what

the last sentence says – in such circumstances, arranging for equal prospects would make things worse for the worst off than they would otherwise be, and could only be justified on grounds of desert which Rawls wants to exclude from determining the allocation of resources).

Does this help make the point clearer?

In contrast, in H802 the tutors act as facilitators and their presence on the conference is much less apparent. Conference contributions encourage the students to be self-reflective learners working directly with their peers:

> Sorry to be slow off the mark in setting up Activity 2. Here are the guidelines I suggest. 1. The aim of the activity is to investigate the experience of 'searching as learning'. Please read the printed course guide and the online description of the activity. The underlying question is, 'When or under what circumstances is searching learning?' 2. It will be quite a challenging exercise in collaboration, as there is a fair amount of liaising to be done in order to finish the activity on time. So, I recommend we retain the same groupings as in Activity 3 of Block 1, and I will assign new roles. 3. Here is a plan of the task with suggested people assigned to roles. Please email me if you have objections to what I have proposed.

Because the conference structure is designed to be student-driven, the written genres of the conference appear to reflect the academic content of the course: an innovative course about learning and technology which in some senses challenges traditional academic concerns.

I am adopting here a similar methodological stance to previous work on academic literacy and academic written genres as evidenced in this volume (Ivanič *et al.*, Chapter 3; Stierer, Chapter 11) and, therefore, make distinctions not merely between academic content but between the different written contexts within which conferencing is being used for learning by students and tutors, and the different practices that are associated with these contexts. Different conference genres reflect the different positions and identities being taken up by tutors and students within the particular conference. Students are making use of these learning environments in their own ways, resulting in specific practices associated with their learning; adopting different practices results in the production of contrasting texts. The conference sites in the two courses focused upon here embed very different academic content in terms of the subject areas and disciplinary genres that are being drawn upon, and being created, by both tutors and students. The academic content of A423 is more traditionally defined, with students having recourse to a body of academic knowledge based upon the acknowledged authority of named authors and philosophers. Although the relationship between issues of pedagogy and the technologies used for teaching and learning is complex, in this particular instance, it is reasonable to make the assumption that the content matter of A423 can, at least at some level, be conceptually separated from the conference. For H802 such a distinction is more difficult to make. The academic content of the course and the use of the conferences for course delivery are not conceptually distinct. For example, students learn about the content matter of 'collaborative learning' or 'on-line interaction' experientially through contributing to the conference and undertaking 'on-line tasks' with other students; this work is then complemented by readings – many accessed only via the Web – by recognized authors in the field.

Epistemic modality and conference contributions

In order to explore the ways in which students negotiate academic knowledge through writing in the conference, I will use here the concept of 'modality' as a tool with which we can begin to examine the ways in which students position themselves in relation to knowledge in the conference. Modality is a term used by social linguists to indicate a speaker's attitude towards a proposition. Focus is often placed upon the use of modal auxiliaries such as 'may', 'must', 'could', 'should' and 'need' in order to indicate a speaker's attitude towards what they are saying. The use of categorical assertions, such as 'it is', indicates strong belief in or commitment to the truth of what is being said. I have found Jennifer Coates's discussion of 'epistemic modality' in speech very useful when looking at tutor and student conference contributions. Coates (1987) makes the point that it is not just the modal verbs that matter but all the different ways in which speakers express commitment to the truth of a proposition. She describes epistemic modality as being 'concerned with the speaker's assumptions, or assessment of possibilities, and, in most cases, it indicates the speaker's confidence or lack of confidence in the truth of the proposition expressed'. Although her own analysis concentrates on speech, I have previously suggested that this work also tells us something about student essay writers, in terms of both their relationship to the academic knowledge that they are writing, and to their perceived relationship to the reader of their essay, the tutor (Knox 1992). In this instance Coates's analysis also helps us to make more sense of conferencing.

Although on both courses students reported how much they had enjoyed contributing to the conferences, they expressed some disappointment with regard to the kinds of debate taking place and, additionally, how these debates were intended to feed into their written work. In A423, students were concerned about the level of academic debate taking place in the tutor conference. As one student put it:

I want more than a discussion I can get down the pub!

They were therefore concerned that conference interactions were in a sense not academically focused enough. Additionally, they were looking for the tutor contributions to get them on the right track. They found it difficult to value the contributions made by other students:

I'm not really interested in what other students think. How do I know if they are right or not?

It seems as if students were adopting a very traditional model of learning in this course: they were looking to the tutor for recognition that conference contributions had academic validity. In this conference we can discern quite noticeable differences between tutor and student contributions in terms of modality and commitments to the truth of the proposition. Whereas students tended to make more tentative and hedged contributions, tutor contributions were generally more categorical in nature, reinforcing the view that the conference tended to reflect a more traditional academic relationship between tutor and student.

Student contributions tended to be characterized by more tentativeness and hedging, with few categorical statements. The use of 'I agree', 'there seems to me', 'I believe' and interrogative forms indicates epistemic modality in Coates's terms. Coates also explores how epistemic modality functions to mediate interpersonal meaning between speakers, or in this case between conference participants. In effect, students are doing two things at the same time when they write their conference contributions. On the one hand, they are using the conference to indicate their own beliefs and understanding about the course being studied. On the other, they are creating relationships with other students and their tutor. Research on computer conferencing has tended to focus upon the latter, the collaborative nature of these texts. Coates's analysis allows us to go further, however, and look at the way in which students can potentially use their writing on the conference to position themselves in relation to the academic content of the course, and therefore negotiate their own personal construction of academic knowledge. The quotes below have been chosen to indicate a general feel for the contributions on the two different courses and to illustrate potential differences between them. I am not suggesting that by juxtaposing only two messages it is possible to make claims of representativeness or to generalize to other settings. I believe, however, that this kind of analysis can help us to think about the ways in which students are positioning themselves in relation to both the academic content of the course being studied and the broader academic context.

The first quote is from a student studying A423, in which students had been using the conference to discuss the notion of being 'arbitrary'.

I agree we should not exclude women from any job. All your arguments denying the defence of normal courtesy can be used against the unstated (and not unimpeachable) principle, which you claim denies men the right to apply for a job opening doors and allocating cubicles to women in changing rooms. If there is a suggestion that the position might be abused that surely applies to women as well as men. If there is no question of this, or if it is a matter of decency, then it is an entirely arbitrary notion of what is fitting for men to do and what is not. There seems to me no direct correspondence between sex and the capacity to conduct oneself in an appropriate manner and it is non-sense to say that women and only women have the qualities required to successfully do this work. This seems a quite arbitrary exclusion of men. There is so much more to this than simply reducing the issue to a logical defence of a non-arbitrary principle. It involves how we want to live, to conduct our lives, interact with each other, and the standards we set for ourselves. I believe, as I think you do, that many women would prefer not to have men in this job. But many men would prefer not to have a woman working with them if the work involved heavy lifting. In both cases the feeling might be that the work was just not suitable for the person so employed. Why should people of normal sensitivity allow those of extreme views to make them feel uncomfortable in their daily lives? Who is being arbitrary in deciding the acceptability of such practices? Is there a majority?

This student uses a number of linguistic devices which indicate his uncertainty about committing himself strongly to a particular 'version' of academic content, or, put another way, to the 'truth' of a proposition. This tentative, provisional approach may, of course, also be reflecting the discourses of philosophy. This indicates how difficult it is in practice to separate epistemology from students' understanding of academic content.

The student begins the message by aligning his views with those of an earlier contributor to the conference: 'I agree we should not'. He repeatedly uses 'if', indicating a conditionality rather than certainty. He goes on to say 'There seems to me' and 'I believe, as I think you do', neither being strongly committed statements and the latter again relating his ideas to those of another. He then completes his message with a number of questions. The use of these different devices seems to indicate both his own personal exploration of philosophical knowledge and, at the same time, the necessity to link his interpretation to that of the other students. In Coates's terms he is expressing doubt about his commitment to the truth of what he is saying while at the same time creating interpersonal meaning with at least one other student. If writing in the conferences can give us some idea of the ways in which students are positioning themselves in relation to academic knowledge, then maybe we can build upon our understanding of this to develop conferences which are more effective in supporting student learning.

I turn now to a contribution from H802. Here conference contributions tend to be of a rather different textual type from those in A423. This might reflect the three factors which make this course rather different from A423: the conference is almost entirely student-driven; its academic content is not easily defined in traditional disciplinary terms; the course is at postgraduate level. The quote below is from a student who, towards the beginning of the course, is exploring the relationship between collaborative learning and prior knowledge:

I contend that without some assessment of prior knowledge that a student brings into a collaborative activity or project, there is no way to assess the extent or even if there has been an appreciable growth in the learner's construction of knowledge. For example, I bring to this activity extensive use of collaborative activities to construct knowledge in my face 2 face classroom. I daresay that I will leave this activity on Collaborative Learning with far less construction of new knowledge than had I been placed in the topic on Course Design of a third generation on-line course as compared to a conventional distance education course, an area in which I have little or no previous knowledge or experience. That is not to say that I can learn nothing from my colleagues here, but that it would have been more fruitful for filling in my gaps to be placed in the other group.

One student could enter this course knowing virtually nothing about our topics, but with tremendous effort leave the course having constructed an enormous knowledge/understanding base, but because of the overwhelming nature of the experience, weak writing skills, and the tough assessment of assignments make a much lower mark than someone who walks into the course conversant and experienced in the field, who writes well, but who constructs far less knowledge. How is this a fair assessment of either person's quality or quantity of constructed knowledge?

. . . Isn't it hypocritical for us to espouse a particular approach to knowledge, claim that knowledge and understanding is/is not being created and to what degree, yet not have a more precise way to show it both to the learner and to the providing institution other than some one person's subjective opinion, not that that opinion is worthless, but, nevertheless, considering the 'prior knowledge' issue, it is very subjective, and I emphasize the 'prior knowledge' issue, by implication unjust? I ask myself this question every day since I use collaborative learning approaches virtually all the time, and I don't assess prior knowledge. However, I do know the extent of my students' knowledge quite well after working with them several months. I'm not so sure about this approach working with experienced adults entering into higher education.

In common with the contributions from the student studying philosophy, this student expresses different levels of personal commitment to the academic course content. She does, however, make linguistic choices which indicate a much stronger commitment to her version of academic content than that of the A423 student. Her opening, 'I contend', sets up a strong case for her own commitment to the version of the content that she then goes on to espouse. She also makes a number of categorical assertions: 'there is no way' and 'I bring to this activity extensive use of collaborative activities'. She does mitigate her statement somewhat with 'I daresay'. When she comes to discuss 'prior knowledge' she again seems very committed to the 'truth' of what she is saying: 'it is very subjective', 'I emphasize', 'I use' and 'I do know'. She appears to be confident about her presentation of academic content because of her own previous experience in this field. Her engagement is with 'collaborative learning' as an academic concept but it also feels as if the conference is giving her the space to contribute with a strong commitment to what she is saying. This appears to contrast with the previous student's exploration of being 'arbitrary'. Of course, on H802 students are not merely learning about collaborative learning; it is exactly what they are doing. They are not having to make distinctions in their conference writing between academic content and 'using the conference', as is the case in courses with more traditional academic content, such as A423.

Linking conferences and assessment

A novel feature of H802 is that explicit linkages are made between conference contributions and assessed written work. In this respect, then, students are expected to use conference contributions in their assignments. They are being asked to reflect upon their own understandings of the academic content and to make linkages between the written texts of the conference and the written texts that they have to complete for assessment. This is in contrast with A423 where, although the intention is that students will make implicit connections between what is learnt in the conference and their assignments, no formal assessment procedures link the two.

Students on H802 did, however, report that they often found it difficult to make the requisite linkage between the two kinds of writing. So why does it seem difficult for students to make connections between the written texts of the conferences and the texts that they have to write for assessment? We have already seen how these texts embed particular relationships between both tutors and students and students and students. Additionally, I have indicated the ways in which the conferences are characterized by different levels of modality, which are related to both participants' commitment to, and their own understanding of, academic knowledge. I have also suggested ways in which the conferences support collaborative learning to a greater or lesser extent. Arguably the conferences embed new forms of writing, new genres with their own distinct features and associated practices. When we come to look at the assignments, in contrast to the conferences, the assignments tend to embed a very traditional academic 'essayist' genre. Even for H802, assessment tasks are presented in familiar ways. Despite the fact that students are encouraged to include references to conference messages in their written work, the assignment questions are still prescribed by a traditional essayist genre:

> Computer conferencing is an ideal medium for collaborative learning. Discuss.

Discuss the following quotation from Ivan Illich (1971):
I intend to show that the inverse of school is possible: that we can depend on self-motivated learning instead of employing teachers to bribe or compel the student to find the time or the will to learn; that we can provide the learner with new links to the world instead of funnelling all educational programs through the teacher . . . 'Network' is often used, unfortunately, to designate the channels reserved for materials selected by others . . . I wish I had another word . . . a synonym for 'educational web'.

Students reported that there was an artificiality about weaving conference messages into assessed writing. This might result from the fact that students are being asked to make connections between two very different written genres – writing on the conference and writing for assessment – the only linkage between them being to attempt to merge one into another. Since the more familiar way of approaching such a question would be by reference only to established authors, this may arguably have made it even more difficult for students to incorporate conference texts into their assessed work. There seem, then, to be no obvious connections between the new genres being explored and developed in the conferences and the old written genres being replicated in the assessment processes.

In order to address the difficulties that students report in making adequate use of conferencing in their learning and ultimately in their writing for assessment, maybe as tutors we need to concentrate our efforts on understanding the relationship between the different elements of learning in these new environments:

- Understanding the specific academic content which is embedded in the learning environment. What disciplinary and subject matter is being explored in the conference? What assumptions are tutors making about teaching and learning the course?
- Understanding the nature of the contributions that students make to the conferences and how these embed particular commitments to and understandings of academic knowledge. As tutors, recognizing the importance of these and building upon students' understandings in their learning. This may or may not mean replicating the features of more traditional face-to-face tutorials, depending on the particular academic context.
- Being clear in course design what kind of environment the conference is or attempts to replicate or substitute for. We need to know if this is meant to be like a seminar, a tutorial, a lecture or if this a new context altogether; this will help us clarify our role as tutor, facilitator or other.
- Recognizing the contrasts and differences between writing on the conference and writing for assessment and trying to help students see the ways in which they can make connections between the conferences and their assessed work. This may mean more than asking students to weave evidence of conference contributions into written assessment. It is more

likely to mean a very different form of assessment altogether – for example, students keeping their own reflexive log (see Creme, Chapter 6) of how their understanding of a content area has developed and changed as a result of contributing to the conference.

- Recognizing the institutional relationships of power and authority that exist between students and tutors and acknowledging that these are embedded in, among other things, present assessment practices. Becoming a 'facilitator' rather than a 'tutor' does little to alter this.

Exploring some of the more obvious textual features of student contributions to different sites in this way might, hopefully, give us some clues as to why students find it difficult to make connections between writing in the conferences and writing for assessment. On the surface there are not the obvious connections for students to make between these texts, of the kind there are, for example, between traditional print-based material and assessed written work. In such circumstances, students often report looking to the printed text to give themselves clues about how to approach their own writing (Lea 1998). In contrast, in the conference there are few of the familiar marks of authority that students are looking for – for example, the referenced author to give validity to the text. This may, in part, account for why students on the philosophy course were looking for the authority of the tutor contributions. It appears that although the conference record has the possibility of being a valuable record of reflection on learning, such a record does not necessarily have an immediate or obvious value for students in terms of their own learning. At the same time, neither is it perceived by students as a record of academic content in the way that they generally regard printed, referenced course material.

Directions

So how can this kind of exploration help us to make better use of computer conferencing for learning? Writing in conferences can be a valuable learning experience but we need to be able to make explicit the connections between the different academic literacy practices associated, on the one hand, with the conference texts, and, on the other, with assessed written work. If we want to make the links between learning, conferencing and assessment we need to start with the processes of assessment and ask ourselves what we are assessing. It may not be enough to encourage students to engage with the academic 'content' of the conference; we need to focus more specifically on developing students' reflexivity in terms of their own learning, which must include a reflexive approach to academic content. There will, of course, be sites such as H802 where it is more difficult to make a distinction between content and the process of reflexivity. In courses such as these it is, therefore, probably going to be easier to develop such an approach. In others, such as A423, where the academic content is more clearly delineated, we need to explore further the ways in which features of the technology are directly implicated in the kinds of propositional knowledge that students are constructing as participants.

Traditional forms of assessment which are, at present, too often embodied in the genre of the 'written academic essay' cannot adequately make connections with the written texts of the conference. We also need to find new ways of helping students to take advantage of the written records that they have access to on the conference. They need to be able to merge together new and more traditional literacy practices: the 'new' in this case reflected in writing to the conference, and 'traditional' being concerned with practices such as printing off contributions so that these can be highlighted and annotated in familiar ways. For example, some students on H802 talked about printing out all the conference postings and keeping them for reference for use in their assessed writing. We have seen that a major advantage of conferencing for students is that it can allow a reflexive engagement with learning through writing. It creates a written record that students can return to at their leisure throughout the course.

I am aware that this chapter has raised questions which have not been answered. In order to harness the potential of using computer conferencing for learning we probably need to understand much more than we do at present about these written genres. One danger is that if students' use of the conference appears ineffective from the tutor's point of view, an undue emphasis may be placed upon enhancing and improving student information handling skills, much in the way that others in this volume refer to the study skills based approaches being taken towards student writing more generally (see Baynham, Chapter 1; Lea and Street, Chapter 2). What we are really beginning to explore here is the relationship between epistemology and writing in these new multimodal learning environments and the consequences that this exploration might have for rethinking assessment. Hopefully this kind of exploration will enable both students and tutors to benefit from these new writing spaces for learning.

5

Making Dances, Making Essays: Academic Writing in the Study of Dance

Sally Mitchell, Victoria Marks-Fisher,
Lynne Hale and Judith Harding

This chapter is concerned with the practice of writing in a discipline where the primary activity apparently has nothing to do with writing – the activity of dance. Dancers are physical. Many would say that they think with their bodies, in the way that sculptors and crafts people claim that they 'let their hands do the thinking'. They invent through the experience of moving in space, in relation to that space, to ideas, to music, and to other dancers within that space; the documentation of those inventions records their experiments. While dance students in a university setting are confident about their own practice, with its starting point of physical movement (and its other strengths of spatial awareness, sensitivity to physical relationships, concentration, teamwork and an experimental approach), they are often uneasy about the formal writing tasks they encounter. The aim of this chapter is to explore the tensions and relations between the creative, physical work of dance and the formal writing requirements of the higher education context in which that work takes place.

The first part of the chapter is based on interviews, observations and essay samples gathered from staff and second-year students in a university school of dance, while the second part draws on the experience of teaching a 'skills' module for first-year dance students. The study reported on first was part of a wider project, the ongoing aim of which is to improve the ability of students to conduct arguments within their disciplinary fields and in particular within certain written forms, such as the essay or research report.[1] As well as exploring the technicalities of argumentation, the project has sought to understand some of the social, institutional, pedagogical and attitudinal factors which influence staff expectations and student performance.

The study in the School of Dance looked at the kinds of writing that students were required to produce, the attitudes of staff and students and the difficulties encountered. In this chapter we look in particular at the writing required within the context of the choreography course. We want to suggest that the disjunction between writing essays and making dances may not be as great as staff and students often perceive. By looking closely at a typical essay title from the course we offer a socially oriented explanation for the choreography and writing tasks, which draws on Harré's model of personal identity formation. We then describe the way writing functions in higher education to legitimize other forms of making. An analysis of a section of essay text suggests, however, that the writing does more than comment on the making of a dance, in fact it creates meaning which is both unique and part of a discourse (Gee 1990). This enables us to draw an analogy between writing and choreographing – an analogy which is then, in the latter part of the chapter, illustrated in practical work undertaken with students. The chapter ends with students' reflection on this work and with our own attempts to see the implications for improving writing support for students.

Writing in choreography

The small-scale study conducted in the university School of Dance looked at the experiences of second-year students taking core courses in critical studies and choreography for both of which an essay was required. For dance students, essay writing is typically regarded with some anxiety. In choreography, it was not unusual to regard the essay as a distraction, an affront almost, to the intense creative and practical work the students were undertaking. In critical studies, however, where students learnt how to analyse dance as viewers, the essay form seemed to 'fit' the task in a relatively unproblematic way. In this chapter we concentrate on the writing required for the choreography course.

Seventy-five per cent of the assessment for the choreography course was accounted for, not surprisingly, by the choreographing of a dance. Each student had to arrange and negotiate time and space for rehearsal with fellow students as dancers, and to develop a dance from tentative beginnings to eventual performance. There were weekly group workshops at which the tutor introduced principles and exercises in choreography. On these occasions, students also had an opportunity to show work in progress and to receive feedback from the group. A video recording of the dance in progress then formed the basis of a more detailed discussion between tutor and choreographer. Eventually the piece was performed to an audience of fellow students and staff and subject to a final assessment.

The remaining 25 per cent of the course assessment went to the writing of an essay. The tutor, who considered the essence of the course to be that the students should 'discover their voice as artists', could see no connection between the writing task and the making of dance. For her the two activities were entirely separate: choreography was a creative activity involving the individual person, and writing was an impersonal formal exercise. It was with a sense of personal conflict that the tutor brought her expectations in line with those she attributed to the academy:

I mean when I started it I expected, what I wanted to see out of it was a passion for their piece. And I marked all the pieces with a passion for their piece with good marks, and the others low marks and I got it all wrong. So now I've learnt the format. So now I look for, like, a good introduction, that it's quite clinically written as a piece . . . the conclusion.

It is one contention of this chapter that the distinction between choreography and writing is as much to do with *perceptions* of the differences as with an actual radical disjunction between the two. There is, for example, a certain irony in the tutor's aversion to giving stylistic and structural advice for writing; when she is helping students to make a dance, it is precisely considerations of style and structure that she brings to their attention. Whereas choreography is conceived as a process of realizing and transforming ideas through the medium of dance, the preference for writing is as a kind of commentary, giving (reporting) an idea of 'how they felt' and 'more about the person, because it's the person that's creative'. The writing advice that the tutor is able to give is not of course equivalent to that which she gives in choreography. There she is an expert, a practitioner as well as a teacher; in academic writing she is a novice relying on a basic, perhaps superficially understood, shorthand: 'don't use "I", have a good introduction, conclusion . . .'.

Such advice only goes so far in helping students understand what making an essay involves; other more elusive regularities govern success. The essay titles students were asked to respond to in choreography provide clues – though no more than clues – to embedded academic rules and rationales. These titles had been set not by the choreography tutor but by her predecessor, and in each case they asked students to consider their own work in relation to the work of others. The title that most of our sample chose was:

> Describe and discuss how you used particular movement vocabulary and movement quality to realise your dance idea. How did you choose and develop your dance language and how best did it service your source idea? Illustrate your answer to this question from known works.

The tutor, along with several of the students, found the final part of this particularly baffling – what had the work of others to do with the work of the individual student choreographer? One of the students in the study, Hannah, remarked about her resultant essay:

> I think I captured most of what the dance was about. But because I had to write about two other people as well, I don't think it was really focusing on my dance. This is my dance, and now I'm talking about two other completely different people who have nothing to do with my piece. They didn't have any relevance, I didn't take any ideas from them, I didn't use their themes or anything. I felt it detracted from *my* idea. It felt as though it was three pieces in the end.

The difficulty Hannah experienced was not concerned with 'beginnings, middles and endings' but with questions about the purpose of the writing, its rhetorical and epistemological orientation. These considerations relate to the ways in which the dance (which is the subject of the writing) is to be *known through* the writing. They also relate to the way the dance itself is thought about: Hannah sees her dance as a personal achievement unconnected with the work of others; to look at other work is to detract from her own.

How to be new; how to be you

A more social perception of making dance begins to make more sense of the essay title. We read it as asking the student to *make a case for* her dance as a successful realization of a dance idea. To do this she needs to show that her dance is 'original', which means it has to be uniquely hers, not a copy, but also to be recognizable, part of the collective 'ways of doing' that constitute the disciplines and traditions of dance. Hence she is asked to refer not only to her own dance but to the work of other choreographers. Making a claim for 'originality' is a particular feature of much academic writing (Kaufer and Geisler 1989), but it is also a way of explaining what goes on in the making of a dance. Both activities can be elucidated through the notion of a 'personal identity project' (Harré 1983; see also Ross *et al.* 1993; Mitchell 1995; 1996b). The project can be depicted schematically as two axes – the public/private and the individual/collective – which when they intersect create four quadrants. In personal identity formation the quadrants are traversed from the public/collective in a clockwise direction by four types of operation: appropriation, transformation, publication and conventionalization (see Figure 5.1).

In terms of making a dance, the dance student appropriates from the public/collective world of dance, knowledge and skills which feed her own peculiar making (transformation) of a dance piece. So, for instance, another of the students in our study, Lisa, described how her increasing knowledge of dance and choreographers liberated her to make dance:

> It makes you braver, I suppose . . . to be just you, which is a difficult thing to do. You'd think it'd be easy, wouldn't you? Just being yourself. But it's not.

Lisa felt able to take risks and to follow her intuition because she knew from her dance history course that this approach was already conventionalized as dance practice. The dance she made was, of course, uniquely hers, a transformation of everything she had appropriated.

When it is performed in front of an audience, the dance work is published – this is when it really reaches completion. The recognition it receives (for example, its grade, whether it is chosen to be included in a university end-of-year show, and also what the student herself learns from it

Figure 5.1   Personal identity project (after Harré 1983)

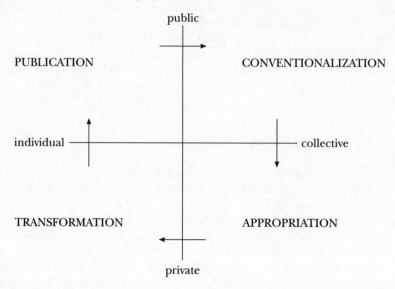

about making dance) are part of its (and her) conventionalization into the discourse (Gee 1990) of dance.

Legitimating through writing

So much for the personal identity project of making a dance and becoming a choreographer; within the higher education context, publication and conventionalization processes are only partly achieved through making in the art form itself. Over and above this, the writing of an essay functions to legitimize the work of the student within the conventions of the academic, largely text-based, institution. Another function of academic writing is to demonstrate, or to argue for, the newness of something (a research conclusion, a philosophical idea, a dance), where 'newness' is understood, as Harré's model suggests, not as '"brand new" or "out of the blue"' (Kaufer and Geisler 1989: 288) but as deriving from orientation to, and distinctiveness from, some established knowledge, conventions, discourses. Kaufer and Geisler note that the academic conventions for making knowledge require both warranting (reference to a conventionalized realm) and transparency (explicitness of assumptions, meanings and reasoning). Transparency in particular is a feature of academic writing, what Olson (1977) refers to as the 'essayist technique'. Kaufer and Geisler (1989: 291) comment that in Western academic contexts 'a system of exploration must be constrained through a system of writing'. Such a writing system makes a claim on behalf of the exploration system (which in this case is the choreography). It publicizes, in explicit verbal form, its newness, or, in Harré's terms, its potential for conventionalization into the public/collective realm.

An extract from an essay by another student, Ellie, makes a good example of how novelty can be claimed through the writing. Her dance is entitled *Here Comes the Sun*:

> This piece [Ailey's *To Bird with Love*] is similar in structure to the second section of *Here Comes the Sun*, Ailey's dancers begin the piece by entering gradually on each side with their focus on themselves rather than on those around them. As more enter, the stage fills and the atmosphere picks up into a lively, swiftly moving scene of dancers ducking in and out of smoothly timed moves and manoeuvres.
>
> Unlike *To Bird with Love*, the actual dance steps of this piece were kept relatively simple, which allowed the use of more complex structuring in its spatial design [...]
>
> What became more and more important in the piece as it progressed, and what helped develop the use of the dance language, was the enjoyment factor that both the audience and the dancers must experience through the piece. By using a strong element of naturalism, both in the general structure of the dance and in the performance of the moves, it allowed more opportunity for real pleasure to be taken from it both by dancers and audience, simply because more pleasure was being put into it. Though most of the time she uses, possibly the most opposite of emotions, this is the same way in which Pina Bausch uses reality in her works. In *1980*, for example, she has one dancer running, circling the stage 50 or 60 times, shouting the words 'I'm tired'. The dancer does not have to feign any fatigue to the audience, because she genuinely *is* tired, and the audience do not have to allow for any kind of artistic licence to be used by the choreographer, and accept that she would be tired – they don't have to because they know she really is exhausted.

Ellie puts her piece into dialogue with the other pieces she has selected. She shows, for example, how Ailey's work is both 'like' and 'unlike' her own. She abstracts from details of Bausch's work to name the principle of 'naturalism' it works by. She has used the same principle in her own work, she says, though with 'the most opposite of emotions'. In making these moves, Ellie is arguing for her dance and its conventionalization within the 'field' (Toulmin 1958) of dance. By 'arguing' we mean the making of claims or statements based on evidence (grounds) that can be justified (warranted) by reference to a rule, principle or authority (see Toulmin *et al.* 1984). Evidence in this case is supplied by description of the dances. Justification comes through the articulation of rules ('if dancers feel a certain strong emotion, the audience will recognize that that emotion is being conveyed') and by invoking authority ('a technique used by Bausch, who is recognized as a highly talented choreographer, is likely to be a good one). There is a strong sense in which Ellie is not reporting, but constructing her justifications, the relationships with dance precedent and authority. Part of the art of essay writing, then, is not so much in choosing material that is similar or related, but actually in *making* relations, whether through similarity or difference.

Recognizing the essentially creative component in essay writing could bring students' perception of it closer to their perceptions of choreography. Essay writing can be a way to make meaning through the manipulation of form. When dance students leave their role as makers of dance, they need to step into a role as makers of essays. Both activities involve a making process; both also have outcomes that are in some sense a commitment, a statement of how things are. The performance of a piece in front of an audience is comparable to the presentation of an essay in its final form – both actions establish a kind of closure and create a certain fixity of meaning.[2]

Exploring correspondences between writing and choreographing

A 'dance skills' module developed for first-year students in the School employed the correspondence between writing and choreographing as a key component. As validated, the module purported to address a wide range of topics to support the dancers' development of physical, information technology and communication abilities. In practice, the approach was less subservient to the institutional notion of 'skills provision'. It was based on a conjecture that the confidence the students experienced in their personal and creative practice as dancers and choreographers could help tackle the unease and distance often associated with formal writing tasks. The aim was to suggest to students that the process of constructing writing shares similarities with the process of making dance. A notion of making, as the playful manipulation of form, could be seen to underpin both activities.

The module involved students in exercises that focused on organization and selection – the way things fit together or do not – as ways of generating meanings. By physically rearranging objects according to particular criteria, students needed to think about ordering in categories, sequences and hierarchies and in patterns that spelled out the relationships of parts to a whole. On one occasion the 70 students in the group were asked to arrange themselves according to the colour of clothes they were wearing. Where white tops were sequenced in terms of coverage and elaboration – sleeveless, with short sleeves, with long sleeves, with long sleeves and collars – elements that did not fit in the overall sequence of colour 'paragraphs' had to be edited out – exit the red plaid shirt. Stripes served as useful transitions between 'paragraphs'; multicoloured prints incorporating all the colour ideas were 'conclusions'. The technique here was to allow students to play with the raw material and make their own discoveries about the way it could be shaped and sequenced as criteria emerged. The students were engaged in processes that the choreographer Laban lists as necessary to the formal construction of dance – 'select, arrange, rearrange, organise, reorganise, combine, recombine', these are things that 'all artists do' (quoted in Heath 1983).[3] But the analogy with academic (or any) writing was also spontaneously recognized – 'That's just like an essay structure!'

Parallels with the process of making dance were drawn out whenever the opportunity arose. For example, when a student was unclear about what constituted a transition in writing she was asked to explain what a transition was in choreography. Could anyone dance a transition? One student did; another disagreed and showed her own version. Again someone disagreed. This dialogue about the meaning of a transition in dance seemed a promising way to explicitly connect corresponding concepts – and, as Laban's comment suggests, terminology – in the two practices. It signalled to students that in writing, as in dance, the maker has certain options available and that these are open to discussion.

A rather more subtle feature of the module that seemed to contribute to exploring the correspondences between writing and choreographing was the setting in which much of the work took place – the students' own dance studio rather than any more formal academic setting. Here the students could be themselves in their dancer personae, flexing, stretching, lying down or sitting cross-legged in an atmosphere that seemed warm, light and welcoming. Tutors, too, were required to follow the studio rules and to remove their shoes. From the written reflections that were a part of the module requirements, it was clear that some students felt surprised at this kind of informality in an ostensibly 'academic' module, but their reaction was appreciative:

> The space in the gym was much better than the lecture theatre and it was noticeable as far as concentration/energy levels were concerned.

Reflections: limitations and possibilities

Students' reactions were generally of this positive kind. Nonetheless, there were some limitations to these experiments in making, in part due to the context in which they took place. When a group of the students who had taken the module in their first year were interviewed in the final year of their course, their wide-ranging responses included a number of reservations. These students, it should be noted, could be assumed to be fairly confident writers since they had opted in their final year for a theoretical module with a considerable writing component.

The students felt strongly that the module came too early, before they had been able to deal with the overwhelming experience of being in a new and confusing situation, and, more importantly, before they had any sense of why they might have any need for this material. Help with thinking about their writing should happen when the writing was happening, so that needs and support could coincide:

> I felt that that was a waste of time because there was no idea, no
> ground at that time of why you needed these skills . . . Actually, having
> it later on when you had essay questions that you needed to work
> to . . . would actually have helped a lot. Even now, when we have to
> develop an argument – I have a 10,000 word dissertation to do and I
> am really struggling with it.

What we know of the difficulties experienced by students writing for the
choreography course bears out this comment: help was needed not with
general essay-writing skills, but in addressing the particular requirements of
the writing task, its epistemological and institutional purpose as well as its
relation to the making of the dance. The student's comment is also a
reminder that essays are not the only text required in the higher education
context; developing an argument across the 10,000 words of a dissertation
is a new challenge altogether.

Some of the group also felt that the module should have been optional,
especially for those who saw themselves as already confident writers and
group participants when they arrived (most of these were mature students).
Some felt it was too basic and unchallenging, reinforcing a stereotype they
resented of dancers who can move but not think.

Although a number of students felt liberated by the opportunity to discuss their formal writing with lecturers from the School of Dance, others
wanted any writing support to come from tutors within their own disciplinary communities. They attributed their own successes in writing to the help
of a tutor who was a dancer, but who also represented academic authority
in an intense way 'because she writes books'. From their descriptions, this
tutor seemed to treat the two practices of choreography and writing as
quite separate activities. Discussions with her had, these students claimed,
never touched on the shared process of creative construction in the making
of writing and the making of dance – a reminder that it is quite possible for
dance students to become successful writers without recourse to analogies
with dance.

Despite this, however, we want to persist in claiming some value in exploring the correspondences between the two activities. For many students,
overcoming resistance to the idea of writing is the biggest hurdle. This is
also recognized by the tutor on the critical studies course who devotes at
least two seminars to detailed, rather technical, discussion of what essay
writing involves. At times, she acknowledges, her clear explanations can be
counterproductive:

> They worry tremendously about the writing. And I think that sadly they
> see it as a different kind of activity from what we've been doing in all
> the sessions [discussion of videos of dance performances]. . . . They see
> it as a different kind of activity which is somehow distanced from them.
> They somehow have to put on a different kind of hat, if you like, and
> engage in something which is alien. And it's very difficult to draw the
> line between helping them with their work, focusing on it, as you know

we try and do, taking them through it, taking them through the structure, making a fuss about it. Which on the one hand is beneficial; on the other hand it makes something really grand and big and difficult. And I'm not convinced I've found the happy medium yet in the status of written work and how large it grows in their mind.

Students' sense of themselves as 'dancers' can become a way of retreating from engagement with the task of writing, but if connections can be made, if only of a metaphorical nature, then something productive may have occurred. Even the confident third-year students we interviewed, when reminded of the incident when students had danced transitions, engaged with the idea and used it to think aloud about particular difficulties they were having with their current writing tasks:

> It's funny you should say that, because just yesterday I was reading my essay, she asked to read it through and I guess something that I really noticed was there were quite a few places where something was missing, you know, like a linking sentence, it just needed that link to get into the next part.

What can our experiences in the School of Dance, both as researchers and as lecturers in other disciplines, tell us about how to address the needs of student writers, not just in dance but in other subject areas as well? A number of key related points seem to have emerged. First, *the timing should be appropriate*. In terms of curriculum design it may be important to provide students with an introductory module of some kind, but this should not be assumed to cater for all the specific and changing needs of the student as she progresses through the course, from module to module.

Second, *timing should be governed by real need*. Again, need may arise at any point during the course brought about by the real demands of interpreting particular tasks and meeting assessment deadlines. To be successful, an introductory module would need to create a genuine initial need and therefore an immediate context for support, by setting a challenging writing task in, say, the first two weeks.

Third, any attempt to help students with writing needs to take account of *their sense of identity and their attitudes to and beliefs about writing*. We have suggested that exploring the links between writing and choreographing can be a productive way of confronting inhibiting perceptions that some dance students may have towards writing. We have also noted the value of situating the act of writing quite literally in a new space, one that was comfortable to the students.

Fourth, it is important to *make links with students' existing knowledge*. Again this belief underpins the bringing together of dance and writing. It should be interpreted also as referring to the knowledge that students already possess about writing and the need to *avoid the perception of low expectations* enshrined in the provision of a 'skills' module. It would then seem appropriate that students should *know the purposes* for which they are writing. In the case of the choreography course, for example, students might expect to engage in discussion about why they are being asked to write and how. This would involve on the part of staff a preparedness to be theoretical and, possibly, political; that is, to talk about writing on a broad level. Our discussion in this chapter of the 'personal identity project', of novelty and of argument in relation to the choreography essay may provide suggestions as to how such talk might be focused.

Finally, all the above points come together in an expressed desire for subject-specific tutors, that is, for *support integrated within students' own disciplinary study*. Although many students do value the freedom from judgement that having lecturers from other disciplines bestows, there is clearly a need to engage subject tutors in staff development which encourages thinking about what writing involves. Such tutors need to be able to convey their understanding confidently to students so that students may also feel confident or at least clearer about what they are asked to do. In dance, such discussion could usefully involve consideration of correspondences between writing and choreographing. It should also involve reflection upon the educational, institutional and epistemological purposes of writing (see Lea and Street, Chapter 2), and the different modes – for example, argument – that students might, directly or indirectly, be asked to employ.

Acknowledgements

Our thanks to the staff and students of the School of Dance. All student names have been changed. Thanks, too, to the Leverhulme Trust who are funding the project 'Improving the Quality of Argument in Higher Education' based at Middlesex University during 1995–99. This chapter is based on a paper at the conference of the Humanities and Arts Higher Education Network on 12 October 1996, and published in conference proceedings.

Notes

1. The project is entitled 'Improving the Quality of Argument in Higher Education'. It is funded by the Leverhulme Trust and based at Middlesex University until August 1999 (see Mitchell, 1996a).
2. It is this fixity that makes the timing of the essay important. In our study we found that, depending on when their performances were scheduled, some students were required to hand in their essays before their dances had reached completion. Hannah expressed the awkwardness of this situation when she commented that before the dance is finished 'you haven't got much to go on apart from what you *hope* it can be'.
3. This list has similarities with that proposed by Heath (1983) in her analysis of the approaches that children who have been told bedtime stories seem to use (explain, break down into small bits, note analytic features and recombine in new contexts). These approaches, she claims, lead to easy adaptation to essay-text literacy – ask questions, take notes, discuss various points of view, write discursive prose, revise and feed back.

6

The 'Personal' in University Writing: Uses of Reflective Learning Journals

Phyllis Creme

Is there a place and space for the expression of 'the personal', and is it relevant in higher education? How is the term used and contested in the study and writing of academic disciplines by students and tutors? These are important questions for students trying to find their own sense of identity as students in higher education, as well as for their tutors who may have various and sometimes conflicting models of their task as teachers. In this chapter I compare the different meanings attached to the notion of the 'personal' in the context of learning journals used in a disciplinary and an interdisciplinary course. By 'learning journals' I refer to what are variously called, for instance, 'reflective journals', 'study diaries' and 'learning logs', which are increasingly used in a wide range of courses in higher education. They are written on a regular, ongoing basis, and focus upon the students' processes of learning and their own relationship to the course material. Their use in higher education brings to the fore the complex issue of the meanings and status of the personal in student academic writing.

The problematic nature of an apparently rather innocuous suggestion to students to make use of their personal position was thrown up by my work in an action research project on the uses of 'new forms of student writing' that were introduced alongside traditional essays in courses taught by social anthropology faculty at Sussex University. The research was funded by a UK Higher Education Funding Council 'Teaching and Learning Development' project administered by the National Network for Teaching and Learning Anthropology in 1997–98. The study was designed to look at the impact on student learning of the new forms of writing, all of which may be defined as some kind of learning journal, although they differed from course to course in important ways. The two courses that I discuss in this chapter are: a second-year, core political anthropology course; and an option on a first-year, interdisciplinary critical reading course, on the topic of 'death'. The death course was included in the research because it was designed and taught by a member of the social anthropology subject group who was based in the School of Cultural and Community Studies; at Sussex, the arts/social studies degrees are divided between major subject and 'school'-based courses, which are broadly interdisciplinary in character.

In this chapter I first briefly describe the research process and some indicators for practice from its findings; I then focus on the particular issue of the different treatment of the personal in the discipline-specific and the interdisciplinary course, which brought out some of the difficulties, ambiguities and opportunities of the new forms of writing. I want to argue that, although the 'personal' was defined, constructed and experienced in different ways, the very fact that it came up as an issue during this research demonstrated that the new forms of writing gave students an opportunity to define for themselves their own pathway within their university courses that many valued highly.

The research

Taking an 'academic literacies' approach, informed, for example, by re-search carried out by Lea and Street (Chapter 2), I aimed to place the students' writing in the context of the pedagogical and institutional setting in which it was produced. From the start, therefore, I was looking at the purposes and rationale for the introduction of the journals and how they were incorporated into the course processes, as well as tutors' and students' epistemological assumptions about their courses, and their attitudes to the journals. I was based in a school along with a number of social anthropology faculty, in something of a participant observer's role, and worked closely with tutors responsible for the courses being researched. I read course outlines and associated documents; attended seminars and course-related activities; used evaluative questionnaires; considered tutors' written – and in some cases oral – feedback to students on their work; and analysed many examples of different kinds of student writing. I carried out numerous in-depth interviews, and had many informal conversations, with tutors and students, both individually and in groups, on their experiences and views of anthropology, of their courses, and of different forms of writing.

Benefits of the use of learning journals

The research indicated that writing learning journals had the potential significantly to enhance and develop the depth and range of student learn-ing, in different ways according to their purpose within their respective courses. However, the extent to which this potential was realized in practice varied considerably – not only for individual students, but also in the extent to which the journals were integrated into the course teaching, learning and assessment processes. Here I draw out some generalizations drawn from the research data which I believe are relevant for tutor practice.

First, journals gave students an opportunity to write regularly and at length, allowing them to develop their ideas and writing fluency. It is a

theme of this book that writing is a major means by which students construct their disciplinary knowledge. The idea that writing discursively,
regularly and at length helps to develop student understanding and build
up a conceptual base recalls Peter Elbow's (1981) work on 'free writing': getting students to write 'without stopping' as a way of 'freeing up the writing
process' has been proved effective by countless teachers of writing and
their students – often to their surprise – for many years. Writing learning
journals is not necessarily about 'free writing', particularly when they
are written as public documents, but it certainly has more of that flavour
than the usual work that students do at university: 'it flows more easily', as
many students put it. In asking students to keep a regular learning journal,
tutors foregrounded the idea of writing as a process and a tool for learning
rather than as a product and occasional demonstration of knowledge. As a
tutor put it, a major purpose of the journals was to 'make the process of
learning visible' both to the students themselves and to those reading and
assessing them.

Second, writing journals enabled students to construct a 'map' of the
complex structures and relationships in a course or range of material. One
of the reasons that tutors gave for introducing learning journals is that
they asked students to 'make connections' between ideas within the course
and ideas outside it, and this was a recurring theme in students' discussions
about their writing. Discursive writing is often more effective than, for example, seminar discussion because it can be a cumulative and progressive
process of meaning-making that produces a visible, substantial record which
can be revisited and, as appropriate, amended. Regular writing, therefore,
enables the student to construct connections and patterns that cannot be
formulated in any other form, such as talking or memory. It allows her to
become her own reader of work in progress and gives her an opportunity to
trace the developments in her learning from an outsider's perspective.

Third, writing journals encouraged the students to think differently. Research into academic writing genres shows how prescribed forms of writing
are integrally bound up with the construction of knowledge of a discipline
and how they determine the ways of thinking a subject. As Bazerman (1981:
10) puts it: 'The problem of choosing which words to put on a page looks
outward to a whole world rather than inward to a contained technology'.
For the students I worked with, the front line of their 'whole world' was
represented by a general consensus as to what kind of writing was expected
of them, gleaned from what tutors said and from written guidelines, both
generic and course- or even assignment-specific. For the first half of their
course the short essay was the writing to which they were accustomed and
by which they were assessed. During a first-year seminar I attended, a list
elicited from first-year students as to what an essay 'contains' included:
'structure; facts/evidence; background to debate; introduction and conclusion; references and bibliography'. The essay needs to have a 'logical flow'
which 'takes your argument from point to point'. The introduction needs
to acts as a signpost to the reader. In the end the essay is about 'trying to

persuade somebody'. This is a list which is unlikely to be contested in most university courses, and it is a formulation that students I have spoken to have internalized, although it does not necessarily obviate the difficulties involved in the complex task of making meaning in any individual piece of writing. Nevertheless, some students did express to me in very formulaic terms how they went about an essay:

> you know, you have a certain number of words, the introduction and conclusion are so long, you can only make three to five points . . .
> I get it all down, then I go back and look to see if I've put in the links.

The traditional student essay is a form that accords well with a positivist perspective where the external world is knowable and questions can be answered: 'yes, you have to come to a conclusion', the students were told in the above seminar. As one tutor put it, the essay is about 'the art of applying reasoned argument in the light of empirical evidence as clearly and succinctly as possible'.

In terms of an anthropology course, it is not clear that the essay alone, as presented above, is necessarily best suited to helping students to 'learn anthropology' which, as one tutor expressed it, involves students 'unlearning', seeing the world differently, questioning their own stances and assumptions. Moreover, ethnographic writing (that is, as done by anthropologists) includes, for example, description (often of a vivid, evocative kind), first and third person narrative with a good deal of dialogue, history, generalization and theory. The learning journals were introduced to allow students to engage in different kinds of writing and therefore in different kinds of knowledge production from the essay. For example, containing more use of a first person narrative and commentary than essays, they allowed students to be more 'provisional' and more 'personal'. The reiterative and reflexive nature of the genre, where students moved back and forth between different aspects of the course, and where the journals were (with exceptions) only 'completed' because the end of the course was reached, called for an 'open' form that suggests a process that continues, without necessarily coming to a fixed conclusion. In some cases learning journals were seen as a stepping-stone to other more formal work, but this, I suggest, should not be seen as their main purpose; by encouraging different ways of thinking, they are useful in themselves.

The discipline: the 'personal' and 'reflexivity'

The introduction of the new forms of writing was related to a continuing discipline-based debate about the status of the researcher and of writing within social anthropology (for example, see Clifford and Marcus 1986). The contested notion of the 'personal' in both anthropology research and education was therefore a continuing motif running through the study. It came up in different guises in different places – for example, in tutors' discussions around anthropology as a discipline, and in descriptions about the new forms of writing which offered students different and sometimes contradictory messages about what using the personal might mean. It emerged as an issue particularly acutely in relation to another highly contested term, 'reflexivity'. Conseqently, as a part of the research project, the subject group organized a staff development workshop on reflexivity, which was debated with regard both to anthropology and to teaching and learning. The discussion was later summarized in a report which compares 'reflexivity' and 'reflection' and then applies both concepts to students' learning of anthropology.

> Anthropologists have always been 'reflexive' in two related senses. First they have concerned themselves with recognising how knowledge about the world is socio-culturally situated – this is, and must be, a foundational principle for a discipline concerned with the relativity of different knowledge systems. Secondly, they have concerned themselves with situating 'themselves' in relation to knowledge and its production. What appears to have happened in recent years is a foregrounding of these processes in anthropological writing combining an intensification of self criticism/self awareness with the making explicit of the politics of knowledge production. This latter development, which can be related to the project of modernity, has led to debate about the status of 'the personal' in the production of anthropological knowledge.
>
> (Mitchell 1998)

The report goes on to question the notion of 'the personal' in student writing:

> The status of 'personal knowledge/experience/opinion' appears problematic in student writing. It is common to state quite explicitly when setting the guidelines for essay-writing that students should develop their own argument – the imperative seems even stronger when dealing with 'new forms' of student writing. However, it is clear that students are not always sure precisely what this means and particularly when an explicitly stated aim is to encourage 'reflexivity' the development of the students' own position soon becomes conflated with notions of individual experience or personal knowledge . . .
>
> There seemed to be overall consensus in the workshop that reflexivity in student writing, and the new forms introduced to encourage it, are not intended to be 'about' personal knowledge or experience . . . rather, the new forms of writing are intended to encourage reflection on and challenge to personal or common sense knowledge, in the pursuit of anthropological knowledge. Again this should be a two-stage process whereby students reflect on both the situatedness of their own knowledge and their position vis-à-vis its production. *By encouraging students to take a critical stance towards their own common sense categories,*

and to their own autobiographies, new forms of writing can enable students to make new kind of connections between their lives, the learning process, the texts they are reading and social science categories. . . . This reflection should implicate both non-academic and academic life . . . explicit reflection on learning creates greater awareness of how learning 'fits together' and how knowledge changes the course of study. This focus on learning itself should ultimately lead to better learners.

(Mitchell 1998; emphasis added)

On the development of the students' 'own voice as scholars' and terms such as 'originality', 'individuality' and 'creativity', which were also the subject of 'lively debate', the report points to a mismatch between students' understanding of 'originality' as 'the input of "personal knowledge"' and anthropology tutors' expectations that this would be 'be firmly anchored within intellectual debate'. This brings to the fore how ideas of the personal are contested, in this case between tutors and students, who were concerned to express their 'own opinion'. The following statement in the report demonstrates how it is the tutor, as the representative of the discipline, who has the power to make decisions about what goes into student writing and what stays out:

A 'creative' or 'individual' essay identifies new connections or original insight and thereby introduces new arguments to the debate. Such argument cannot be forged from purely personal opinion or individual experience alone.

(Mitchell 1998)

I have quoted this report at length because it points very clearly to the difficulties students can have in negotiating discipline-derived terms, and because, within this framework, it makes a judgement as to how students' personal experiences might be relevant – or not – in an anthropology course. The report reflected debates that had an impact on the tutors' attitudes to their students' writing, and in turn influenced the students' approach.

The issue of the personal in terms of writing is given a different gloss by Ivanič (1998), who posits a way of conceiving the (student) writer's 'identity' as different writing 'selves': the 'autobiographical self', comprising the identities the writer brings to an act of writing; the 'authorial self', which is the sense of authorship and authority that can be discerned by the reader, and which may be experienced by the writer as 'ownership' and control of the text she writes; and the 'discoursal' self that is inscribed in the genre and linguistic features of the text itself. Ivanič describes some of the discoursal characteristics of acceptably 'academic' writing that appear in students' essays, such as nominalization and abstraction, and, on a broader textual level, the presentation of a case and the answering of questions. The adopting of such features in academic writing positions the writer into taking on particular ways of knowing and thinking that do not invite personal knowledge or experience. In these terms, the question for my purposes here is how far the introduction of different forms of writing made a difference to the 'writing self'. The purpose of learning journals may be to introduce the writer's autobiographical selves (for these are multiple) into the texts that students write at university, as a way of facilitating the development of the authorial self. Another way of putting this is that offering different forms of writing expands the range of the discoursal selves that students can assume, and that the more 'personal' discourse of the journal eases the transition to the adoption of the new autobiographical self involved in being a university student.

Different courses, different journals

These issues surrounding the diverse meanings of the personal in the new forms of writing emerged in a focused way in my study of the two courses on political anthropology and death. I do not want to suggest too great a difference between the aims of the new writing on the two courses, for they had much in common in their intention of engaging students with the course material. Nevertheless, the differences were marked and had important effects on the student writing.

The 'new writing' on the two courses had different titles that rather neatly reflected their different purposes as the tutors saw them: the *Record of Study* and the *Death Journal*. The second-year political anthropology course was seen as an important theoretical foundation to the final-year options that demanded a greater degree of independent work on the part of the tutor than the course had done so far. It was here that the process towards helping the student to 'think like an anthropologist' (as the aims of the degree had been expressed) seemed to come to fruition – tutors spoke of qualitative shifts in student work at this point. The death course was seen as foundational in a different sense: as an interdisciplinary course in 'critical reading' in the first term of the first year of the degree, its major aim was to introduce students to academic practices, which also involved a shift in students' conceptual position. Making use of the 'personal' in student writing had different meanings according to the different values and epistemological framework of the discipline-specific and the interdisciplinary course. To some extent – as a course taught by a social anthropologist – these differences were also apparent within the death course itself. These different ideas of the 'personal' were discernible in how the two courses were presented, taught and assessed, and were clearly present both in the rubrics for each of the 'new forms of writing' and in the way in which the tutors discussed them, as I consider later. The *Record of Study* was seen as a way of using the personal to develop students' anthropological understanding, whereas the *Death Journal*, set within the interdisciplinary course, gave more scope for an exploration of the personal – the student's 'autobiographical self' – in its own right.

The *Record of Study*

The political anthropology course handout introduced the *Record of Study* in the following way:

> The Record of Study is a summary of the reading and other research you have carried out on the course along with notes on your views of the material you have encountered in the reading in the seminars, and the lectures. It is a kind of history of the work you have done on the course and a Record of what you have read and how your ideas have changed. . . .
>
> It is designed to encourage reflexivity about your own learning.
>
> It is a record of all aspects of the course – lectures as well as the reading.

This indicates how the *Record of Study* was intended to reflect its title: its major purpose, as the tutors expressed it, was to develop the students' understanding of the concepts presented in the course – concepts that themselves changed and were contested over time, in accordance with changing theoretical positions. The tutors' thinking in introducing the *Record of Study* came out more clearly in an interview I had with the course convenor:

> We wanted students to start their records of study with a statement about what they expected of the course, and what their first understandings were of concepts like politics and power, then to keep this record of study up to date at least every two weeks. Through that we wanted them to see that their own understandings of those concepts running through the course were evolving. [We expected that] this would give them some sense of achievement, some sense of confidence in their own learning and also provide a vehicle for reflecting and connecting similar arguments found in different contexts and seeing that there was some cumulative aspect to their learning. Finally, we wanted them to be reflexive in another sense, in that they could incorporate evidence from their own personal experience into the record of study showing that their understanding had evolved through engagement with the analytical issues which the course was dealing with.

What this seems to be promoting is the idea of the student as thinker and opinion-holder, trying to grasp new ideas, and as a 'reader' who thinks about her own position with regard to the course material. In this context the personal is to do with the students' intellectual stance and their social/political identity; one aim of the journal was to enable them to bring this identity into a relation with the course material. The fact that some students had a more clearly defined sense of this identity than others had an impact on how easily and effectively they were able to take on the task of writing the records of study, as a number explained to me in discussion. Here is an extract from one record of study:

We had great difficulty in defining what a society was and weren't sure, for example, whether travellers were a part of our society or whether they had their own. This is where the now famous bubble theory was born – maybe an individual can be part of a 'sub-culture' or 'sub society' within a much larger society structure (a small bubble inside a much larger one)....

... one of the problems I have is concentrating on the subject. I tend to wander off at times (maybe you've noticed that in my record of study here!) although my marks on the whole have been very encouraging. So I suppose having to write a 1,000 word piece on a pretty wide subject forced me to collate relevant information, group similar and opposing concepts and avoid wandering off.

The writer is 'talking through' his thinking about the ideas presented in the course, which are interspersed with comments about his way of studying and doing the assignments, his attitudes to the readings and to the course generally. In the first paragraph he expresses possibilities and doubts about terms, and in the process reworks a definition of the 'bubble theory' which is encapsulated in his image of the bubble inside a 'bigger' one.

The aims and assumptions of this core anthropology course, as expressed both in the course convenor's remarks and the subject group's report on reflexivity quoted above, which particularly stressed students' conceptual development, influenced what was written in the aptly titled record of study: this student does not write generally about his own life 'experiences'; rather, the relevant (personal) experience in this context is the course-specific process of reading, seminars, reflecting and writing pieces for assessment. The autobiographical self, to use Ivanič's terminology, that comes through in this writing is that of an engaged student of the course. Even the history of this self is recorded in terms of studying and learning in the passage about the writer's problem in 'concentrating on the subject'. The extract also demonstrates a confident authorial self – the writer's sense of authority – which is expressed, for example, in the slightly playful use of language in his own framing of the fragment of the bubble theory, and the almost intimate address to the reader/tutor: 'maybe you've noticed I tend to wander off the point'. The difference between this writing and the essay, as students and tutors perceived it, is that the writer is more able to bring in aspects of an autobiographical self to this context, and through the use of the different kind of writing, construct a new kind of discoursal self. He is writing differently in a way that encompasses his reactions to the reader as well as to the course material and with a confident sense of an authorial presence in his study.

The *Death Journal*

The critical reading course in the School of Cultural and Community Studies, of which the death course was one option, was designed to enable students to 'read across a range of texts' from different disciplines. In the 'Handbook' the courses are described as:

> programmes which compare the approaches of different disciplines to particular topics or problems . . . The course aims to introduce students to a range of themes central to the School . . . It seeks to understand the individual in society through modes of imagination and comprehension of the social sciences, literature and the arts.

The rubric for the *Death Journal* said:

The purpose of the journal is to provide a space where students can:
- record and reflect on representations and explorations of death . . . in various forms of the popular media . . . literature . . . artistic work [a 'scrapbook' format was suggested].
- consider contemporary issues surrounding death and their own thoughts on this.
- reflect on 'personal' encounters with death or dying.
- reflect on assigned readings.
- 'read across' texts . . . make links between different readings on the course . . . The journal's shape, content and style will vary a great deal depending on its author and I hope that students will make it their own.

The use of the first person here may be a signal of the writer/tutor's approach. She referred a number of times in the seminars to her belief in the need for a writer (in this case a researching anthropologist) to acknowledge her own subjectivity and her own presence in a research project. At the same time, her intent was also a 'critical' and 'scholarly' one. In a conversation, she elaborated on what she hoped students would get from the course and particularly from the experience of writing their journals:

> One of the main things I'm trying to get them to do is to challenge, denaturalize, . . . to challenge common-sense views about there being a single and right way to do things and getting them to realize there are all kinds of ways . . . and I see that as a necessary step to a critical viewpoint . . .
>
> I ask them to think about the different writing genres . . . I try to encourage people to read beyond the individual text to get some of that excitement of being a scholar.

In terms of the use of the personal, she added another dimension:

> I like being surprised by the creativity of my students. . . . I think I'm also interested in helping students to find their voice. I'm trying to get them to get the confidence of seeing that they don't just have to say what someone else has said.

The use of the terms 'voice' and 'confidence' suggest a more person-than discipline-centred approach than the discussion of similar terrain in the reflexivity report quoted above. Throughout the death course there was a kind of to-and-fro movement between a disciplinary (anthropology) and an interdisciplinary stance, and between a focus on what might be perceived as 'scholarly' and 'personal' experience. However, this is to suggest a contradiction, whereas the purpose of the course was precisely the integration of these two ways of knowing. At the first seminar the tutor presented her reasons for teaching the course: it was an anthropologist's perspective that set the course in the context of the social construction of death. However, this was not an *anthropology* course and this 'dominant' orientation was countered by several factors that opened up discussion of other perspectives: the choice of books, which included fiction and psychology, and the encouragement to talk about 'personal' experience, enabled divergent approaches to be introduced. Here are some quotations from students about their reactions to the course and to writing the journal:

> It helped me to feel that what I think is legitimate. Now I will be more confident about putting my own opinion into my essays.

> The journals are expansive – you work outwards from one idea. In an essay you have to select, whittle down.

> I had never thought much about death but one time I had an experience and realized how lonely death would be.

> It was nice to have an opportunity for self-expression in this setting.

> It was like having a conversation with myself.

The tutor expressed her pleasure that students felt 'comfortable' with being able to talk and write about experiences – in this case about a premonition of death and life after death – that were not a part of her own conceptual framework, that she would not have introduced herself, and that would not have appeared in an anthropology course.

The relatively free-flowing structure of the seminars was reflected in and consistent with the requirements of the journals, which also gave students an opportunity to make choices about content and to make connections between the texts read, the representation of death in the public domain and their personal experience. The notion of 'understanding' became a more integrated matter than is often the case in higher education, one that neither ruled out the personal nor allowed it to dominate. Personal thinking and experience were seen as valid in the academic setting – not just as a means to a different 'academic' kind of understanding, but in their own right, to be articulated, refined and developed in ways that the writer herself decided.

The following list indicates the range of areas the death journals dealt with but does not give a sense of how integrated different aspects could be:

- Friends' and relatives' deaths.
- 'Will I continue?'
- 'My longings for death'.

- Conference on Death and Diana, Princess of Wales.
- An art exhibition.
- How the gay community coped with AIDS.
- The Holocaust.
- Humour and death.

In the example below the writer has used a reading as a trigger for a narrative about her own experience: here she moves from a reflective section about deaths in her family to a reference to one of the course texts, and then moves back again to her experience that is now informed by the work she has read, so that it becomes difficult even to know whether she is referring to her own experience or that of the author. She is using the text for her own purpose to make sense of her experience and, reciprocally, also explicitly uses that experience to interpret the text. In this way, a holistic, autobiographical self that includes an articulation of her feelings and reflection is brought into the writing. In this example from a death journal the incorporation of an autobiographical 'reading self' is quite distinct from that of the record of study quoted above:

> I don't want to let him go, why should I, he's still my boy even in his death. Just as my mother is still my mother despite her death. I can move on – I have moved on – but I will not let go of what they are, that will remain with me always.
>
> While reading *Patrimony* for this course on Death, I felt unsure about Roth's feeling about his father's actual death. He writes beautifully about that pre-death feeling that certainly I experienced while nursing Mama though her cancer. . . . But when it comes to the point when his father dies the book ends. Maybe it was too soon to look at it. Maybe too painful, at a deeper level than the pain felt at illness, the pain felt at impending loss when you can still do something to help, or at least, reach out and touch a fragile but pulsing wrist, make contact with the living. After death nothing. They are gone . . . Roth writes about his father's own grief at his wife's death, and the depth of it, but it's almost as though he expected to be able to deal with the death itself artfully, and when it comes to talking about his own ultimate pains he can't. Maybe it wasn't what he expected and it threw him. I wonder if death, the finality of it, throws us all . . .

The interdisciplinary nature of the death course, the topic itself and particularly its accompanying journal opened up a space for students that allowed for their 'personal experience' in a way that was not relevant in the records of study: 'You could say what you wanted', one student believed of the death journals. This seemed to suggest to the students a different model of the personal that was something to do with a sense of self – perhaps of their 'own voice', as the tutor had put it. This partly came from their realization that their own experiences could be relevant in a university course, validated as they were both in the seminars and particularly by being included in the death journal course-work. Partly it was an evocation of the Romantic view of an authentic, individual self that persisted even in this course concerned with the social construction of selves. As Graham (1991) points out, a sense of the 'personal' as an 'authentic' individual voice was strongly present in work on writing in education in the UK in the 1970s (for examples, Britton 1970). Graham associates this with the idea, now in retreat, of an authentic, unique and unified self waiting to be released and expressed, usually through imaginative writing. This way of thinking about writing in education influenced generations of English teachers in the UK and particularly in the USA.

The notion of the authentic single voice has tended to have been replaced by, for example, the 'subject' in post-structuralist literary theory, or by the notion of multiple identities, in the way that Ivanič explores it. From this point of view, every act of writing, which can never escape the assumption of a discoursal self (in Ivanič's terms), is an interpretative construct – and conversely, every language act also positions the writer. As Usher (1993: 123) puts it, 'even the most personal meanings, where "I" seems to speak most authentically, are discursive articulations, interpretations though which tradition speaks and the "I" is spoken of'. This view of language as a means of constructing knowledge and identity also fits in with the notion of writing as a social practice that informs this volume. Indeed, it fits with some of the student experiences of writing the journals. Nevertheless, as Ivanič points out, the possibility of, and the need for, 'authenticity' in writing is strongly felt by student writers, whatever its source might be.

The death journal was not strongly presented in terms of an individual voice but both the journal and the death course itself had marks of that approach, as I have explored. Notwithstanding the fact that the tutor was an anthropologist and that the students on the course readily spoke of differences in their different writing 'I's, the impression of 'writing for myself' in the journals contrasted for many with the need to adapt to 'academic' ways of writing. That sense of 'writing for myself' might be variously interpreted – for example, in terms of a sense of an 'essential' self, or in terms of identities that felt more 'real' to the students, perhaps because they were more long-standing and entrenched, than the 'academic' self that they were in the process of constructing. As the students expressed it frequently in discussions about their journal writing, 'I could put my own opinions down', 'I felt I mattered'. With regard to the journals, the students took their assumption of being able to 'be myself' to mean that they could write as they liked in a way that felt empowering and liberating. This did not necessarily mean that the writing was 'easy' and in practice it was hedged around with their different senses of appropriateness. In some cases, in fact, writing a journal posed as many difficulties as any kind of writing might, and students sought guidelines on 'what to write', which they had to consider in relation to their readers and the course setting. There was therefore sometimes a tension for them between their sense of operating as an 'individual' and the demands of a particular writing task. All the same, the impression of being able to express the personal remained for them, and it was frequently validated by a strong authorial voice in their journals. The death journals explicitly invited aspects of the student's own experience to be brought in as a 'legitimate' part of the teaching and learning setting. Since death is, as the rubric for the course put it, a 'universal experience', it was a topic that everyone could, if they wished, engage with and relate to. One student expressed her belief that 'everyone who chose this course has a story to tell'. For this student – and it was true to a greater or lesser extent of many of the students on the course – the death journal was a place for telling these personal stories in a context that attempted to integrate the personal and the academic approach.

Directions

I am suggesting that the careful use of learning journals can offer a rather liberating opportunity for students to chart their own route through their studying in higher education. The records of study and the death journals were different from each other because their contexts were different, but they also had elements in common. By giving greater scope for the personal in the academic setting they allowed student writers to incorporate into their university writing ways of knowing that are usually absent from it, and opened up a different kind of space for their engagement with the course. By inviting students' 'autobiographical selves' to appear centrally on the academic stage, the journals offered a way of fostering the development of a confident authorial self that claims the right to write as a university student. By asking students to write differently, the journals allowed them to think differently. In this way the new forms of writing have a potential not only for enhancing student learning but also for expanding tutor and student perceptions of the boundaries of higher education. There are many courses for which learning journals would be useful. However, the different uses of the idea of the personal in the two courses I have looked at demonstrate how the introduction of learning journals needs to be thought through as carefully as any other curriculum innovation within any particular course. Among the issues to be considered are the following:

- How do the journals fit with the epistemological assumptions and purposes of the course?
- How will they be integrated into the teaching, learning and assessment processes?
- How much 'freedom' do the journals allow students in practice to negotiate their own relationship to the course?

It will be important to enable students to use the journals flexibly for their own purposes in relation to the course and to give both themselves and their readers the opportunity for enjoying their range and diversity. As the tutor on the death course put it: 'I like being surprised by the creativity of my students'.

Acknowledgements

I should like to acknowledge the help of Sussex University social anthropology tutors, particularly Jane Cowan, Jon Mitchell, Jeff Pratt, Alexander Schulenberg, Richard Wilson and Ann Whitehead; and of the students who took part in the 'New Forms of Student Writing' project. The views expressed here, and any shortcomings, are my own.

7

Writing in Postgraduate Teacher Training: A Question of Identity

Mary Scott

There are a number of professions in which entitlement to practise may depend on the acquisition of a vocationally oriented postgraduate qualification. Schoolteaching provides an obvious example, and initial teacher training at the postgraduate level is the immediate context within which student writing is considered in this chapter. To be more specific, the writing to which I shall be referring was produced by students on the one-year Postgraduate Certificate of Education (PGCE) course. As the word 'postgraduate' indicates, the students already held degrees of relevance to the subjects they wished to teach in the secondary school.

However, while the particularities of postgraduate teacher training are my primary focus, I would hope that they do not represent the limits of this chapter's relevance. In fact, I would suggest that teacher training can provide illustrations of wider issues and controversies which are likely to be pertinent in one form or another to any postgraduate course which includes time spent both in the university and in the 'real' world of a profession – a pertinence which may also encompass, to some extent, those undergraduate courses which are sited both in and outside institutions of higher education.

The field of education is characterized by a 'web' of dichotomies – dichotomies that apply equally to law, librarianship, nursing and business administration, to give but four examples. The metaphor of a web has a further usefulness, too: it suggests a generative centre. In this paper that location and function is given to 'theory' and 'practice' which are viewed as the dichotomy from whose substance other dichotomies are spun.

Popular discourse offers many examples of the antithetical evaluations which 'theory' and 'practice' currently tend to generate – the 'useless and the 'useful'; the 'half-baked' and the 'commonsensical'. Practice as learning by 'doing' in the 'real world' is not infrequently associated with 'high standards', while theory is regarded as remote from the 'real' and thus as failing through irrelevance to prepare learners for their future roles and tasks. In this way the perception of higher education institutions as far removed from the concerns of the 'real world' is reminted in forms which derive at least some of their emotive power from that deep-seated cultural myth of the 'ivory tower' in which reflection is held to be a nebulous and inadequate substitute for the concrete immediacy of action.

Politicians in the UK have criticized educational theory along these lines for some time. As early as 1983, for example, Sir Keith Joseph, Secretary of State for Education, referred to 'jargon-ridden theorizing' (Joseph 1983). Such attacks became more vehement in the early 1990s, culminating in the statutory requirement that schools play a greater role in the training of teachers. Thus it is that schools are now linked to training institutions in formal partnership arrangements whereby student teachers spend two-thirds of their time in the partnership schools. The partnerships vary considerably in their day-to-day detail and especially with regard to the components of the PGCE course to which teachers in schools make their greatest contribution.

However, even within this new context, the preferred mode of training continues to be reflection on practice (Wilkin 1996: 174). Like most teacher trainers, Carson (1995: 151) defends this focus against its critics: 'Reflective practice does signal an attitude of thoughtfulness that is necessary for teaching in these uncertain and changing times.' A consequence of this view is that the individual student is encouraged to think of herself as a 'reflective practitioner'. This image, which seems to confer a definite identity, is, however, highly problematic. In fact, so overused has it become in teacher education that, as Carson (1995: 151) himself has commented, it tends to be no more than an empty cliché:

> The phrase reflective practitioner has been abroad in the land. So much so that student teachers will roll their eyes at the very mention of the 'R' word. Surely it is a term that has been over-used in teacher education and students are right to object to its endless and often empty repetition.

This comment matches my own observations as a tutor. Consequently, in this chapter I attempt to put back into 'reflective practitioner' some of the complexity which is too often emptied out – a complexity which carries important pedagogic implications especially in relation to student writing. To pursue that aim I shift the focus from 'reflective practitioner' to the broader issues which it encapsulates – issues of *agency*. In other words, I base my change of focus on the fact that the primary purpose of reflection on practice is the promotion of the trainee teacher's agency. As I shall shortly indicate, this entails questions of identity and subjectivity.

New contexts have, however, led to new conceptions of the kind of agency, and so of agent, which the PGCE course should foster. In order to lend those new conceptions visibility in their relation to PGCE student writing, I next provide a contrasting background in the form of a brief discussion of PGCE student writing in the early 1990s. I base my comments on a study which I carried out in my role as a PGCE tutor on the 'education component', as it was then called.

A brief retrospect

Before the introduction of formal partnerships between schools and institutions of higher education, PGCE students were offered few written guidelines concerning the assignments they had to produce for assessment purposes. The main requirement was that they should relate theory to practice in an 'enquiry'. This specification had as its implicit corollary an idealized identity for the teacher trainee. The PGCE student was assumed to be an active and independent learner who would benefit from considerable freedom to pursue her own particular areas of interest – this being regarded as the pathway to the enhancement of her identity as an active, creative and autonomous practitioner, her *agency*. In other words, the student writer was expected to possess those dispositions which progressive pedagogy advised her to foster in learners in schools. This perception of learners as active and autonomous constructors of knowledge correlated with a view of writing which reaches back to the Romantic period and emphasizes creativity and individual expressiveness in meaning-making.

The final assessment of the students' assignments was consistent with this emphasis. Though the provision of minimal criteria might seem to allow students a number of possibilities, the assignments which were awarded high grades were usually strongly interpretative in their orientation. To be more specific, the students tended to follow the same basic pattern in which the abstractions of theory were teased out of concrete data such as vignettes from classrooms, or transcripts of recorded talk, or excerpts from policy documents. Consequently, though the assignments were referred to as 'enquiries', the most successful tended to be more like essays in which the students used theory in order to develop an individually distinctive and personally relevant perspective on some aspect of educational practice. It was, furthermore, a perspective which avoided simplistic conclusions; instead it showed an awareness of complexity and an abstention from easy answers.

The examiners' comments on the highly rated assignments added another dimension to this emphasis on individual and personally relevant meaning-making. The assignments were treated as if they were mirrors of the writer's subjectivity – a subjectivity regarded implicitly, if not explicitly, as constituting the trainee teacher's ideal identity and the source of her agency in the classroom. The examiners referred, for example, to students' 'maturity of understanding', and to their being 'sensitive and knowledgeable', 'imaginative' and 'insightful'. There were some references to traditional academic criteria such as 'this is a cogent argument', 'there is evidence of wide reading'. Such criteria were, however, usually shaped into personal qualities – for example:

> he demonstrates an ability to synthesize, compare, sustain an argument with evidence of originality.

A particularly graphic illustration of the extent to which an assignment could thus become identified with the individual who wrote it is provided by the following examiner's comment:

> This is clearly an enthusiastic and hardworking student with consider-able imagination and promise who should do well in her future career.

This tendency to treat the students' texts as indices of their identity is problematic. However, the problem should not be seen as deriving solely from a possible mismatch between the qualities suggested by an individual student's assignment and those the student might be said to demonstrate in the classroom. Such an explanation would not challenge what most needs to be questioned, since it would reinforce certain assumptions concerning the student's subjectivity – assumptions which can be captured by borrowing those aspects of Bernstein's (1996: 56) characterization of 'competence' which identify the latter with an 'in-built creativity, an in-built virtuous self-regulation'.

'Competence', as thus described, serves to make visible the alliance that was being forged on the PGCE course between, on the one hand, progress-ive views of the learner, and, on the other hand, the view of student writing as the expression of inner capacities implicitly regarded as the source of a teacher's agency in the classroom. The visibility of this alliance helps in its turn to bring into sight, and so to open up to discussion, what has been edited out – any suggestion that writing does not come naturally even at the postgraduate level. Once we attempt to address that omission and so begin to focus on student writing as potentially assisted by teaching, we are inevit-ably confronted with issues relating to language. I do not, however, restrict language in this context to its lexical and grammatical forms. Few of the PGCE students had difficulties of that kind. In fact most of them were fluent and experienced academic writers. My focus is rather on a student assignment as a text being shaped by the writer; in short, as an example of written discourse (Bazerman 1981). This, I would suggest, is an approach which could address what the students themselves perceived to be their most pressing difficulty. As one of them put it:

> The difficulty I had with the assignment was really not knowing . . . what reflecting on practice would be like as a piece of writing.

In more recent years, students have been provided with detailed written guidelines intended to help them know 'what it would be like as a piece of writing'. However, as I shall demonstrate below, the new context of teacher education has created its own tensions and problems.

A new context: teacher training as a partnership

When the examiners' primary criterion was an interpretative focus in which the writer developed an individual set of meanings, arts graduates, and especially those with degrees in English, tended to obtain higher grades than did science or maths graduates. This is not surprising, since the students could transfer to classrooms and schools the kind of close interpretative reading with which they were already familiar.

The recognition of how the written assignment advantaged some students while disadvantaging others was one factor which led to the development of new, more detailed guidelines. However, as I shall indicate below, the introduction of the statutory requirement that trainee teachers spend two-thirds of their time in schools was a more immediately pressing influence: teachers in schools were to be involved in advising students on their professional studies assignments. Because they did not have a shared understanding of what was expected of students, a more detailed and explicit specification was required. Adopting an even wider perspective, I see a possible link between the more detailed character of the new guidelines and a change in the general perception of learners and learning in higher education. The new guidelines can be said to reflect a growing emphasis in UK universities on the importance of pedagogy – an emphasis which has led to an insistence that assessment criteria be made explicit to students. A selective plundering of Bernstein's (1996) theories once again helps me to crystallize this change of focus: 'performance', a term which subsumes 'specialized outputs' and the 'explicit rules for realising them', has replaced 'competence'. To put it another way, by drawing on the current government-coined language of teacher training, 'competence' has been ousted by 'competencies'.

However, in the institution in which I work the greater involvement of schools in the training of teachers was largely viewed as a welcome opportunity to develop an improved PGCE course in which theory and practice could be more closely integrated. To emphasize the value of the extensive participation of trainees in the life of schools, 'student teachers' were renamed 'beginning teachers'. For similar reasons the 'education component' is now the 'professional studies' programme. This programme is currently based on the recognition that a teacher is engaged in a wide variety of educational aims and objectives beyond those demonstrated within curriculum areas. Lectures and seminars thus cover cross-curricular topics such as the history of the education system, language and learning, pupil learning and differentiation.

In accordance with the aim of partnership between schools and the higher education training institution, beginning teachers are at present required to carry out a 'school-focused enquiry' as well as a 'research and development' project under the tutorship of teachers in their placement schools, these enquiries being partly intended as a contribution to the school on the part of the beginning teacher. The questions or problems to be addressed are decided in discussion with the teachers, but the assessment criteria are provided by the training institution. These criteria are designed to indicate the 'postgraduateness' of postgraduate teacher training, an aim which I shall comment on later. Students have to relate theory to practice, construct an argument, appreciate the usefulness and limitations of their research methods and assess the value of their research. The two pieces of writing can (and in the case of the research and development project, usually do) become the basis of the professional studies assignments which the beginning teachers submit at the end of their course.

The trainees are now given detailed written guidelines which break down the school-focused enquiry and the research and development project into component parts. The following excerpt from the abstract of one beginning teacher's final assignment illustrates the pattern that frequently results:

> The first section deals with the formulation of the investigation. It begins by posing the main question of the study . . . and why it is important. . . . The second section explains the methods employed to obtain information and examines the findings of the investigation. . . . The third section . . . seeks to discern . . . what strategies could be employed to remedy the situation, and the degree of support for them. . . . The fourth section includes an appraisal of the limitations of the data . . . and the methods used to obtain information.

In short, the guidelines offered to students represent a move towards 'performance', that is, towards 'specialized outputs' requiring 'specialized skills' and 'explicit rules of realisation' (Bernstein 1996). In this instance, a successful display of 'performance' requires the student to adopt an empirical-positivist view of 'research' – a view which the training institution identifies with 'postgraduateness'. In practice, this research paradigm can lead to a rather mechanical application of the guidelines, with the beginning teacher offering a few generalizations about the limitations of questionnaires or interviews (generalizations which could be found in any textbook on research methods), and then tagging on brief summaries of vaguely relevant theories. This is hardly a demonstration of 'postgraduateness', if 'postgraduateness' is taken to mean an understanding of research paradigms and the importance of 'methodological integrity' (Brown and Dowling 1998).

However, most assignments use the guidelines less slavishly and in ways which point to the students' individual interpretations of the relation between theory and practice – interpretations which turn on what the students make of the partnership between training institution and school. In the next part of this chapter I analyse two assignments which I have selected as illustrations of very different approaches and which together show how two beginning teachers position themselves in relation to the competing discourses of competence and performance; that is, in relation to the unarticulated but clearly evident parameters of their conception of their agency in the classroom.

A framework for analysing students' written texts

I base my analyses on the four interrelated contexts which Bazerman (1981) identified as shaping written academic discourse. Those contexts are: the object under study; the literature of the field; the anticipated audiences; and the writer's own self. Bazerman was analysing papers by well-known academics (J.D. Watson and F.H.C. Crick, Robert K. Merton, and Geoffrey H. Hartman) who were intent on presenting new knowledge, but the difference between professional academic writers and students is actually an advantage in this instance in that it throws into relief the particular contours of the students' situatedness as writers. In other words, as this reference to situatedness indicates, I seek to avoid the Romantic view of the writer which I outlined above and associated with 'competence'. In place of the decontextualized, creative individual whose writing is viewed as the expression of certain personal qualities or dispositions, I propose a text in which the writer is primarily visible in the connections she makes with, and between, the object of study, the literature of the field and the anticipated reader(s).

In Bazerman's paper the four contexts both impose a coherence on the three examples of academic discourse which he discusses, and simultaneously illuminate the differences in the shaping of the three texts. The 'objects under study' – the structure of DNA, the ambivalence of scientists, and Wordsworth's later poetry – are differentiated in terms of their modality: DNA is an object that exists in the world; the ambivalence of scientists is, however, a concept which has to be argued for; and Wordsworth's later poems are the medium of Hartman's 'subjective recreation of the poetic moment'. It is from these differences in the 'object under study' that Bazerman largely derives his account of the differences in the other contexts. The use of the literature of the field and the role of the anticipated audiences (in this case the writers' peers) mainly differ according to what is regarded as accepted knowledge in each case. Thus Crick and Watson do not need to rehearse the literature relating to DNA but only that concerning its structure, while Merton has to show that ambivalence is a significant absence from the literature about scientific behaviour. Hartman, on the other hand, does not need to refer to other critics' readings in order to persuade his peers that his interpretation is both plausible and enriching of their response.

It is not my purpose to evaluate Bazerman's paper in terms of its adequacy as an account of academic discourse or to use it to develop a theory of writing. What Bazerman offers me is a theoretical orientation or convenient comparative frame within which to discuss student writing. In fact, the value I derive from Bazerman's paper rests finally on the contrast between the smooth coherence which he discerns in the examples of academic discourse he analyses, and the tensions in the PGCE students' assignments which are made visible by attention to these four contexts.

As already indicated, those tensions point finally to questions of agency which turn on where the students locate themselves in relation to theory and practice, a positioning which corresponds to where they see themselves in the partnership between the school and the institution of higher education, and how they interpret 'beginning teacher'. Thus the 'writer's own self', which tends to be a neglected context in Bazerman's paper, becomes the central, albeit largely implicit, context in the beginning teachers' assignments.

The two assignments which I have selected for discussion were each given high grades. They are representative of different approaches, but together they bring into focus what it means to write about education from within the new context of a partnership between school and higher education institution.

Beginning teacher A's assignment

The 'object under study' seems clear at first glance. The writer tells us in her brief abstract that the assignment 'looks at some of the theories in the areas of language and learning, language acquisition and bilingualism in the mainstream, and their common currency'. However, 'in the mainstream' signals that her primary concern is not with theory as theory, but rather with theory in its capacity to serve practice. Practice comes more sharply into focus in the next sentence of the abstract: beginning teacher A states that she 'also looks at the ways in which the partnership school provides for its bilingual learners' needs, and at the school's policy statement and recommendations for good practice'. The emphasis on practice is intensified when, in the sentence that follows, A tells her readers that she is in search of 'models of good pedagogy' which can inform her future teaching. This hint of autobiography recursively draws theory and practice into an alliance within a subsuming and personally pertinent object of study – the nature and sources of the teacher's agency in the classroom. As will emerge later, agency (and so also identity) here turns on a clash of discourses in which the meanings and values which A finds in her reading compete with those which she encounters in the world of the school.

At this point a return to Bazerman's paper can serve to highlight the problematic and demanding nature of the beginning teacher's task as an assignment writer. Bazerman's academics each dealt with an object of study which they defined in relation to procedures and knowledge in their well-established fields. The beginning teacher, on the other hand, has to create the object of study within the demands and expectations of the higher education institution and the school.

The implications of this dual situatedness are more clearly traceable within A's assignment when her use of the literature of the field is brought into focus. It is there that she finds her theoretical perspective – a perspective which matches Bernstein's description of 'competence'. This is evident in the assignment's full but concise summaries of the emphasis on personal meaning-making which is to be found in, for example, Barnes *et al.* (1990) and Levine (1990) – an emphasis which offers a view of knowledge as constructed by active learners. The assignment outlines in general terms the pedagogic corollary of this view of knowledge and its implications for the teacher's agency in the classroom – teachers can promote learning by valuing the experience which the learners bring to their learning and by helping them to make links between that experience and the new knowledge which the teacher is introducing.

Beginning teacher A invests her sources with considerable authority. This is evident in the reporting verbs which she uses – 'point out', 'show' and 'demonstrate' – and in her use of generalizations that appeal to accepted wisdom. For example:

> The importance of providing opportunities for pupils to continue to develop literacy skills in their first languages is now well accepted.

Furthermore, the authority she gives to her sources is invariably located in the authors themselves. Thus sentences like the following which begin with a personal subject are the most frequent form of reference: 'John Wright shows'; 'Wright points to . . .'; 'Marion Williams and Robert L. Burden . . . identify'; 'Torbe explains'. In short, the educationists to whom A refers are treated as mentors offering her insights which she feels she needs to be able to translate directly into practice. Consequently, ideas are not treated as ideas to be set against other ideas in the development of an argument or a personal philosophy of education. She has found a philosophy ready-made in what she has read, and she implicitly ascribes the teacher's agency in the classroom to an ability to convert that competence-oriented philosophy into a recipe for practice. However, that practice is located in a school where the national curriculum and national assessment have introduced a different discourse – a performance-oriented discourse. This has implications for A's realization in her text of the other two contexts which Bazerman proposes – the anticipated audience and the writer's own self.

The sense of audience which the assignment suggests is further evidence of the emphasis on personal meaning-making which A saw as defining the teacher as an agent in the classroom. In that she refocuses her own experience in the light of her reading and acknowledges her needs and interests, the assignment takes on some of the qualities of a personal narrative or diary: she writes for herself perhaps more than for others. For example:

> I wanted to know more [about language and learning] . . . I now realise that my sensitivity to low levels of fluency may have masked my need to understand far more about the ways in which cultural identities are constructed. I remind myself that there are many ways of doing this which do not involve academic text and enquiry.

Beginning teacher A is, of course, also writing for the examiners and the teachers in the partnership school. However, it is clear that she expects a sympathetic audience since she entrusts her readers with the kind of self-reflectiveness illustrated by the comment above.

Bazerman's fourth context, the writer's own self, is woven into A's text in ways that spring directly from her experience in the classroom. The primary identity which is adopted is that of a beginning teacher, and it is an identity which she finds difficult, as she states several times. For example, she writes:

The need to know has to be created cooperatively by teachers and students in ways that are personally meaningful to learners. This reality is a tall order for beginning teachers.

This positioning of herself in relation to experienced teachers is a theme that keeps surfacing. However, what it serves to conceal is the actual nature of A's problem. While increasing experience will no doubt bring greater expertise, I would suggest that her difficulties currently derive from competing identities which turn on a conflict between competence and performance. On the one hand, she endorses competence-oriented discourses which locate agency in an empowering personal meaning-making (in fact, in view of her enthusiasm her identity might be said to be that of a disciple); on the other hand, she is also a practising teacher encountering performance-oriented concepts such as 'transferable skills'. However, since she assumes that competence discourses should translate into rules for the realization of specialized outputs, she sees no contradiction between 'personal meaning-making' and 'transferable skills' or between Levine's (1990) competence view of communication and the performance strategies of the communicative approach to language teaching to which she refers approvingly in the descriptions of actual lessons which she includes in her assignment.

At this point I need to emphasize that I do not see the problems which I have described as originating in the student. Her assignment is thoughtful and perceptive, and the bedrock values which she expresses (for example, valuing each student's language and culture) are ones which all teachers should surely hold. What I am suggesting is that the pressures associated with being a beginning teacher who spends most of her time in school inevitably result in a strongly felt need for 'answers', and too little time for reading. Thus, whereas in the early 1990s the PGCE students with high grades developed a personal perspective out of theoretically focused analyses of exemplars of practice, the assignments of the high achievers among the beginning teachers now tend to demonstrate an understandable desire to plunder a narrow range of theory in a search for solutions to immediate problems. However, as I shall argue later, there is a way forward which would not imply going back to the past.

Beginning teacher B's assignment

Beginning teacher B experienced the same dual situatedness as beginning teacher A, but handled it differently in her assignment. Whereas A is primarily concerned with the application of theory, and wants practice to be in line with it, B concentrates on practice. In fact, she implicitly, and almost immediately, presents practice as more 'real' than theory. Thus, although the 'object under study' is initially 'differentiation targeting different abilities', the meaning of that concept is dealt with briefly – a definition drawn from Capel *et al.* (1995) soon getting it out of the way:

Differentiation targeting different abilities is about 'raising the standards of all pupils in a school not just those underachieving. It can
be conceived of as within a whole school policy . . . [and] is a planned
process of intervention in the classroom learning of the pupil. It
takes into account prior learning and the characteristics of the individual.'

(Capel *et al.* 1995: 121)

Having thus disposed of problems of definition, B turns to her primary
object of study – 'differentiation', not as a concept but as a practice. Keeping within that focus, B investigates the extent to which differentiation is in
place in the school where she is teaching. Having established that it is in
fact a school policy which is implemented in most classes, she arrives at her
main concern, 'bad behaviour'. Following the pattern of research provided
in the assignment guidelines, she then frames a question:

To what extent can differentiation targeting ability and learning styles
help to alleviate bad behaviour?

This question suggests that the object under study derives from anxieties
relating to her actual experience in the classroom either as an observer or
as a teacher.

The emphasis on practice also influences her choice of relevant literature. She chooses texts which she sees as having a direct bearing on her
empirical question. Furthermore, she places what she takes from her reading alongside the comments of members of staff whom she interviews,
treating the two sets of sources as similar in kind – both are open to question.
This is strongly indicated in her choice of reporting verbs coupled with a
personal subject: for example, 'Gardner proposes'; 'she (a support teacher)
believes'; 'Topping claims'; 'according to Reid *et al.*'. However, in referring
to her own research, she draws on a positivist paradigm, attributing the
status of the real and certain to her results and conclusions. She 'discovers',
she 'shows', she produces 'findings'. She admits to responding to Gardner's
theory of multiple intelligences with enthusiasm, and declares that she will
not abandon her interest in the theory even though it has been strongly
criticized. She is, however, no disciple: she states that she will put Gardner's
theory to the test in the future, using a larger, more carefully selected
sample of students. She thus indicates once again that she holds an instrumental view of theory: it should serve practice. However, she assumes that it
can only do so if legitimated by the results of research that uses recognized
quantitative methods. This assumption can be said to place the teacher's
agency firmly within 'performance' as defined by Bernstein (1996): agency
now depends on having the specialized research skills which will enable
specialized outputs – findings which can be applied in the classroom.

In contrast with A, who writes primarily for herself, B can be seen to
regard her main audience as the teachers in the partnership school. She
acts as an informant, as is evident in her didactic mode of presentation. For

example, she asks questions such as 'What is mixed ability?' and 'What is differentiation?', and then provides the answers.

As the discussion above has already suggested, the image of the 'writer's own self' which emerges from B's assignment is primarily that of an apprentice researcher. However, the day-to-day business and concerns of beginning teachers do not allow a place for a training in research or for detailed planning and discussion of a proposed project. Beginning Teacher B has thus finally to conclude that her procedures were inadequate and that none of her findings have any significance. Paradoxically, it is in her detailed account of the limitations of her investigation that the merits of her assignment lie.

The general significance of the above analyses of the two assignments can be summarized in the following way: each assignment finally points to the tensions and problems associated with the current siting of the PGCE course in both the school and the university. However, whereas beginning teacher A does not perceive the conflict between 'competence' and 'performance' (Bernstein 1996) perspectives on the teacher's agency, B identifies agency in the classroom with an exclusive, performance-oriented emphasis on what is testable within a positivist paradigm.

Conclusions

To conclude this chapter, I turn finally to issues of pedagogy which rest on my selective borrowing and recontextualizing of 'competence' and 'performance'. In so far as it is identified with an 'in-built creativity', 'competence' can imply that writing cannot be taught. 'Performance', on the other hand, can suggest that all aspects of writing can be acquired as explicit 'rules of realization' or 'transferable skills'. As tutors we need to question the 'competence' view of the student writer, while also resisting the extremes of 'performance'. Steering between that Scylla and Charybdis is no easy task since there are no detailed maps; each of us, like each of our students, has finally to find her own route, but an awareness of the need to find a route can only help, as can discussion with colleagues (in both the school and the university) of possible ways forward.

Such discussion should not, of course, be seen as uniquely appropriate to teacher training. It should have a place, too, in other professions, such as business administration, nursing, law and librarianship, where students also move between the workplace and the university. In fact, I would argue that students could be in a better position to understand and negotiate the tensions deriving from those two contexts if tutors gave writing a more prominent pedagogic role. What I have in mind is a series of seminars in which the numerous issues pertaining to each of Bazerman's four contexts would be addressed in relation to samples of writing which would include published texts from the course reading lists as well as the students' own coursework in draft or final form. As the analyses of the beginning teachers' assignments have indicated, such an approach could accommodate attention to the particularities of linguistic choice within the competing discourses of the workplace and the university.

No matter what their precise content, such discourses tend to dichotomize theory and practice. Within the context of seminars such as I am suggesting, however, the notion of the 'reflective practitioner' would fill with newly minted meaning, since its complex relation to individual conceptions of agency would be visible and open to discussion. In other words, students would address and crystallize for themselves those issues of identity and subjectivity which would inevitably shape not only their writing but also their mode of response to the pressures and demands of learning both on and away from the job.

8

A Question of Attribution: The Indeterminacy of 'Learning from Experience'

Simon Pardoe

Introduction

Reading and marking texts that students have written can be a dispiriting experience. Sometimes it seems that key points of the course have not registered in the students' minds. Often the texts seem even to lack a basic knowledge of writing 'that surely should have been acquired long ago'. In the words of one concerned university tutor whose course I researched, and describe here, "you can sometimes wonder what planet they are coming from".[1]

Criticism of student writing, by employers and politicians, and within higher education, is all too familiar. The difficulty is that such criticism, and accompanying calls that 'something should be done', is not actually helpful either to tutors or to students in understanding the difficulties they face in moving forward. Understanding *unsuccessful* student writing, in a way that offers practical insight and ways forward, is one of the key challenges for writing research.

What is fascinating about researching student writing as a participant observer is the opportunity to hear students' talk around their writing, and accounts of their writing. In this role, not immersed in the teaching and marking, it is possible to gain a quite different insight into the students' texts. In cases where, as the tutor, I would find their texts apparently confused and 'lacking', as a researcher I have the opportunity to explore *why*. This is the opportunity to try to understand the *origins* of the unsuccessful aspects of students' texts.

Like many other researchers, I often find that apparent problems in student writing do not simply represent a *lack* of skills, knowledge or understanding by students. Unsuccessful texts are often the result of students drawing on familiar ways of learning and writing that have served them well elsewhere, in their previous education, or in other areas of their lives. In the words of Shaunessey (1977) the students' unsuccessful texts potentially have a 'rationale' or 'logic'. We need to understand this if we want to know what further guidance students may need. And in doing so, we may find that we abandon the common view of any teaching of writing as somehow 'remedial' – as teaching only what students should have learned before (Hull and Rose 1989; Swales 1990; Hull 1997).[2]

What I find particularly striking from being a participant observer in a course, and from talking to students about their writing, is just how difficult it is, for the novice or outsider, to work out what is required in a new context. A task or instruction may seem very clear when you are already very familiar with what is being learned, or are simply a passive observer. But the same task may be very unclear and very ambiguous to the student who is trying to use it to guide their actions and writing.

Equally, I am struck by just how difficult it is for tutors to make explicit what is required. Firstly, what is required seems so familiar and obvious to the tutor. Indeed, most of our own learning has been 'on the job', and may have remained very implicit. Secondly, there *is* actually no recipe to writing, say, an 'essay' or a 'financial audit'. For good reasons such texts are not all the same. Thirdly, even when we become aware of the students' need for more detailed guidance, we can feel that we are walking a tightrope between giving this guidance, and feeling we are 'spoon-feeding' the students. In most courses, there is a belief that part of the challenge is that students should work out what is required. Within vocational courses in particular, part of the *intention* is that students learn how to work out what is required within a particular professional scenario.

In this chapter I focus on a potentially major source of misunderstanding between tutor and student, that can lead to students writing texts considered unsuccessful by the tutor. I call this the "question of attribution". It arises when students are involved in 'learning from experience'. More generally, it arises when students are attempting to develop some general understanding from a particular case.

My argument is that learning from an experience in any context involves working out what aspects of it can be taken as generally significant, and what should be regarded as more particular. We cannot assume that the significance of an experience is self-evident. For example, within vocational education, where an activity or experience is inevitably linked to both the educational and the professional contexts, the process of learning from an experience involves working out what aspects of it can be taken as offering insight into the profession, and what should be regarded as being a consequence of doing it within the classroom. The implication is that for students to understand a particular activity or experience in the way we intend, we need to make explicit the significance that we attach to it.

The examples I will offer to illustrate this are taken from a vocational MSc course in environmental science: the students were learning to carry out and to write an "environmental impact assessment" (EIA). But first I want to argue that the "question of attribution" is an important issue in any context of 'learning from experience', both within and beyond education.

Figure 8.1   Attributing an experience of academic debate

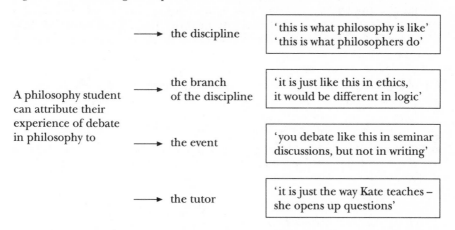

A question of attribution

Within traditional academic education

Within traditional academic education, in which there is an explicit and primary focus on *learning about*, there is nevertheless an important process in which the students 'learn from experience'. They learn at least some of the practices of the discipline through the activities within the course. For example, philosophy students may experience the practice of philosophical debate through the seminars they take part in. However, what they actually *learn* from this about philosophy (that is, about the practices of the discipline) depends on *a question of attribution*. I explain this in Figure 8.1.

What the students learn about philosophy from their experience of debate therefore depends on the way in which they attribute this experience. Crucially it affects whether they think they should reproduce the practices of debate within their essays, and in other courses. In other words, the absence of debate in a student's essay may not 'show' the author's lack of skill or understanding of philosophical debate. Rather, it may reflect their view or assumption that this is not required in an essay. (If debate is indeed required in an essay, students therefore need both explicit guidance that this is so, and guidance on *how* to debate in writing, rather than only in speech.)

Similar questions also arise within other disciplines, and particularly when students are studying in several disciplines at once. For example, sociology, philosophy, English and linguistics embody different views about what 'counts' as evidence and argument. Students who manage to work out what 'counts' in one course may attribute this to the particular course or to the discipline, or may assume it has broader significance for all academic writing. Without guidance, they may sometimes appear to 'fail' to draw on what they have learned elsewhere, and at other times apply practices that were successful in one context to other contexts in which they are seen as unsuccessful.

This applies also within 'study skills' courses which prepare students for academic study. In such courses the students are often engaged in activities in groups of mixed disciplines, and the tutors are under pressure to claim that the activities and experience they provide have the kind of general relevance implied by the notion of 'skills'. There can therefore be some ambiguity in the attribution of particular activities (within, say, an 'essay' or 'seminar') to 'academia in general' or to specific disciplines and sub-disciplines.

Within science education

Within science education, the notion of 'learning by doing' or 'learning by experience' has become almost the dominant pedagogy. Students learn not only the practices of science but even the course content by 'finding things out for themselves', by doing experiments, by 'discovery'. For example, even in school, physics students may measure the gravitational pull of the earth for themselves, by conducting an experiment to measure the way an object accelerates when dropped. They learn both about the practices of experimentation in science, and about gravity.

However, this learning process involves a process of attribution. If students measure an object's acceleration to be, say, 10.5 instead of $9.8 \, \text{m/s}^2$ (as it is recognized to be), they have to attribute this wrong result to their own inaccurate measurement or limited equipment and time. In other words, they have to attribute their result to the constraints in the classroom, rather than to actual variations in gravity!

The point is that this attribution, and the basis for it, may never be explicitly discussed. Through recording teacher–student and student–student conversations in science classrooms, Edwards and Mercer (1987) and others show teachers caught in the difficult position of believing students should 'discover' for themselves, but also wanting them to know the 'right answer'. They show teachers attributing significance and insignificance to the students' different measurements, guided by their own knowledge of what the result *should* be. They show students acquiescing with judgements made by the teacher, and accepting or rejecting measurements and hypotheses, "on no basis that is ever explained to them" (Edwards and Mercer 1987: 124). The implication is that students learn to attribute significance and insignificance to their measurements, often arbitrarily, to produce what is expected. (Ironically, in doing so they miss experiencing the intended practices of science – of pursuing and testing observations so as to produce empirical findings that are accountable to their evidence.)

Figure 8.2 Attributing the significance of scientific observations

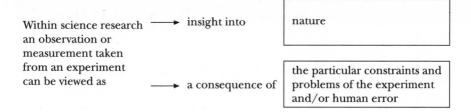

Within science research

Beyond education, attribution is also required of scientists themselves. One of the key observations in sociological studies of the construction of scientific knowledge is of the ways in which research scientists, in doing research, have to attribute variations in their results either to the experiment or to nature. They have to ask whether a particular result, which may be different from what they had expected, is due to experimental problems, or is actually telling them something new about the atoms, cells or whatever they are experimenting with. This is a process of assigning significance to the observation or experience (see Figure 8.2).[3]

Within the workplace

Attribution is also an issue for those involved in learning professional practices from their experience in the workplace. A new employee who is, say, dealing with procedures on the factory floor, writing letters for the boss, or compiling a financial audit, and learning from this experience 'on the job', is involved in a process of attribution. They are involved in learning general practices from particular experiences. Yet aspects of these particular experiences may or may not illustrate general and potentially repeatable practice: they may equally represent practices that are particular to the company or institution, or particular to a single case. Moreover, rather than representing the aims or ideals of the profession, they may represent the response of professional practice to certain constraints of time and resources. I show this in Figure 8.3.

Without guidance on understanding the significance of their experiences, the learner may attribute an experience in ways that are quite different from the understandings of their employer. Moreover, their attribution of the experience has implications for their developing understanding of the profession. It has implications for whether they will repeat or modify particular decisions and actions in a subsequent case, and in a subsequent text. (It has implications for whether they will be seen as personally successful in learning the job, and as either 'bright' or 'slow'.)

Figure 8.3 Attributing the significance of an experience in the workplace

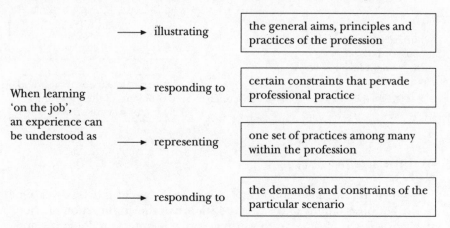

Attribution within vocational education

What is interesting about vocationally or professionally oriented education is that it seems to bring together all the questions of attribution that I have described in these other contexts. The difficulty for the student, and the potential for misunderstanding and 'unsuccessful' writing, are even greater.

Typically, vocationally oriented courses aim to engage students actively in the kinds of professional practices that they need to know and understand in a future career. The familiar teaching process aims to echo the process of learning on the job, to create a situation in which students are learning by doing and 'learning from experience'. In particular, such courses engage students in actually producing the kinds of professional documents (such as reports, audits, letters) that they would produce in the workplace. In some cases this is explicitly called "simulation". In others it is not. Students may simply be asked to carry out, and to write, say, a financial audit or an environmental impact assessment (EIA), as if they were in a professional context.

On the one hand, this 'learning from experience' demands the same process of attribution as I described for those learning 'on the job', with the same potential problems and implications. Students are involved in learning aspects of general professional practice from the experience of particular examples. They have to infer what, say, financial audits or environmental assessments are like in general (that is, the genre) from the particular text(s) they may have read and written. Aspects of the experience may illustrate general and repeatable practices, or they may represent merely one set of practices among many, or a response to a particular scenario and particular professional constraints. Students' attribution of the experience is central to their developing understanding of the profession.

Figure 8.4   Attributing the significance of an experience within vocational education

In learning from experience, within a vocationally oriented course an activity or experience can be construed as:

illustrating	the general aims, principles and practices of the profession
responding to	certain constraints that pervade professional practice
representing	one set of practices among many within the profession
responding to	the demands and constraints of the particular scenario
constituting deviations from professional practice due to	the constraints, practices and priorities of the educational context

Within education, this potentially problematic process is often made more difficult by the pedagogic practice of using single large course-work assignments for both learning and assessment. Students are often involved in learning professional practice from the experience of only one simulation or example activity. This is, of course, particularly problematic when professional practices are not singular or universal, but achieve subtly different functions in different settings.

On the other hand, learning from experience within vocational education poses an additional question of attribution. In parallel to the research scientist learning from a scientific experiment (above), students are engaged in learning from a classroom activity that has been set up in a context removed from the professional context in which this activity is more usually carried out. This means that tutors and students have the potential to attribute an activity or experience to either context. They can view an experience as offering insight into the practice and experiences of the profession, by attributing the experience to 'the real world out there'. Alternatively, they can attribute it to the 'here and now', and view the experience as being merely a consequence of doing the activity within the constraints and priorities of the educational context. I represent this in Figure 8.4.

As before, this attribution is a very fundamental process of *assigning significance* to an activity or experience. If the tutor or students attribute an activity or experience to the wider profession, they will see it as significant insight and learning. If they attribute it to the 'here and now' of the course, they will see it as insignificant or irrelevant to 'real' professional practice. They will also see it as not worthy of inclusion in their professional text. This attribution is therefore central to the students' developing understanding and learning, and to their writing.

If you are familiar with vocational education you will recognize the link here to the familiar classroom talk about whether an activity is 'real' or 'not real'. In a climate in which 'academic' is often used pejoratively to mean 'removed', or even 'irrelevant', the very legitimacy of a course can be construed in terms of the links to the 'real' profssional practices of the workplace. Course information and publicity often emphasize these links: this serves to construct the identity of the department, discipline and course as 'in touch' and 'relevant' to the 'real world' of employment. It also serves to attract students who are making choices within increasingly modularized degree programmes.

Even within the lectures, talk and handouts of the tutor, there are often claims that the activity is 'real' or 'realistic', and that the students will be writing, say, 'a proper report', as they would do in a professional context. It is also common to hear students talking to each other in these terms. They may come to a course with an interest in learning about the kind of professional activity in which they might be engaged in a future career. They may even be quite dismissive of an activity as 'not real', and may draw on their prior knowledge and assumptions of 'real' professional practice in guiding their writing.

I have come to be interested in this kind of talk, of tutors and students, because of its power in legitimizing and delegitimizing educational activities and experience. On the one hand, it is part of a view of education in which 'relevance' is seen narrowly in terms of preparing students for employment. On the other hand, it is part of the fundamental process of attributing significance to experience, and learning from it. Such talk can reveal different understandings by the tutor and students, both of the course activity and of what was required of the students' texts.

Two examples of attribution

I will cite two examples from a study of an MSc course in environmental science. The research was carried out in collaboration with the tutor, who was concerned that previous students' texts were frequently disappointing: this was despite his offering students both tutorial support and an example of a professional text. Significantly, the study was therefore an opportunity to research the issues and difficulties in learning and guiding professional writing that arise even within 'good practice'; even when the tutor is interested in writing, recognizes the kinds of demands he is making on the students, and already offers students additional support.

I say this because there is an unfortunate habit within education of attributing unsuccessful student writing first to students' lack of effort, understanding or ability, and second to the tutor's lack of expertise or 'poor explanation'. These may often be issues but, as readily available and rather easy 'explanations', they are ways of avoiding recognizing the complexity of teaching and learning academic and professional writing, by blaming individuals. In the short term they involve an unhelpful denigrating of the efforts and expertise of tutors and students. In the longer term they prevent real improvement in our collective professional practice and understanding, and undermine the expertise and value of education.

The challenge for researchers and educational managers is to avoid simply blaming individuals, and to recognize and explore the difficulty (for the tutor) of describing and explaining the kind of writing that is required of students, and the difficulty (for the students) of attempting to understand and (re)produce academic or professional texts from these accounts. The challenge is to try to understand the sources of difficulty and what can help.

In vocational education tutors are often criticized for a lack of experience in the 'real world' beyond education. In this case, the tutor was himself a practising professional in environmental impact assessment. He had considerable experience of the 'real world' of the profession. This is partly why his course was so interesting in terms of the question of attribution. He frequently described his own professional experience, and told the students that this course activity offered them a 'real' experience of EIA. In other words, he frequently and explicitly attributed the course to the professional context.

EIA is an activity which has to be carried out under UK and EU legislation. The function of it is to investigate and predict the likely environmental impact of a proposed development, such as a road, supermarket or airport runway, and to communicate this to the local planning authority. In the UK it is simply called environmental assessment (EA). The course I researched involved some traditional introductory lecture input, but the focus was on students learning about EA through actually doing one, and writing one. They were given a scenario, and a copy of a provisional development proposal – in this case to extract gravel from beneath a local estuary. They were also given lots of data about the estuary itself, to use in their environmental assessment.

I joined the course as a participant observer: I attended and recorded the lectures, field trips, seminars, practicals and tutorials. The students were writing in teams of six, to simulate professional practice. With their permission I joined their meetings, in which they were discussing what they were going to do, generally liaising, and collaborating in producing the final text. I also interviewed both the students and the tutor during and after the course.

In the analysis I explored the apparent origins of aspects of the students' texts that the tutor had criticized in his assessment. I went back to the recordings of the student discussions, and to the moments when they discussed these particular features or aspects of their texts. I was interested in the assumptions, the understandings and the ways of talking about science and texts that they drew on in these discussions, which when combined seemed to guide them in unsuccessful directions. I was interested in the origins of these, within their previous education and their experience beyond, or within the course itself and the EIA literature.

Example 1: Experiencing and attributing uncertainty in the scientific data

In interview, the tutor told me that one of the key intentions of this course was:

> to undermine the idea that in science you always have the data you want.

He argued for the importance of understanding the often uncertain and provisional nature of claims that are made in science – especially within environmental science and EIA:

> you see with most of what we teach . . we definitely give students the idea that science is in itself . . . something which is entirely under control / which is not true / because . you can only . . draw conclusions which are as good as the data you've collected / and the bit of data you collect tomorrow may invalidate all you've done already.[4]

Interestingly, he did not actually *tell* the students this within the lectures, seminars or tutorials. Instead, he wanted to *show* them this. Echoing his own experience, he wanted them to learn about the uncertain and provisional nature of EIA from the experience of trying to do one; from the challenge of trying to understand the workings of a particular local estuary from the typically limited data available, and then of trying to predict the likely environmental impacts of a future development.[5]

His critique of most of the students' final texts was that despite this uncertainty their calculations were reported with certainty, as fact, and their conclusions were categorical, as the following examples demonstrate:

> At high flows the concentration of sediment is so dilute that oxygen levels would remain static, and thus the effects should be considered negligible.

> (Nick)

> Thus it is seen that scouring will be more pronounced nearer the pit with only a maximum increase of depth of 1.12 ft.

> (Helena)

There was no discussion of the evident uncertainty in the data and methods. In his written assessment comments on their texts he often asks:

> How do you know?

and describes their texts as:

> a collection of assertions without any discussion.

He concludes his comments on one report by saying:

> there has been little if any attempt to . . . provide a basis for a serious discussion of . . . the effects of uncertainty about the operation of the natural environment.

Going back to my recordings of the students' group discussions, and to their accounts at the time of what they were doing (from interviews), it is possible to suggest several factors that appear to pull the students in the direction of being overly certain about their data and conclusions. The issue of attribution was one important element. What is clear in the student's earlier discussions and interviews during the writing is that they *did realize* the uncertainty in the available data. What is interesting is that they attributed this uncertainty to the classroom context, and not to the professional context. Here, for example, are Robert, Nick and Helena explaining their sections of the text to me:

Robert: I'm sure you could sit down with your numbers . . and you could give a calculation to say that the fish would be all right /

Me: by doing what? /

Nick: well different interpretations . . different ways of looking at the results /

Robert: you can . . I don't know . . you can get anything you want really / to an extent [he laughs]

Nick: but I think that was to do with the way the background information was presented / . . . [the tutor] gave us a choice of . . of er what figures to choose / . . . I reckon in a . in a proper report / then you would have done your own . . . er analysis / you would have got a certain set of figures / and er . . . the answer . would be more defined I think /

Robert: yeah / you'd be doing your own experiments on the river / [Nick: yeah] / because we didn't have the time or the equipment to go out to the river . and do all these . . . kind of things / we just had to use the things that we were given /

Helena: everything is not exact enough / because they don't really know where exactly the aggregate is / there's not been enough . . research done anyway / [. . .]
if they were . really going to propose . to . . dig out the aggregate they'd have had . far more research done /

In other words, far from learning about the uncertainty within professional practice from the experience of uncertainty within the course, the students discounted this experience as being merely a consequence of doing it within the educational context. They therefore wrote their documents *as if* their data and their conclusions were certain.

Looking again at Figure 8.4, we can say that the tutor viewed the uncertainty within the data as representing a constraint that pervades professional

Figure 8.5 By attributing all constraints to the classroom context the students sustain an idealized notion of professional practice devoid of uncertainties and constraints

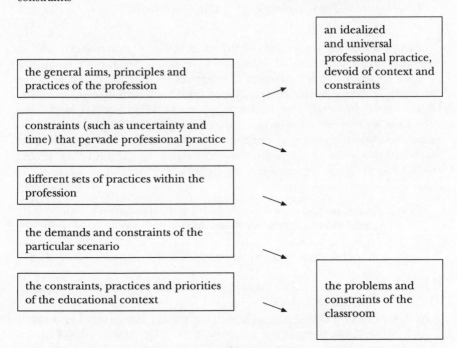

practice. He attributed it to the professional context. However, the students understood the uncertainty as a consequence of the constraints, practices and priorities of the educational context. They attributed the lack of time and resources, and the uncertainty or inadequacy of the data, to the educational context. They therefore do not 'experience' this as insight into professional practice. Instead, they sustain a rather idealized notion of profes-sonal practice, somehow devoid of contexts and constraints (see Figure 8.5). (Ironically, when they later enter professional practice, and are confronted with such constraints in 'the real world', they will look back on their educa-tion and critique it for being idealized and not 'real'.) Significantly for the students' writing, if they view the constraints such as uncertainty as belonging in the classroom, while trying to produce a text in the voice of a professional within the professional context, then it becomes impossible for them to articulate the uncertainty within the text.[6]

What is interesting here is the potential of this kind of talk of what is 'real' and not 'real' to derail the *intended* learning from the experience. Crucially the students have to view an experience as 'real' in order to view it as significant insight into the profession and to learn from it. In this case, for the students to understand that the task involved dealing with uncer-tainty, they needed to see it as significant: they needed to attribute the experience of uncertainty to the professional context, rather than the educational context.

It is clear that the students needed guidance on their attribution of the experience of uncertainty. However, the tutor's response to this is that he had already given it. He had told them that the set of data they had was exactly as they might find as a professional. He told them it was 'real'. He told them it was what the environmental impact assessors would be using if this development actually went ahead. It is therefore important to explore how these claims may be heard.

First, his assertion to the students that "this is real" can function, and can be heard, in different ways. In their discussions the students talked about whether aspects of the course were 'real'. They were evidently very familiar with claims from tutors that courses were 'real', and regarded these quite sceptically. They saw them as part of the tutor claiming legitimacy for the course; the claims refute the assumption that the course is removed from the 'reality' of professional practice. Indeed, information about vocational courses is often precisely about how they offer 'real' experience. The students did not perceive the claims of this tutor to be serving any other function: they did not identify these particular comments as offering potentially useful guidance for writing the text.

Second, as the tutor had anticipated (above), the students conversely brought to the course an idealized view of science and professional practice. They drew on experiences of science at school, where apparently they were always given enough data to make claims with certainty. This combined with a wider belief that science necessarily achieves certainty, rather than also involving uncertain and contentious claims within the process of developing knowledge. They also drew on an assumption that a 'real' report would find enough data to achieve certainty (quotes above); it would not make uncertain claims from limited data. What the tutor had not anticipated is the resilience of these assumptions – the way in which they could be sustained by a practice of discounting experience within education as 'not real'. In effect, the students' idealized assumptions could withstand the experience of uncertainty that he could offer. They were even able to withstand his very explicit accounts of uncertainty in examples of professional EIA in his lectures. The students saw these as examples of 'what should not have happened': they individualized them, rather than taking them as indicative of a wider 'reality' within the profession.

To guide students' attribution of an experience within vocational education would therefore seem to require more than an assertion that an experience is 'real'. It would seem to require a recognition that talk of what is 'real' and 'not real' is actually central in developing understanding, and it is already pervasive in the students' thinking and understanding. It would therefore seem to involve anticipating and responding to the students' own attribution. It would seem necessary to address in some detail what aspects of the activity or experience we want them to recognize as insight into the professional practice.

In this case, the tutor needed to be explicit not only that the data were real, but also that he saw the *lack* of data and the uncertainty as real. Even if this did not challenge the students' idealized view of science or EIA, it would indicate that within this activity he wanted them to attribute the uncertainty to the professional context, and to learn to deal with this in their text. Such explicit instruction would seem necessary to get them to engage with the limitations of the available data, rather than producing the kind of report that they assume to be 'real'.

Example 2: *Understanding an instruction/activity*

In Example 1 I looked at the students' attribution of an *experience*, when the tutor considered that his own attribution of this had been made very explicit. In this second example I look at their attribution of an *instruction*, and the difficulty students faced when the tutor's own attribution was less clear. Once again I identify the implications for the students' text. This example requires some explanation of environmental assessment and the scenario. But it makes an important point, with wider significance, about the need to make explicit the rationale for a course activity within the classroom and professional contexts.

The scenario
As is typical of professional texts, environmental assessments are complex, and can have subtly different functions within different scenarios. In this course, the tutor therefore set out a scenario, and contrasted this with other scenarios they might encounter.

In this scenario (an actual case), the landowners of the banks of a local estuary had made a very provisional proposal to allow a developer to extract gravel. The proposed *method* of extraction had not yet been decided. The planning authority was nevertheless interested in knowing what the impacts might be. The students were to take the role of independent consultants working for the planning authority at this early stage. Their task was to inform future decisions about *how* the gravel might be extracted with minimum impact, and *whether* this was even possible.

The problematic instruction/activity
As consultants in this professional scenario they could, of course, assess the likely impact of every possible method of extraction. But clearly it would be a more productive use of their time to focus on the method(s) of extraction most likely to be proposed by a future developer. (The tutor explained that this could be chosen on the basis of being cheaper, or of being least environmentally damaging and most likely to gain planning permission.) *The act of choosing was therefore partly attributable to the professional context.* However, as students, within the time constraints of the course, they could realistically assess only one method. *The act of choosing one was therefore also attributable to the educational context.*

The tutor asked the students first to "think what a probable extraction technique might be", and then to focus their assessment on the likely environmental impact of this. (Because the initial 'choice' was only a preliminary task, he articulated it only once, within an introductory lecture.) If we look at what he actually said to them, we can see that he started, as we might expect, by explaining what they had to do in terms of the professional context. He explained how the task was "legitimate" in terms of professional practice. He said they needed "to think what the most probable extraction technique could be". But then, at the point I mark with a ◇, he began to shift:

> it's only then after discussions with a variety of interested parties that the extraction technique is finally . decided / so it's quite legitimate . asking you in producing an independent environmental assessment . . to think . what the . most probable extraction technique could be / ◇ you could if you wanted . if you've got time . think of a variety of techniques . and balance them against one another / but we don't have that time / what I want you to do as a group / before we start talking in the workshop two weeks today / is to . sort out who is going to do what / agree among yourselves what the extraction technique is going to be / because that has implications for everybody

After the point marked ◇ the instruction progressively lost the link to the professional scenario. His use of "you" became ambiguous as to whether he was addressing them as consultants or students. His explanation "we don't have that time" was ambiguous about the context (classroom or profession) to which he was attributing this time constraint. But then his talk of the "group", and the deadline in the "workshop two weeks today" shifted the account firmly into the classroom context. In other words, he starts by explicitly attributing the choice to professional practice and the professional context, and then shifts towards attributing these to the educational context. There is a dual attribution, in which the rationale for the choice is therefore ambiguous. Finally, with "agree amongst yourselves what the extraction technique is going to be" he reformulated the instruction merely as a procedure (Mercer 1995: 93), increasingly separate from either rationale.

In the students' discussions, in trying to understand this instruction, their own articulations similarly identified the procedure without the rationale. The most common reference to the instruction was:

> we've got to pick a dredger by Friday.

Interestingly, the tutorial discussions did not clarify the rationale for the choice. The tutor asked about, and the students described, the extraction method they had "chosen to use", and their reasons. Their discussion was equally ambiguous about the context of the "choice", and the capacity in which they were choosing. Yet neither the tutor nor I saw this ambiguity at the time.

The students' confusion, and the implications for their texts
Within the students' meetings, when they were trying to work out exactly
what to do, the act of choosing an extraction technique became increasingly confusing. Without a clear understanding of the rationale for this
"choice" within either the classroom or professional context, it was possible
for both the status of it, and the capacity in which they were taking it, to
shift freely within their discussions, and finally in their texts.

The students did retain the notion that the choice of extraction method
was made prior to writing the text. However, in trying to understand the
choice of method within the professional context, the students lost touch
with the tutor's original scenario, and developed quite different professional scenarios in their minds in which they might also be producing a
report with the choice already made. In particular, they shifted into another possible scenario in which they had worked with a developer to choose
a method, and were now presenting the method and the likely impacts of it
to the planning authority.

The tutor's written comments on their texts reveal the significance of this
in terms of the different function of their text. He critiqued their texts for
announcing decisions as if they were already made, rather than informing
future decisions.

> You have adopted the role of hard-line developer with only one pos-
> sible scenario not that of an independent arbiter whose role is to find
> an acceptable way for extraction, or if this is even possible.

> ... it is being introduced as a summary of decisions already made not
> as a basis for an open discussion of the merits of different approaches.

The shift is apparent if we look at extracts from their texts. Here, for
example, Alan makes categorical and authoritative statements about the
decisions and future actions of the developer, as if those decisions are
already made, and as if he is actually party to these decisions and actions:

> Section 2: Project description
> The extraction of the aggregate <u>will be done</u> using a clamshell
> dredger ... Three silting ponds <u>are to be dug</u> first ... Work <u>will be
> initiated</u> in the north end of Block 5 ...
> Once the dredger has excavated a sizeable pit <u>it will be loaded</u> onto
> a pontoon ... The channel bank <u>is not going to be</u> breached ...
> The main alternative to the chosen method of a clamshell dredger
> was extraction using a cutter suction dredger but <u>was rejected</u> due to
> the following short-comings: ...

This contrasts with a previously successful text (given to me by the tutor as
an illustration of what he wanted) in which the authors – as independent consultants – instead *describe* "the main decision" that will need to be taken, *report*
the "possibilities", *choose* one likely method for their own further analysis,
and from their analysis *identify the key issues* that will need to be addressed in

this future decision about extraction methods. They therefore offer information and criteria to *inform* the reader in making a decision, and they maintain the distance of an apparently independent third party.

The implications for the students' learning

Since the general function of EA is to *inform* decisions (both by the developer and by the planning authority), the students' own shift away from this, and towards the activity of *making* and *announcing* them, represented a major loss of a learning opportunity.

It is significant that *making* and *announcing* decisions is perhaps linguistically easier than seeking to *inform* the decisions of others. If the students were to recognize and take on the more challenging function of *informing* decisions, then they needed that crucial understanding of the status of their "*choice*" of dredger within the professional scenario. They also needed a recognition that the form and function of their text was something new and unfamiliar, which they needed to learn. It involved more than 'reporting what they did' in the way that they were used to doing within lab reports. They would seem to have needed a guided look at how environmental assessment texts *inform* rather than *announce* decisions. Yet this is precisely the guided analysis of examples that is usually missed in higher education courses.

The students' reaction to the tutor's comments (quoted above) was one of confusion and disbelief. These effectively threw into question both what they thought they were doing and what they thought EA was about. Their own reactions confirm their shift into a very different scenario, and a different understanding of this text: rather than informing decisions at an early stage, their text had become part of the final submission for planning permission, in which all the decisions had been taken.

> Robert: but if this is an environmental assessment . . it shouldn't be open for discussion anyway / you should have made your decisions from the alternatives /
>
> Alan: this is what I did /
>
> Robert: it's what that's what you put in an environmental assessment / you don't go for planning permission ... and say "oooh I've left all these other things"! /
>
> Alan: I thought our job was to pick which we thought was the best / that's what I thought /

By this time, the students had in effect done what was expected of them within a pedagogy of 'learning by experience': they had made sense of the activity by developing an understanding of what a professional would do. The critique meant they left the course in confusion.

Problems with general claims that the activity reproduces 'real' professional practice

Crucially for the students, as they had shifted into their different scenario, they had nevertheless been able to sustain their actions with the knowledge that this was what a 'real' consultant would do. There are indeed environmental assessments of the form they produced. However, *the assumption that what is 'real' must be acceptable is a dangerous one*. It implicitly assumes a rather singular (as well as uncritical!) view of EA.

In retrospect, the students needed guidance on the ways in which the different scenarios within EIA that they had been told about in the lectures (involving different relations between people and between documents) actually demand different EA texts. They needed to look at the ways in which, for example, environmental assessments achieve different functions within different scenarios. Only then could they consider the implications of their particular scenario for their text. Only then could they realize how their own text might actually need to be *different* from 'real' examples they may find or be familiar with.

Significantly, this need to focus on the diversity of practice and texts therefore runs directly counter to the temptation in higher education to make the general claim that an activity is 'real', or reproduces 'real' professional practice. This kind of simple claim (that is common in course publicity, and in tutor and student talk in vocational courses) is inadequate and potentially misleading. It involves a very general attribution that may actually mislead the students in understanding the significance of particular instructions and actions. It encourages students to put aside the diversity of professional practice, to pursue practices that are 'real', but which were nevertheless not required, not functional and not appropriate in this particular instance.

Implications for researching student writing

I started by arguing that one of the key challenges for writing research is to understand unsuccessful student writing, in a way that offers practical insight and ways forward. I have tried to illustrate the importance of researching students' *accounts* of their texts, rather than simply the texts themselves, and of trying to understand the potential 'rationale' behind unsuccessful aspects of their texts. This can offer practical insight into why these might have been unsuccessful, and can offer the tutor practical ways forward. It challenges the assumption that students' difficulties in writing are simply an issue of their 'skills' in writing. Instead it focuses our attention on the understandings that have guided them, and the practices they have drawn on.

In a short chapter such as this, one can only focus on a particular issue. However, it is important when exploring the origins of unsuccessful writing not to claim a single 'cause'. This is likely to have underestimated the complex and subtle demands of the writing task, and to be simply rejected by the writers themselves. As I have argued elsewhere (Pardoe 1997; 1999) it is important to explore a potential network of factors that *together* may have enabled, prompted and sustained the students' unsuccessful understandings and writing. The question of attribution is likely to be one important element.

The way in which I have addressed the question of attribution has an important implication for how we view talk between tutor and student, and between students, about what is 'real' or 'realistic'. It is important to analyse the functions and the effects of these claims within the classroom, rather than simply joining in! By this I mean that it is not helpful for researchers simply to react to the claims of vocational education (that the activities are 'real') by counter-claiming that they are 'not real'. I see this as a potential danger when, for example, Bernstein (1990) argues that knowledge and practices are inevitably "fundamentally transformed" by being "recontextualized" into the classroom; and when, for example, Freedman *et al.* (1994) argue that student writing within professional simulations needs to be seen not as a process of bringing professional practices and texts into the classroom, but as types of texts in their own right, quite distinct from the "real" workplace.

By asserting what is 'real' and 'unreal' themselves, their analyses miss the negotiation of this within the classroom. They miss the ways in which making links to professional practice beyond the classroom is part of the process of attributing significance to activities and experience, and learning from them. They miss the way in which separating off educational experience and activity from the 'real world' is already a pervasive practice. They miss the way in which students have a highly sceptical view of claims that activities in education are 'real'. And therefore they miss the need for tutors to anticipate and respond to assumptions and talk of what is 'real' as an integral part of developing shared understandings within their classroom.

Implications for tutors in higher education

I now summarize what I see as the practical implications of this research for tutors. My concern is where students are learning the general practices of a profession or discipline from particular examples and experiences provided by a course.

First, we should not assume that the significance of an experience is self-evident. As I have shown in Figures 8.1–8.4, learning from an activity or experience in any context involves working out what aspects of it can be taken as more generally significant, and what should be regarded as more particular. Within vocational education, where an activity or experience inevitably involves links to both the educational and professional contexts, the process of learning also involves working out what aspects of it can be taken as offering insight into the profession, and what should be regarded as being a consequence of doing it within the classroom. In order for students to understand a particular activity or experience in the way we intend, we need to make explicit the significance that we attach to it.

Second, we need to bear in mind that students may come to vocational and science courses with an already sceptical view of claims that an activity or an experience is 'real'. They may bring an established practice of dismissing aspects of an activity and experience as being simply a consequence of it being within the educational context. If the observations of Edwards and Mercer (1987) and others (above) apply more widely, they may have learned from school science sometimes to dismiss their actual data or results, and report what they think 'should have happened'. If we want students to experience constraints on a professional activity (such as time, resources or accuracy) as a part of their experience of professional practice or science research, then we need to make the status of that experience explicit. We may need to articulate explicitly that this is a part of the intended learning. Conversely, if they need to understand some aspects of the activity or experience as being a consequence of the educational context, then we need to make that clear, too. (This does not undermine the way in which other aspects of the activity can nevertheless give important insight into professional practice. After all, the educational context provides an opportunity for developing exactly the kinds of explicit understanding that get missed in 'on-the-job' training in the workplace.)

Third, as Edwards and Mercer (1987) have argued for science education, within courses where students are learning the practices of a profession from the experiences provided by the course, we similarly need to be very wary of slipping into explaining an activity solely in terms of the immediate classroom procedures. This fails to give students the understanding that they need of the rationale for the activity within the profession, and/or within the course. In particular, if students are to report their activity within a professional document, in the voice of a professional, they need an explicit understanding of this activity as a part of professional practice.

Equally, as tutors, we need to be wary of the general claims (common in vocational education) that a whole activity is 'real' or 'realistic'. These simply encourage students to assume that if they have followed 'real' practices, and a 'real' text, then their own text must be acceptable. Instead, we need to develop their understanding of how the task and their text link to particular scenarios and sets of practices within the profession.

Finally, and most importantly, we need to make explicit for students the implications of the professional scenario for the text. This is likely to seem self-evident to the experienced tutor, but it is exactly what needs to be learned. If there are new challenges involved in their writing, such as articulating uncertainty, informing a decision, or even using evidence and previous research to produce an argument, then students need some guidance about *how* this is done. They cannot simply deduce the linguistic form and strategies of a professional text from the task or from the scenario, and they cannot reinvent it from first principles. Without guidance about the new genre, and how it may differ from those in their experience, students may simply reproduce old familiar practices. Without guidance about the ways in which individual texts need to differ from one scenario to another, they may feel it is acceptable to refer to any 'real' professional text they find in an attempt to work out what is required. To go beyond the reproduction of their existing practices, or of available examples, they need to be offered a range of chosen example texts, and they need explicit guidance in seeing what is both common to these, and significantly different. Only then can they begin to understand what is demanded of their writing, and recognize and understand the subtle strategies and wordings that make texts functional in different scenarios.

Acknowledgements

My thanks to the EIA tutor and students whose teaching and writing I researched, and whose collaboration and insight made the research possible. My thanks also to Roz Ivanič and Greg Myers for our discussions on the research, and to Kate Rawles for her detailed comments on earlier drafts. An earlier version was presented at the British Association for Applied Linguistics Annual Meeting at Manchester University (September 1998); my thanks to the participants for their comments. The phrase "a question of attribution" is taken from the play of that title by Alan Bennett.

Notes

1. I am adopting the practice of using single quotation marks around a term or phrase that is not in my voice; thus I distance myself from the term/phrase or the assumptions and values behind it. Double quotation marks are used for an actual quotation.
2. Further studies that pursue an understanding of unsuccessful student writing include David Bartholomae (1985), Mike Rose (1985; 1989), Roz Ivanič (1996; 1998) and Rachel Rimmershaw (1993). See also Pardoe (1993; 1994; 1997; 1999).
3. Particularly readable and interesting accounts of this within sociological studies of the construction of scientific knowledge include Latour (1987; 1993) and Gilbert and Mulkay (1984).
4. Transcript symbols used:

   Speech
   ..   indicates a pause or hesitation, roughly half a seocnd per dot;
   /   indicates an apparent break between units of speech, indicated by the speaker through a change of tone or a pause;
   [...]   indicates that at this point in the extract some of the original utterance has been omitted;
   underlined indicates author's emphasis;
   Written text
   ...   indicates that at this point in the extract some of the original text has been omitted.

5. The tutor's account of uncertainty in EIA drew on his experience as an environmental assessor, constantly faced with the demand to make predictions from limited data, and his knowledge of the way in which EIAs are usually based on the very limited data available about a particular local area. His account would seem to be supported within the environmental assessment literature. In a key introductory text on EA, Bisset and Tomlinson (1988: 126) summarize the situation as follows:

EIA is intended to provide decision makers with an understanding of the environmental consequences of a proposed action or project. This objective is achieved by the use of environmental information which is often characterised by scarcity and uncertainty, predictive techniques with unknown error margins and evaluation methods which assess and present information to decision makers in a variety of ways.

Despite this 'scarcity and uncertainty' of existing information about a local environment, the 1989 UK government guidelines for EA say that: 'While a careful study of the proposed location will generally be needed (including environmental survey information), original scientific research will not normally be necessary' (Department of the Environment 1989).

6. A further contributor to this process was that the students drew on the practice that has been observed in the talk and writing of professional scientists, of addressing uncertainty more in the informal spoken interactions than in the final written text (see Gilbert and Mulkay 1984). The tutor similarly discussed the uncertainty of EA in his spoken lectures rather than in his written handouts. This shows the need for more explicit guidance if they are to articulate the uncertainty in writing.

Part 3

Contexts of Writing and
Professional Learning

9

Writing for Success in Higher Education

Janice McMillan

Introduction

Writing in higher education is a challenging task for many students. Such 'literate acts' or individual constructive acts, are, according to Flower (1994: 19):

> sites of construction, tension, divergence, and conflict. They happen at the intersection of diverse goals, values and assumptions, where social roles interact with personal images of one's self and one's situation ... [they] are often sites of negotiation where the meaning that emerges may reflect resolution, abiding contradiction, or perhaps just a temporary stay against uncertainty.

To understand learning as a 'site of negotiation' is a useful way of exploring students' experiences of writing in higher education. This is particularly so in South Africa, where many adult learners cross the formal boundary into higher education with relatively poor previous experiences of formal education or schooling. Recent literature highlights the barriers or feelings of 'disjuncture' facing non-traditional mature learners once they have crossed the formal, institutional boundary (Weil 1986; James 1995) and it has been argued that there is often a tension between formal institutional access, and curriculum or epistemological access.

While significant, this view neglects an important component of learning, namely the role students play in this process. The quote by Flower above attests to this, and highlights how complex a process it can be. This chapter sets out to examine these issues from a particular perspective. While many students do struggle to cross epistemological boundaries in higher education and we need to be mindful of this, others succeed, often against all odds. In order to understand successful learning, this chapter draws on research exploring the learning and writing experiences of first time non-traditional mature learners. The main question it examines is what the process of constructing a 'successful' learner role entails, and how this becomes visible through writing practices. The question is addressed through qualitative case-study research of adult learners – writers – on the Certificate in Adult Education, Training and Development at the University of Cape Town (UCT). I explore experiences of learning and writing for success and the complexities involved in this. While I use the term 'success' in this study, I am aware that it is not unproblematic: both who and what determines success within and across contexts. Theoretically the chapter draws on a sociocultural/constructivist framework, arguing for an understanding of learning which takes account of contextually located processes of meaning making rather than decontextualized accounts of learning.

Background and context

At UCT, certificate-level adult education provision has traditionally been non-formal. From the mid-1980s until the end of 1994, the Department of Adult Education and Extra-Mural Studies offered two year-long non-formal programmes: the Community Adult Education Programme (CAEP) and the Adult Learning in the Workplace Programme (WLP). While there was substantial overlap between the two programmes, there were important distinctions in terms of student groupings. Whereas students on CAEP were predominantly community-based adult educators, Xhosa- or Afrikaans-speaking and predominantly 'black' (used to denote both 'coloured' and 'African' apartheid racial classifications), the students on the WLP were a mixture of 'CAEP-type' students and corporate- or industry-based trainers. There was thus a strong representation of white, English- or Afrikaans-speaking students on the WLP courses over the years.

Provision on both these programmes was non-formal, access to the institution being granted on the basis of previous experience. Given that the courses lacked formal accreditation, assessment took on the same non-formal status, although certificates were awarded to students who had a high attendance record. The aim of such courses was to provide access for the further development of practitioner competence – students thus entered with the role of practitioner firmly in place, and this was built on during the programme. They were provided with an opportunity to reflect on and further develop the skills and experience they already possessed. The notion of the 'critical reflective practitioner' (Schön 1983; 1987), explored by Elizabeth Hoadley-Maidment in Chapter 10 of this volume, guided the thinking behind curriculum design and development and the teaching approaches adopted, allowing us to integrate learning and experience, and to facilitate critical thinking and problem-solving. In this way, increased possibilities for practitioner development and, I would argue, 'successful' learning were put in place. However, with the move to formalize the certificate course, the relationship between roles and learning became more complex.

Shifts: from non-formal to formal

Inequities in access to higher education as well as problems in the relationship between higher education, national reconstruction and human resource development are currently high on the agenda in South Africa. The African National Congress's (ANC) Education and Training document (ANC 1994), on which the government White Paper (Department of Education 1995) is based, continually links issues of access to the need for redress and equity. Access is thus viewed as providing equal opportunities to those who have found education inaccessible in the past.

Many providers have responded by formalizing provision. UCT responded to such calls in 1995 by introducing a new formal Certificate in Adult Education, Training and Development. Many of our students – mature adult educators/trainers – now entered the certificate programme without the normal formal requirements for entry to university study. We initiated a policy of 'alternative access' and encouraged any of our students who had completed one of the two previous one-year non-formal programmes in our department to apply for the new programme. This qualification, therefore, together with their experience as practitioners, provided them with formal access to the university. However, while we retained a policy of institutional access on the basis of prior experience, the course now offered formal accreditation, and formal written assessment was introduced. The course thus had a twofold aim: the further development of practitioner competence and the development of academic skills and competencies.

During 1995, while conducting the research reported here, student numbers more than doubled, from the usual 30–35 students per course to over 70. This move also brought a very diverse group of practitioner students on to our course, including both community-based educators and trainers and those located within a corporate or industry setting. The latter grouping included some students who already possessed undergraduate and even postgraduate university qualifications. What interested me, therefore, was to investigate and explore what possible 'innovative combination of conventions' (Fairclough 1992a) students might be adopting in the process of learning in order to be successful; I wished to understand these through the students' experiences of learning and writing.

In thinking about writing and assessment on the certificate programme, we saw the need for it to serve two parallel purposes. First, given the fact that the course targeted adult education practitioners, there was a need to allow them to draw on that work experience through assessment tasks – to enable them to become 'critical, reflective practitioners' (Schön 1987). While writing is by no means the only way in which this can be done, assessment is an important component of formal learning, and we attempted to incorporate assignment tasks which would require a reflection on their own work (see Appendix 1).

Second, we understood, given that many of our learners had no experience of formal higher education, that we needed to allow for them to develop 'academic literacy practices' which would hopefully enable them to 'acquire the discourse' (Gee 1990), or at least an important component of it. We recognized, however, the difficulties that students have with academic writing for assessment (see also Lea and Street, Chapter 2). Many studies exploring learning in higher education allude to this (Chiserie-Strater 1991; Flower 1994; James 1995). James (1995) also argues that many studies of adult learners highlight the immense significance of assignment grades, yet he argues that we often overlook the role that both assessment and lecturers play in 'legitimizing' higher education studies. This emerged in students' accounts of their learning. One student interviewed, Nomzi, when asked what she felt about assessment, said that she felt it was a good thing because:

> you know where you stand and if you want to take it further, you know what your [weak points are] . . . it's how you can learn.

Another, Yasmine, when she did not do as well as she thought she might on a task, blamed us as lecturers:

> I felt it was sort of your fault that I rewrote the whole thing because you didn't make it clear to me exactly what you wanted. If I had known, I could have . . . sort of got 80% for it.

Understanding learning: meaning-making and negotiation in context

Learning and writing: negotiating academic literacy demands

Thesen (1994), working from a sociocultural/sociolinguistic position, looks at second language students' experiences of writing at university. She argues persuasively for an approach to learning which attempts to look at 'voice or subjectivity . . . [locating] meaning in the individual' (Thesen 1994: 56), yet without losing the tensions and contradictions this poses. Thesen believes we need to ask ourselves where we think meaning can be found – and believes a discourse approach should be concerned with the interactions between people in a given context rather than relationships to text. This then allows for meaning to be located in the user or individual rather than the system. Discourse is therefore 'a process of meaning exchange, via language, in a given context. Individuals have differing access to these patterns of exchange in different contexts' (Thesen 1994: 25). She sees this interpretation as an attempt to bring together the view of discourse as negotiated meaning 'with the fundamental recognition that individuals do not have equal access to this process of negotiation' (Thesen 1994: 25). Thesen argues that learning within this perspective assigns a stronger role to the individual as agent, acting sometimes from the centre, and at other times from the margins. What is important is to understand that students are continuously making decisions in their learning. In particular, she argues that:

> this perspective makes it easier to track and understand the way dis-
> courses rub against one another, and what individuals do about this.
> Locating meaning in the individual does not mean that I am down-
> playing the social, but trying to find a starting point that is more pro-
> foundly social, in that it deals with human action, which must surely be
> at the heart of the social.
>
> (Thesen 1994: 56)

Highlighting some of these issues in relation to student writing, Flower (1994) expands on the notion of discourse and the role students play in their own learning. She points to the importance of understanding learn-ing as 'negotiating meaning' and argues that we need to understand social cognitive processes as being a source of tension and conflict among the many forces that act to shape meaning: the demands of the learning con-text as well as learners' own goals and knowledge. As a response to this tension and conflict, learners rise to the active negotiation of meaning, thereby creating meaning in the intersection of alternatives, opportunities and constraints. For Flower (1994: 18), a literate act is 'an individual con-structive act . . . [which] can call for the orchestration of diverse, seemingly incompatible practices . . . [these] also reflect the complex, even contradic-tory, goals and purposes that often drive meaning making'. This implies, following Clark and Ivanič (1997), an understanding of the relationship between writing and social context. They argue that it is important to bear in mind the relationship between writing and context. In addition, in any particular context of situation, the context of 'culture' provides the range of possibilities which are competing for dominance. What the writer brings to the task, in terms of his/her own attitudes towards it, beliefs about what is expected from the task and the purposes behind that particular task, links to the broader context of culture and affects the process and out-comes. The context of culture therefore, affects writing practices and, in response, Clark and Ivanič argue that writers may either resist or conform to the patterns of privileging within the context of culture.

Drawing on theories of academic literacy, Lea (1998) further explores the conflicts and contradictions students experience as they negotiate aca-demic knowledge in relation to the more familiar worlds of work, com-munity and home. Lea (1998: 4) believes that 'a central part of the learning process for students is concerned not just with the struggle between other familiar "ways of knowing" and "academic ways of knowing" but with the different literacy practices that are associated with these'. In particular, she argues that adult learning often involves contestation and challenge as students interweave prior knowledge and ways of writing and reading texts with course requirements. In this process, students are both constructing new meanings and constituting new knowledge bases. In trying to understand this process, she looks at three adult learning domains and the interrelationship between them: the domain of cultural/social contexts which situate the circumstances in which individual student learning is taking place; the learning texts domain which is concerned with the texts that are produced and the ways in which students construct their academic knowledge through the production of these; and the domain of academic literacy which mediates the relationship between the other two domains. In considering these three domains, Lea argues that we are better able to understand the different interpretations of text production and the ways in which these are embedded in cultural and social contexts.

Within this frame, she highlights two approaches to learning – reformulation and challenge. The former approach is one whereby students try and reproduce course materials, thereby attempting to 'learn the discourse', while the latter is often an explicit attempt on the part of students to relate a course to their own wider life-world context. Adult learners in higher education, Lea believes, are thus trying to do two things simultaneously in producing texts: they are trying to construct their knowledge in ways which make it appropriate for assessment, yet at the same time they are trying to maintain a sense of their own identity and the validity of other ways of knowing.

Learning and writing for 'success': the construction of roles

This brings us to the notion of 'role'. It is a useful and important concept in understanding learning as it can be argued that it is within roles that meaning is made and negotiated – it is 'meaning-making made active'. As different people relate differently in the same role, it is the acting out or social construction of a role that relates the individual to society. Furthermore, within a specific role, there is also space for 'sub-roles' such as 'best student' and 'stupid one' – all of these are taken so as to establish a position in relation to other members of the group.

Kasworm's (1990) study of adult learners in formal higher education settings highlights the importance of role in interesting ways. Drawing on and extending the sociocultural theory of Vygotsky and others, she explores adult learners' patterns of interaction with the higher education context. She identifies four patterns of interaction – conflict, withdrawal, accommodation and transformation – all of which look at the kind of learner–teacher relationship, the kind of learner role students identify for themselves, as well as their own perceptions of what higher education learning is about.

Both Lea and Kasworm appear to imply an 'either/or' approach to learning and writing – in other words, that students exhibit one particular approach to their learning and writing experiences. I believe we need to understand that there are often multiple and even contradictory patterns which emerge in each student's experiences of learning. Negotiation and meaning-making often involve the construction of multiple roles and these then become visible through the practices of writing in particular contexts.

The study

My research involved working with four women students with whom I had a fair amount of contact in various ways throughout 1995. The students share many similarities with other adult learners in South Africa: disrupted or poor schooling, impoverished backgrounds and broken family lives. Two are ex-DEC students and two ex-DET. In their own ways however, they are all strikingly different. Two are Xhosa-speaking, one English and one Afrikaans. Their ages range from early 30s to '60+ with one foot in the grave' (as the eldest herself put it).

My data consisted of interviews, informal group discussions, observations and pieces of assessed student writing. I adopted an ethnographic case-study approach in order to collect 'thick descriptions' of what was happening with some of my students. While my approach was, obviously, not a full ethnographic study in the anthropological sense of a total 'immersion into cultural issues', I developed an approach that allowed me to incorporate culture and context as ways of understanding learning (see Chiserie-Strater 1991; Thesen 1994). I conducted two interviews with all four students – one which foregrounded their experiences as students in the class, while the other foregrounded their lives outside the class: as adults, as practitioners and as learners. During the first interview, I focused my questions on the two aims of our course and specifically their experiences of writing assignments, working in groups and relationships with others, both learners and educators. While my original study involved four students, for the purposes of this paper I have selected two which highlight contrasting patterns of interaction and meaning-making.

I will present each case separately as I believe this better captures the specificity of each student's process of learning. I begin by providing a brief life-world synopsis for each; I then discuss each of their experiences of learning and writing on the certificate course. Given that I am interested in the different ways in which students construct roles and how this shapes their perceptions and experiences of writing, my analysis will focus more on their *understanding* of writing than on their actual writing practices.

Yasmine: 'maybe I'll quit . . . tomorrow'

Yasmine, aged 37, is a single (widowed) parent of two children who lives in Mitchell's Plain (formerly a 'coloured' township) with her sister and her sister's husband and their child. She says that Mitchell's Plain is divided by a railway track and that she lives on the 'wrong side' where:

> gangsterism is rife and the unemployed sit around on the street corners.

Having grown up in Diep River, her family was moved to Manenberg during the height of the Group Areas forced removals. When I asked her about the effect of political events in her life, she said that while she was not directly involved in political activities, she was made aware of them through her experiences and her family. After leaving school at the end of standard nine, getting married and having a child, Yasmine started working in a clothing factory as a machine operator. Nine years later she had her second child and decided she was not going back. I asked her if this was because she wanted to get involved with helping people:

> no, not helping people. Helping myself . . . I was fed up with being a number [on the factory floor].

At the time of the interview she was employed at a youth volunteer centre as a satellite branch organizer but felt that she would like to start an office where she could work on her own. Yasmine's experience of learning and the ways in which she dealt with the writing demands of the course was tinged with contradictions and turmoil yet ultimately with success. Writing played a big part in helping her to work through much of this conflict – both inside and outside the certificate course.

The primary pattern of engagement I identified in Yasmine's learning experiences was that of conflict (Kasworm 1990) – she also adopted in many ways a challenge approach to her learning (Lea 1998). However, there was also evidence of withdrawal and accommodation (Kasworm 1990) or reformulation (Lea 1998) in her account. Given strong linkages between her personal and learner identities, Yasmine's experience demonstrated a fairly high sense of anxiety and conflict:

> I wanted to give up at some stage.

Students who find learning a site of conflict, often experience life difficulties and, according to Kasworm (1990: 11), 'they are unique in the intensity and breadth of their personal life difficulties'. In terms of the kind of learner role she saw for herself, Yasmine felt that she was:

> more on the outside, I think, sort of looking in.

This seemed to be a case of the 'solo learner', a pattern of engagement Kasworm argues is indicative of the withdrawal pattern. This was clearly evident in her relations with other students, with the lecturers and with her processes of writing. While the role of lecturers was important in her learning, she felt that:

> there'll always be this power thing.

Yasmine spoke of the conflict between herself and the 'professionals', other students on the course, whom she perceived as thinking they were superior to her because of their formal job status. It appeared that some students were 'in the discourse' and she was 'outside it'. This relates to Thesen's comments about the different ways in which discourses 'rub up against each other' and how students deal with the conflict this causes; it is highlighted in the following extract of a poem by Yasmine:

DISCOURSE
We are being told about
The roles we play
The discourse that we follow
As if we didn't know

There's groups that feel they've been there
Others feel they'll never get anywhere
It's clear to them, but what about the rest of 'em
I'm lost!!

Through all of this, assignments follow,
Handouts to read and books to borrow
I think I'll quit . . .
Tomorrow.

It is in her writing that she seemed to find a way to express some of her anxieties and to make meaning out of her experiences. Writing plays an important role in her life even outside the classroom, and she indicated in the interview that she finds it easier than talking. In addition, it had become an important way of working through difficult issues in her life:

If I feel strongly about something, I dream it. Then I get up and write it down . . . I would like to write a book. Not just any book – my life story because lots of interesting things happened in my life so I would like to put it down on paper.

However, it is not without conflict either. Given that she sees herself as a perfectionist – 'practice makes perfect, but I'm not perfect yet' – she often feels disappointed. This is both with herself and with the lecturers:

like if I did an assignment and didn't get the marks I thought I would I get very upset with myself.

What is interesting, however, is that when Yasmine wrote assignments, while she might resist writing them, she managed in some ways to 'suspend' the inner turmoil and anxiety she often felt. On the coversheet of her Assignment 4 (see Appendix 2), she indicated that:

I nearly didn't write this assignment because it dealt with politics

(it was concerned with the Reconstruction and Development Programme (RDP), a key piece of legislation aimed at addressing socioeconomic transformation and redress). Her assignment however, was lucid, well argued and a coherent piece of writing for which she received a high mark. She was able to discuss the views of others towards the RDP together with her own. In addition, she was able to do this in a way which did not reflect the ambivalence she expresses towards the topic initially. There is thus a third pattern that emerges in this account, namely accommodation (Kasworm 1990). While she adopts a stance of challenge to the course demands and finds this causes conflict for her, her need to see herself as 'student material' gives the course – and writing in particular – 'authority' for her in shaping her experience.

While I have argued that withdrawal was also demonstrated by Yasmine in her account of her learning experience, particularly in her experience of assessment, this did not totally obscure her success. In other words, while Yasmine's experience was difficult and often tinged with turmoil and conflict, she found ways to negotiate meaning – she saw herself as being able to rise up above this conflict. This was particularly through writing on the course. Her pieces were lucid and very little, if any, of the turmoil she spoke about in her learning comes through in her writing. So in some ways, her writing exhibited a reformulation approach while at times she grappled with a challenge approach towards her learning (Lea 1998).

Nomzi: the multiple roles we play

Nomzi, aged 48, is a single mother of three children. She grew up in Cape Town, one of 11 children, and describes her life as very 'in and out', something she feels is related to her difficult family relations. Her 'in and out' identity also relates to periods spent in both the urban and rural areas, separated from her mother and brought up by her grandmother. She sees this as an important part of her identity and experience; she sees herself as both urban and rural – these identities are balanced for her and help her work with people from different communities:

> You must be careful how you work with rural women otherwise they won't come to you. You must be flexible.

This issue of 'flexibility' is important for Nomzi and something which she brings into her learning on the course. Nomzi currently works as a sewing trainer for a large non-governmental organization. While she loves her job and working close to people, she is also very clear that by doing things for her community she should not create dependency:

> you should teach her how to make food, not give her food.

For Nomzi, an important issue on the certificate course was being able to reflect critically on what she was learning. This was important for her as she felt that she could transfer what she had learnt back to her work and experiences in life. She felt that independence was important – the course presented a place where it was expected of her to:

> think, do your own things.

While she enjoyed the diversity in the class, she often felt that group discussions were intimidating. This emphasis on group work, an important part of the course and strong feature of the discourse of much adult and experiential learning, was something that was contrary to her preferred learning process.

When asked if she felt she was coping with the demands of the course, this unease was evident:

> ya, I think I am into that . . . although I might not be . . . I would put myself in writing, group discussion and reading but . . . I don't contribute much in class discussion. I contribute only in writing.

Nomzi's processes of meaning-making and negotiation had, therefore, to take place largely outside the social context of group learning and within her own writing. However, it was not all negative for her. While she found talking in groups difficult, she absorbed their ideas and often found an answer to her own question – she learnt to use the group processes to her advantage and overcome a potential barrier to learning. It is at the moments of recalling her past experiences – work and life more broadly – that learning really had meaning for her and, I would argue, she used this to negotiate success in her own assessed writing.

According to Kasworm (1990), the primary pattern of interaction is that of transformation, and this is the most integrated and yet complex pattern of engagement. Students engaging in this way are uniquely oriented to broad world-views concerning the nature of higher education and the undergraduate learning process; they speak to a prominent, definitive perspective of their own internal value of learning, their involvement across their life work in learning, and their commitment to learning as a broadening of values, perspectives, and beliefs. Elements of this pattern were strongly visible in Nomzi's account. For her, the importance of the relationship between her identity as adult and community worker, on the one hand, and that of learner, on the other, meant that she constantly made reference to the role that the course played in her own practice, as well as the role that her world of practice played in her learning. Nomzi also showed a high degree of critical reflection on herself as a learner and on how learning related to work and life. As a student, she thus had clear expectations of herself. While she valued lecturers as mediators, she also saw herself and her life experience as important in guiding her learning.

The notion of 'self-reflection' was also present when Nomzi spoke of her assessed writing. She acknowledged that such writing is about argument and that:

> you don't write something like a story.
>   You must argue . . . you say what you want to say and then you reflect it on the outside and look at it on the other side . . . you must reflect on your everyday life, your own experience.

However, it is also important for Nomzi in her writing to reflect on past experience and to express her opinions:

maybe there is an argument which you must reflect on from what you are reading. You say 'I agree with this but in other ways, I disagree'. You reflect again – as if you are talking to someone else. I then repeat it to myself until I can hear it – it must make sense to me before I can write it.

These feelings about the importance of reflecting on her own experience were brought into her writing of Assignment 4. Unlike the other three students, she chose the first of the two choices (4A), mainly because:

I wanted to say what I think of RDP, not what other people think. It's where I could express myself about what's happened and what must be changed – to redress the past.

A secondary pattern that also emerges in her account is that of accommodation. While she felt that 'life experience taught you a lot', she did see the university as having value and the usefulness of the curriculum and transmission process: witness her indication of the importance of written assessment as telling you 'right from wrong'.

In many ways, Nomzi exhibited many of the attributes of a 'critical reflective practitioner' (Schön 1983; 1987), in that her role as a practitioner was continually under personal scrutiny. The way she engaged with her learning – linking her experiences outside the class with what she was learning – are highly indicative of this:

I learnt to think deep and also to add to my experience about how this happened the previous time . . . more especially, I have worked out how to do the right things.

Her assignment reflected this strongly. She comments:

My general knowledge of apartheid laws during the years has given me experience of what has changed and what has not. This assignment will be based on community understanding [and] needs and what impact the RDP principles would have on the community.

For Nomzi, therefore, success on the certificate was made possible by a complex process of self-reflection and meaning-making through writing for assessment. The context of the course allowed her to build on her previous experiences, but she felt that she had to actively link her learning on the course with her outside world(s). She also showed flexibility in her learning so that where at times she might have felt on the margins of the course (for example, in group work), she was actively engaged in the process of border-crossing and making meaning for herself as a learner (McMillan 1998). This emerges particularly in her strong feelings about the need for critical reflection, as well as in her belief of the importance of argument in the process of writing assignments.

The practices of writing were experienced differently by the students: for Nomzi, on the whole, they seemed more positive experiences than for

Yasmine. However, what emerges clearly is that each of them found ways to take action and exhibit agency in their learning which allowed them to successfully negotiate potential boundaries to acquiring the discourse.

Conclusion

In exploring these two students' experiences of learning and writing, I have argued that the ways in which learner roles are constructed and the contexts within which learning takes place are crucial to understanding success. Success in turn needs to be understood as a process of boundary negotiation and meaning construction. For Yasmine, this was through her writing, finding a way to deal with her personal feelings in ways which did not obstruct her learning on the course; for Nomzi, this was in being able to reflect critically on both her life and student experience, integrating both. While this is a unique process for different learners, it is at the intersection of the individual and the social and through the construction of learner roles that meaning is made and success attained (McMillan 1997).

However, if we acknowledge that learning contexts involve specific discourse communities, and that both life-world and learning experiences impact on opportunities for success, it is clear that success in one context will not necessarily guarantee success across a range of other learning contexts. A key issue, therefore, for further research is assessment and the role such practices play in shaping learning experiences across contexts, particularly if we are serious about widening opportunities for students to access a range of higher education contexts.

We need to be mindful of the 'signals' that are given out through curriculum and pedagogical practices, particularly through assessment tasks. These are the clues that students use in their attempts to engage with otherwise unfamiliar academic literacy practices. Furthermore, if we wish to make 'challenge' and not just 'reformulation' approaches (Lea 1998) a reality in higher education as a way of fostering the development of new voices and identities among our students, our approaches to curriculum and pedagogy need to make explicit opportunities for this. So, too, do our assessment tasks and the ways in which we judge student writing. Neglecting to do this could set students up for failure; or at the very least, feelings of disjuncture (Weil 1986) which could lead to disappointment and even possible withdrawal from higher education.

Note

1. DEC and DET are the abbreviations under which the education departments of the apartheid era were known. DEC was the Department of Education and Culture for 'coloured' students, and DET the Department of Education and Training for 'African/black' students.

Appendix 1: Question paper for Assignment 4 of the Certificate Programme

CERTIFICATE IN ADULT EDUCATION, TRAINING AND DEVELOPMENT

CONTEXTUAL STUDIES (EMS105W)

ASSIGNMENT 4

PLEASE NOTE:
* This assignment should be between 3 and 5 written A4 pages
* YOU MUST CHOOSE EITHER 4A OR 4B
* DUE DATE: 4.00 pm, TUESDAY AUGUST 15

ASSIGNMENT 4A

What do you think the RDP would look like if it was successfully implemented in your community or workplace?

EXPECTED OUTCOMES:

In order to complete this assignment successfully, we expect you to:

* show that you have a good understanding of the development needs of your community/workplace
* demonstrate that you have some understanding of the underlying principles of the RDP
* show the ability to interpret these principles in relation to the situation in your own community/workplace
* put forward a clear argument of your view on the meaning of the RDP.

ASSIGNMENT 4B

'The RDP means all things to all people.'

Do you agree with the above statement? Make a clear argument, backed up by evidence, as to whether this statement is true or not. In order to answer this assignment, you will need to research the different views, understandings and meanings that people bring to the RDP. You should interview a minimum of 3 people, and they should be as different as possible (in terms of culture, language, class background, occupation, gender, etc.).

EXPECTED OUTCOMES:

In order to complete this assignment successfully, we expect you to:

* show that you understand the significance of the issue or question raised by the above quote
* show that you are able to do some simple research, present your findings clearly, and to interpret your findings
* argue your own viewpoint on whether the above statement is correct or not
* make a clear argument as to whether your research findings support your own views on the above statement, and if not, why not.

Appendix 2: Cover sheet for Assignment 4 of the Certificate Programme

CERTIFICATE IN ADULT EDUCATION, TRAINING AND DEVELOPMENT

CONTEXTUAL STUDIES (EMS105W)

ASSIGNMENT COVER SHEET

Name: **Student Number:**

ASSIGNMENT NO. & TITLE:

Date:

Please answer the following two questions in as much detail as possible:

1. To help you establish your own patterns of learning, reflect and describe the process you followed to complete this assignment (this could include an estimate of the time it took, who you talked to, what you read, how many drafts you did and the order that you followed).

2. How successfully do you think you have dealt with this assignment? Give reasons for your answer.

ASSESSOR'S COMMENTS:

MARK:

10

From Personal Experience to Reflective Practitioner: Academic Literacies and Professional Education

Elizabeth Hoadley-Maidment

Introduction

Professional education is an expanding area of university work. As professions such as nursing, physiotherapy and social work achieve graduate status, courses are being fundamentally restructured and there is a growing literature on the nature of professional education (Bines and Watson 1992; Eraut 1994). Most of this literature focuses on the development of professional competence and academic understanding and how this is achieved through a combination of traditional academic learning and experiential learning gained in the workplace. Areas of interest include the role of mentors, the relation between competence-based outcomes and academic learning, and examining the ways underlying academic disciplines such as biological or social sciences are presented within courses designed around professional frameworks.

The role of academic literacies in professional education has not been addressed in the same detail as these broader issues. They are important, however, not simply because of the written nature of much university education, but more particularly because so much assessment in the university system requires students to write. Some disciplines – for example, medicine – minimize the role of written assessment by using systems based on multiple-choice questions, oral examinations and practicals, but many professional programmes use assessment strategies based on those associated with the underlying academic disciplines. The social sciences, for example, are core to a range of professional courses including nursing, teaching, social work and management. Social sciences are traditionally assessed through essays, experimental and project work presented in report form, and by timed written examinations. When these disciplines are taught within professional courses which aim to develop professional competence, we must consider the relationship between the types of writing required and the aims and objectives of the course. The question for those teaching professional courses is how to ensure that they are designed in ways which will ensure that students learn to make the links between academic concepts and theories and professional practice.

In this chapter I want to examine the connections between models of professional education and academic literacies, as well as the practical implications of these for teaching and assessment. My interest in this area arose from work I undertook in the School of Health and Social Welfare at the Open University. The Open University is a distance-learning institution which until recently has taught mainly through written texts. This throws into sharp relief the potential contradictions between linguistic approaches to academic learning and literacy, and practice-based models of professional education. Although the issues discussed here arose in the context of distance learning, they apply to all forms of professional education in which students are expected to write at length and are, I would suggest, particularly pertinent to developments in computer-aided learning (CAL) and open learning where students may have less face-to-face contact with their tutors and more demands made on their use of the written word.

The chapter begins by outlining relevant theories of academic literacy and professional education. I then report on how these issues were perceived by a group of academics working in the area of health and social welfare. The last section considers the implications of my findings for the teaching of academic literacies within professional education.

Academic discourse, academic literacies and professional education

Linguistic approaches

As a term, 'academic discourse' is problematic. It is widely used, but in differing ways by individual disciplines. Any discussion of students as writers must start, not with a discipline-based definition but with a linguistic one. Sociolinguists such as Swales (1990) regard individual academic disciplines as discourse communities, each using language in particular ways. There are commonalities between them, however, so that it is also possible to talk of academic discourse as a general form of English. All academic communities use written communication a great deal. This is a result both of the tradition of academic publishing and because communities are very widespread geographically. The language of a discourse community consists not simply of technical language in the sense of individual words or jargon, but also systems of rules for using these in spoken and written forms. In this sense each academic discipline – for example, psychology or sociology – is an individual discourse community. However, academic disciplines also share certain linguistic patterns and forms which serve to identify pieces of writing as 'academic' regardless of the subject. Although some of these rules are breaking down, academic English is generally marked by an impersonal style created by the use of abstract nouns, passive verbs and a tendency to avoid the use of pronouns such as 'I' or 'we' which identify the writer. It is also common for sentences to have grammatically simple forms but to include large numbers of nouns and adjectives whose main function is to make meaning more precise. Sentences are frequently 'front-loaded' with noun phrases or clauses illustrating the main subject appearing before the main verb.

In addition to these grammatical features, academic writing adopts easily recognizable forms. These range from academic papers and books aimed at highly knowledgeable members of the discourse community, to apprentice pieces such as essays written by undergraduates. Pieces of writing which share both forms and linguistic features are described as 'genres' by some linguists, with different forms of academic writing, such as essays, projects and reports of different kinds referred to as 'sub-genres'. While students are not expected to have the same grasp of the concepts and theories they are writing about (Biber 1988), student writing is still recognizable as academic writing and is unlikely to be confused with vocational writing which mature students, in particular, may already use fluently because of their previous professional training and experience.

Accordingly, students are generally expected to learn three things linguistically: the language of the subject or subjects they are studying; the rules and conventions used by individual disciplines; and the more general features of academic writing which make it instantly recognizable. As apprentices, students learn the language of subjects they are studying as an integral part of learning its concepts and theories, but they also undergo more general socialization into writing in an academic way. They are frequently expected to learn the general conventions of student writing very quickly on the assumption that they have already begun this process at school. But many students on professional courses are mature students who followed vocational rather than academic paths on leaving school and consequently find it diffiicult to grasp the importance of conventions such as the organization of essays into introduction, body and conclusion, the use of sections with headings in scientific reports, and the rules followed by different disciplines for citing references and attributing quotations. A good example of this is the frequent complaint from lecturers that students fail to give reference lists. This problem is so common that we must ask why it occurs. It would appear that students fail to pick up the functions of a reference list, not simply as an indication that they have read around the subject, but also as an indication that they realize the importance of acknowledging sources and not plagiarizing. In other words, learning to write reference lists in an acceptable form is one of the 'professional' skills of a university education which is independent of the discipline or professional course being studied.

Students also need opportunities to practise using the new academic language. This occurs through informal use of the discourse in class and in written course work. Mode of study is important here. Full-time students obviously have greater opportunities to practise new discourses but may be learning two or three different discourses simultaneously, depending on their programme of study. Part-time students generally study only one or, at most, two subjects at once, but complete fewer pieces of written work so tend to learn one discourse, and possibly one genre, at a time. Finally, there are students studying by distance learning. Their main disadvantage is the lack of opportunities to use the new discourses informally. Where students are following courses closely related to their professional work, however, close links between the two may help to alleviate this problem.

Social science approaches

Those of us whose interest in academic literacies is grounded in sociolinguistics and language teaching are familiar with the practical implications of linguistic approaches for teaching more generally. A second group of academics, however, has been greatly influenced by a separate but related approach to academic discourse, which draws on the work of the French philosopher Foucault (1972). This model focuses on how knowledge is 'framed' and is concerned with the expression of the abstract ideas which make up the concepts and theories of academic disciplines. The focus is on the development of skills of analysis. Entry to the discourse communities occurs as the student learns to reframe ideas in relation to concepts and theories and to use the language of the academic community appropriately. In the social sciences the evidence to support the theories is taken from everyday life, requiring students to redefine everyday experience by creating a frame drawn from the concepts and ideas they have learnt in the course (Northedge 1992). At some point students become overtly aware of this change, described here by a student who had just completed the Open University social sciences foundation course:

> It was a whole new way of looking at everyday life, to see everyday objects even, to be described as concepts and/or situations and you had to get your brain into that mode of thinking to understand it. There were specific concepts within individual disciplines such as geography and politics and then the last stage of the course was all about drawing on these individual pools of ideas. It was exciting and fun knowing that you could just pick out from any pool you wished. That's where I'd say my confidence really came.
>
> (Hoadley-Maidment and Mercer 1996)

Occupational discourses

Finally, when we look at the situation of students on professional courses, particularly mature students who have already undertaken vocational training, we need to consider how the academic discourses they are learning relate to the specialist language they may already know and use in the work setting. Occupational groupings are another example of discourse communities. If we are to value and build on students' experiences as users of occupational discourse, we need to examine the commonalities between the writing done by, for example, nurses and social workers, and undergraduate academic writing. In many cases, students will be fluent writers of reports, case notes and care plans, but these follow conventions and use language differently from academic essays. Closer examination, however, may reveal that vocational genres share some linguistic features with forms of student writing such as project reports. It could be argued that academic literacy is best approached through forms such as these, since students will be building on skills they already have.

Reflecting on personal experience

In developing a theory of professional education, the caring professions have been strongly influenced by two explanations of adult learning. Kolb's (1984) learning cycle focuses on the acquisition of knowledge and provides the main educational framework in the Open University courses I considered. At the same time, these courses aim to teach reflective practice by drawing on Schön's (1983; 1987) model of the reflective practitioner. This is concerned with *process learning* in the development of professional competence. The basic premise of Schön's work is 'learning in action' in which students carry out an action and then think consciously about it. Through 'reflection' they gradually learn to reframe problems and solutions within the discourse of the profession. As there are interesting parallels between Schön's ideas and the Foucault-based approach to discourse outlined above, it is worth considering how this may inform the development of academic literacies.

Schön's theory is rooted in the concept of the 'reflective dialogue' taught in face-to-face teaching situations such as practical workshops. He describes in detail the one-to-one conversations that occur between teacher and student while the student is engaged in practising a professional skill, for example drawing an architectural ground plan, in a setting where the teacher acts as *coach* rather than imparter of knowledge. This kind of teaching is familiar to most of us. It is the basis of adult education teaching in hobby classes such as arts and crafts, of sports coaching, science laboratory work and individual music lessons. It is also widely used in professional courses such as schoolteaching, nursing, social work and medicine where people are taught 'on the ward' or have periods of 'teaching practice'.

The theory emphasizes communication, although Schön himself does not address the role of written communication. He describes the student–tutor dialogue as having a number of feedback loops. The 'language' of these dialogues may not consist solely of spoken or written words, however. In architecture, for example, there is a combination of visual language (drawing of ground plans, elevations and so on) and spoken language which the professional needs in order to explain the visual language to clients and people such as surveyors, engineers and builders. In other words, each profession needs a language for *talking about* practice. A dialogue while carrying out a piece of practical work is likely to start with a problem. Students ask for help from the tutor because they are stuck and a conversation ensues which proceeds through questions and answers accompanied by drawing, demonstration or musical performance. The conversation provides opportunities to practise the language of the profession and to reframe the professional knowledge appropriately.

Although popular, the reflective practitioner model has been heavily criticized (Greenwood 1993; Eraut 1994; Boud 1995). Eraut draws attention to Schön's overwhelming interest in the creative aspects of professional development and is concerned that in real life there are few opportunities for deliberate reflection as Schön describes it. Eraut concludes that the theory is most useful as a theory to describe metacognition in skilled behaviour. He is not, however, concerned in this critique with the role of language or communication in professional learning. If we turn to the way in which students develop the discourse to communicate professionally, there are two other problems with Schön's theory.

One is his failure to take into account the *collective* learning that occurs in face-to-face practical classes. For the individual student the dialogue with the tutor/coach occupies only a small proportion of time – perhaps five minutes in a two-hour session. In-between times students get on with their own work: they practise the skills and ask for help when they get stuck. More importantly, they interact with other students: they wander round the room and learn by observing what others are doing, they discuss their work and provide help for each other, and they learn by overhearing the dialogues between the tutor and other students. In other words, learning in a 'practicum' of the sort Schön describes is a social dialogic experience in which students are part of a collective experience which enables them both to use the discourse and apply it directly to practice, albeit in a sheltered situation. An analysis of work-based learning settings would doubtless show similar patterns.

The second failure relates to the particular role of communication in the caring professions. Here communication is not simply for talking about practice but also a vital way of carrying out practice. (The same is true of teaching.) Students therefore need feedback on their communication skills in the same way that a student architect needs feedback on his drawing skills or a trainee surgeon on his use of surgical instruments. In face-to-face teaching this is often done through videotaped role plays. However, writing also plays a part. Professional courses in areas such as teaching, social work and youth and community work increasingly use reflective diaries or log-books to help students develop these skills. Students are given questions to focus their reflection on practice and asked to complete a diary, usually on a weekly basis. This may then be referred to in discussions with tutors or in assessed written work. In distance-learning courses, diaries and logbooks can substitute for some of the tutor–student dialogues which occur in face-to-face teaching. One important consideration, however, is that the diary itself is not seen as a device for developing competence in academic writing but as a private form of writing in which students can use notes and abbreviations and include confidential material. The aim of these diaries is to develop professional competence through reflective thought, not to practise writing as preparation for academic assessment.

Academic attitudes to writing in professional education

The School of Health and Social Welfare at the Open University has developed its courses for professionals in the health and social care fields using the distance-learning model originally developed by the university for its under-graduate programme. This uses a core of text-based teaching consisting of course workbooks which encourage active learning through problem-solving activities, supplemented by 'readers' containing academic papers, videos and audio-cassettes. The School emphasizes the value of courses aimed at a wide range of people working in the fields of health and social welfare rather than at one professional group, and has successfully developed a number of self-contained courses and, more recently, diplomas for this audience.

One of the main features of the courses is the opportunity for students to draw on their personal and work experience both in understanding aca-demic concepts and issues and as illustration and evidence in written assign-ments. There is, however, a lot of anecdotal evidence to suggest that students have difficulty in using this experience 'appropriately' in their written work. This may partly be explained by the fact that courses were developed initially at an academic level equivalent to second-year undergraduate study (so-called second-level courses) but taken by many students who were new to university study. Most students enrol because the courses are work-related and enable them to link academic learning to their professional lives. However, this raises questions as to how the academic writing students are asked to complete relates to their work experience and previous education and training. The demands and assumptions of the assessment strategy, because it was taken from that of the originally more traditional under-graduate programme, did not take into account the starting points for this group of students.

In 1995 the School of Health and Social Welfare began preliminary work on the development of an introductory course at first-year undergraduate level. There was a lot of informal discussion among academics as to the links between traditional academic assessment and work-based learning. There was a feeling among academics that students with no previous experience of university study failed assignments on the School's existing courses because they lacked the ability to write 'academically', but it was difficult to ascertain what lecturers meant by this. I therefore decided to carry out a small survey of academics' views on academic writing and the use of personal experience in the School's existing second-level courses. I was particularly interested in how those responsible for setting assignment topics and examinations regarded the development of academic writing and its relationship to the assessment strategy in ostensibly practice-related courses. The survey was carried out at the end of the 1995 academic year so that respondents were able to draw on the examinations and projects they had just marked when responding.

At that time the School offered eight second-level courses, each worth 30 Credit Accumulation and Transfer Scheme (CATS) points. All the courses had a workload of approximately 6–8 hours a week over a 30-week teaching year, during which students completed four written assignments. The assignments varied, but most courses asked for three essays and one longer piece of work (an extended essay or project) which provided an opportunity for students to undertake a small investigation related to their job, or alternatively to pursue a topic through library research. This longer piece varied in length between courses from 2000 to 5000 words. There appeared to be little consensus among staff as to the value of projects, other than that they provided opportunities for students to draw on their personal experience and relate it to the academic concepts and theories taught on the courses, and there was also some confusion over the difference between projects and 'extended' essays.

Six lecturers responsible for the overall co-ordination of individual courses (the School offered eight at the time) completed a questionnaire, designed to elicit their views of the students' strengths and weaknesses in relation to academic writing. The respondents were people with academic expertise in social sciences and professional expertise in health and social care: none of them described themselves as having expertise in academic literacy although, like the majority of Open University teachers, they had experience of working with mature students who needed support in this area.

They were first asked to rank the competence of students as academic writers. Using a four-point scale, two indicated that most students needed help and four that some students needed help. Three said that most students started at a low level but were fine by the end of the course. Given that help with writing would be provided by part-time tutors, the respondents were not able to indicate whether this was as a result of help from the tutors or, if so, what form this took.

The lecturers were also asked to rank different types of writing competence in order of importance to their course on a three-point scale from very important to not important. This revealed that academic argument was considered to be the most important form of writing, closely followed by the ability to draw on personal (including work) experience in assignments – the latter being seen as either 'very important' or 'important'. In most cases there was an assumption that students understood what was expected when asked to combine personal experience and academic argument.

Five said that students had particular problems with the reflective project. The weaknesses were given as a failure to understand the need to analyse, together with a lack of understanding the handling and interpretation of data. The latter is not, strictly speaking, an academic writing skill, but in a distance-learning course the only way students can indicate that they have learnt research skills is through their written work.

All thought that many of the students were taking the course as their first Open University course and commented on the implications of this. For example:

> we attract people direct from the field. They are often steeped in practice, but unused to academic study and writing.

The questionnaire provided space for additional comments. Detailed comments were made which showed that many concerns were common ones. Comments such as the following were typical:

> have difficulty in using personal experience in an appropriate way (as a vehicle to organize course themes and issues, etc.).

> ... reflect on own experience and then use it to illustrate a point of argument rather than just 'fill the page'.

> The use of personal experience as an exemplar is actually quite a sophisticated process and I don't think that often people can see that the personal experience cited in the course has already been very carefully structured and so we get a lot of stream of consciousness stuff where insights are deeply embedded and not pulled out to support an argument.

In one case, however, those teaching the course had over the years decided that they could not assume students had these skills and had adapted the assessment strategy to take this into account. The difficulty of providing academic socialization on courses such as these was also commented on. One person considered that it was more difficult for students to:

> challenge and innovate in the face of a set of materials as opposed to a person,

and felt that when this was coupled with low levels of experience in presenting arguments, this resulted in problems. This respondent was particularly aware of the impact of distance teaching methods on the development of academic literacy and the skills which are associated with 'graduateness'.

Issues raised in the survey

Although the questionnaire was brief and relatively unstructured, the results it produced were valuable for the common concerns that they revealed. The importance these academics gave to the development of skills in expressing academic argument reflects the centrality of written academic argument to teaching in the UK university system. In social sciences (and arts and humanities), essays presenting academic arguments are regarded as the best way of judging whether a student has understood the concepts and issues of a course and developed higher-order cognitive skills such as analysis and synthesis. At the same time it has been shown that knowledge and argument are differently defined and constructed by different disciplines, and that 'new' disciplines related to professions such as nursing also have individual characteristics (Bines and Watson 1992). In professional education the emphasis on traditional forms of academic writing has to be questioned, particularly where programmes have a substantial practice component, increasingly measured in terms of competences. This in turn raises questions about the relationship between vocational training and particular forms of academic writing.

When we turn to the skill of linking personal experience to theory there is an added dimension. The way we normally talk or write about personal experience is in narrative form. Students on professionally related courses need opportunities to practise linking narrative to argument. This operates at a number of levels, from organizing ideas to the use of appropriate grammatical forms. The difficulty identified in the survey is that of turning the (narrative) experience into a form which illustrates an academic argument based on abstract concepts, issues and theories. One way to teach this is to begin with forms which students feel competent in using, such as reports and case studies and small investigative projects. These often enable students to draw on work experience for content and to write about this experience in narrative form initially, while at a later point, for example in a discussion section, they have to analyse and synthesize this in academic terms.

The main concern of the academics is summed up in the word 'appropriacy'. The responses point to a desire for students to integrate practice and theory in a context where the assessment strategy is based on traditional academic measures. In addition, it is important to consider the distinctive features of supported open learning and how these may affect students' development as academic writers. Mitchell (1995), writing about the development of academic argument, says that the basis of most learning in the UK education system is spoken language. This is seen as 'open and transformative' while written language is 'the site of closure; the assignment which marks the end of a period of study' (Mitchell 1995: 133). Spoken language provides opportunities for students to try things out. For most students this means discussing concepts and issues, both inside class and informally. Academic discourse is learnt within a social and collective setting, involving both tutor–student and student–student interaction. The importance of spoken language in the development of writing by adult students is well documented at levels from basic education (Baynham 1995b) and return to learning (Gardener 1985) to language support for university students (Clark and Ivanič 1992).

In the Open University, as in most distance-learning institutions, not only is the bulk of teaching material in written form, but so is the support system. Tutorials are optional and the main form of communication between students and tutors is a highly sophisticated system of written messages around the exchange of written materials, especially students' own writing and feedback on this. Because students lack informal discussion opportunities, they generally do not practise using ideas and concepts in spoken language before they have to write about them. In other words, written language has to fill the role of open and transformative learning which Mitchell and others ascribe to spoken language. While aspects of Open University teaching, such as the inclusion of activities in the text, increase the interactive nature of study, this does not replace the oral practice at using academic discourse which occurs in informal discussions. One teaching issue is therefore how written language is used to provide practice at using academic English and subject-specific discourse.

The challenge in text-based learning of this sort is building up a steady dialogue of reflection with sufficient feedback loops when there are only limited opportunities to use spoken language in the ways described by Mitchell and Schön. Because it cannot be assumed that all students will take advantage of the interactive nature of the text (there is evidence that many students skip activities) the only dialogue that is guaranteed is the one between student and tutor around the student's assessed written work. Reflective diaries are useful here because they help students reframe their existing professional experience as they make the links between their practice and the theories, concepts and issues contained in the courses, within a private form of writing which will not be assessed.

Text-based learning must also assume that students are, or will quickly become, confident users of written text. Students who enrol on health and social welfare courses for work-related reasons often feel uncertain about expressing themselves in writing at the beginning of the course, especially if they have no background of university study. At the same time, because of the importance of text, they often feel under great pressure to become confident writers quickly, both in order to complete their written work and more generally because they may need to communicate with tutors and other students in writing. In a text-based learning system, learning to write about personal experience, as opposed to drawing on it in spoken discussion, becomes a priority. Computer-based learning, especially the use of asynchronous tutorials, makes similar demands.

Additionally, courses frequently ask students to develop higher-order academic competences while not explicitly showing them the links between these and the professional education and expertise they already have. It is therefore apparent that students need to know at the beginning of the course what they will be expected to be able to do in written form by the end. This in turn should influence the assessment strategy. Adopting an approach which develops students' academic literacies, by building on those they already have, may mean rethinking the academic genres in which they are being asked to write early in the course. It also means making sure that students recognize where an academic task such as a project may differ from projects they have done elsewhere. For example, it is not always clear to students how projects differ from essays. Open University students receive assignment booklets containing guidance on completing the written assessments. These often refer to 'argument' while at the same time failing to say explicitly that projects must relate the data collected to the issues and concepts presented in the course. Since many professional students are familiar with descriptive reports and probably write them regularly themselves, they may feel that the only conclusions they have to reach are those drawn from the data themselves. In other words, they approach an academic assignment in the way they would prepare a report for a case conference, without realizing the difference in both discourse and genre.

Another issue which arises in health and social care courses is how students indicate that they have understood the value base of a course. Equal opportunities and anti-discriminatory practice are central to study in the caring professions. Guidelines are frequently laid down by professional bodies. For example, at the time of the survey the School of Health and Social Welfare offered a course, 'The Disabling Society', which presented a model of disability expressed through a very specific discourse, based on the politics of equal opportunity. It was easy for students to appear to have understood the ideas and concepts being taught because they used the discourse quite confidently in their written work. However, it was also apparent that many of them had understood only at the surface level (Morgan 1993) because when asked to illustrate their answers from their experience they were unable to do so. In other words, the relationship between reflection-in-action and academic understanding was not made.

Practical implications for professional courses

My main concern was initially with distance learning, but I am aware that the rapid growth of open learning and information and communication technology (ICT) means that the issues I identified at the outset are increasingly relevant to all professional university courses. I would particularly draw attention to the following.

There is a need to develop systems for part-time and distance-learning courses which substitute for the kind of communication experience gained in a practicum so that students can begin to reframe their experience using academic discourse in a less formal way than an assessed assignment. This should begin by being more explicit about the positive value of studying part-time, particularly the opportunity it provides to feed back the academic learning into professional practice on an almost daily basis. Computer conferencing, for example, has potential to serve as a practicum by providing a 'protected' situation in which students communicate with each other and with the tutor, learning and practising the academic discourse. Through the setting of appropriate discussion topics it is possible to provide opportunities for students to relate these to practice in a very immediate way. (See Lea, Chapter 4, for further discussion of the relationship between conferencing and learning.)

It is also important to use written tasks for learning rather than conflating the learning and assessment function. Reflective diaries, taping experiences and using questionnaires as frameworks for the analysis of critical incidents can all provide opportunities to practise academic discourse and establish feedback loops between academic concepts and professional practice. Course designers must then consider how the assessment strategy can best evaluate the type of learning, choosing methods of assessment for their ability to link theory and practice, rather than simply using already existing methods which suit institutional systems and regulations.

Finally, there are staff development implications. Tutors on professional courses are generally recruited because they have appropriate academic knowledge and relevant professional expertise as well as teaching skills. Few, however, see themselves as language or communications specialists, assuming that students should have learnt such competences at an earlier stage and often not feeling confident to undertake what is often perceived as remedial teaching. But the increasing emphasis in universities on developing students' general cognitive skills and the concept of 'graduateness' points to a changing role for tutors. This means that tutors must feel confident to teach students how to make the links between practice and academic study. For many years in the United Kingdom there has been a movement concerned with 'language across the curriculum'. Although rooted in schools, this is equally relevant to university education. While professional education programmes with practice elements are increasingly tackling these issues (Bines and Watson 1992), they must also be addressed in relation to more traditional open and distance-learning courses.

Conclusion

The real challenge for many professional courses, as teaching methods change in response to new technology, is ensuring that the aims and objectives drawn from the professional requirements of the course are attainable within systems designed for academic learning. Courses such as those I have described bring together two approaches to learning: 'traditional' academic learning of theoretical academic knowledge and 'reflection-in-action' whereby the doing informs and is informed by the learning. The first is concerned with developing a range of higher-order cognitive skills such as analysis and synthesis, while the latter focuses on improved performance comprising communication, observation, the performance of technical and scientific procedures and the exercise of professional judgement (Eraut 1994) The literature indicates that the two have many principles in common. In particular, there is a desire for students to acquire the discourse of the professional or academic community. The ability to communicate effectively within that community is seen as an indication of professional or academic success. But there are particular implications for the support of students who have few opportunities for using spoken language in their studies.

11

Schoolteachers as Students: Academic Literacy and the Construction of Professional Knowledge within Master's Courses in Education

Barry Stierer

Every year, thousands of British schoolteachers begin work towards a master's degree in education, based in a UK university or college. Their studies typically require them to read research and scholarship about aspects of education, to carry out practical activities and research projects, and to prepare written assignments. Their reasons for embarking on such courses vary. They may wish to improve their job security, or their chances of promotion, by adding to their existing qualifications. They may wish to improve their professional effectiveness and confidence, by gaining a greater understanding of certain aspects of their work as teachers. They may wish to learn about an aspect of education which is new to them, perhaps because they would like to work in that area in the future. They are highly motivated students. Most of them pay their own fees for what is, at least in part, a form of professional development. Most of them work towards their degrees in their own time: indeed, few are given time off from their teaching commitments in order to attend sessions or to make progress with their studies.

This chapter discusses the results of a research project that examined the kinds of writing schoolteachers are required to produce as part of their work within master's-level programmes in the field of education. The Master of Arts in Education programme at my own institution, the Open University (OU), was used as the main case study for this project during the 1997 academic year, based on an analysis of course materials, interviews with MA students and tutors, and an analysis of students' assignments and the written feedback they receive from their tutors.

Issues and questions framing the research

The Open University's MA programme in education is described as follows in the OU's own prospectus (Open University 1997: 31):

> The MA has developed a reputation for being both intellectually challenging and professionally relevant:
>
> • intellectually challenging because you will be asked to address complex issues and come to terms with advanced literature;
>
> • professionally relevant because you will be encouraged constantly to identify the significance of your study for your everyday work and concerns.

This description neatly encapsulates the two traditions, or 'orders of discourse' (Foucault 1972; Fairclough 1989), which I would argue our MA programme – and indeed many MA programmes in education – attempt to incorporate. The first of these places particular value on the traditional intellectual competences of 'the academy', at least in the humanities and social sciences: the construction of a *coherent argument;* appropriate *uses of evidence;* the privileging of *analysis and criticism* over description; and so on. The latter places particular value on aspects of professional development typically associated with *training:* the ability to *reflect* upon one's practice, and upon the implications of that reflection for *changing practice;* the ability to demonstrate the *professional relevance* of one's learning; and the need to link the results of study to *professional competences and practical outcomes.* Whether, and how, these competing discourses can ultimately be reconciled within a single programme of study was one of the main issues in the research. A key assumption underpinning the research was that it is within the 'literacy practices' associated with these courses – and especially in the writing requirements – that these two orders of discourse are most acutely focused.

Most teachers studying within an MA programme are doing so – at least in part – for professional reasons. Moreover, the courses are – at least in part – about their professional work. Consequently teachers approach the courses – not unreasonably – with the expectation that their professional experience will provide them with many of the resources needed in order to produce assignments and thereby successfully fulfil assessment requirements. One of the starting points for the research was an observation that many teachers studying within the MA programme experienced considerable confusion over the expectations they were attempting to meet, with respect to writing, sometimes leading to fraught conflicts with their tutors. They experienced this confusion despite the fact that Open University course materials are generally considered to be exceptional in the extent to which they make such expectations explicit. I suspected that this confusion was due in part to a conflation of professional discourses and academic discourses in the way writing tasks were described, coupled with a lack of explicitness about the way in which students are expected to negotiate these ways of using language.

Starting points and frames for analysis

The research project represented an attempt to apply some of the theoretical ideas and practical insights arising from recent research into aspects of academic literacy, which has concentrated mainly on undergraduate teaching within traditional academic disciplines, to the comparatively under-researched area of professionally oriented teaching at postgraduate level. The project also sought to apply some of the ideas, emanating from research into the nature of professional training and knowledge, to the specific context of writing – an aspect that tends to be overlooked in such research.

With respect to the field of academic literacy, the project is located within, and seeks to make a contribution to, a growing area of research into aspects of academic writing in higher education based on a 'critical' perspective on discourse and literacy practices, or what Lea and Street (Chapter 2 of this volume) call an 'academic literacies' model. Within this perspective, academic writing is conceptualized as a set of social practices embedded in networks of culture and power. Rather than viewing academic writing as a transparent medium for representing knowledge, or as a set of rules to which students need to accommodate, this perspective views academic institutions as sites of power, and academic writing as a point where power is exerted and contested. This perspective problematizes these practices, and recognizes that students' so-called failures as academic writers may be explained by, for example, their struggle to reconcile their own identities, and purposes for studying, with the authority and control of the institution (Ivanič 1998). Such a perspective has provided a helpful explanatory framework for research into the academic writing carried out by schoolteachers within master's-level courses in education, for reasons which will be discussed at the end of this chapter. For a more detailed elaboration of this perspective on academic literacy, please refer to the Editors' Introduction to this volume.

Another field of research and scholarship is pertinent to this investigation, and that is the area of 'professional knowledge', or 'expert knowledge' – and *teachers'* professional knowledge in particular. A lot of work has been done in this area, which is essentially concerned with the relationship between training, conceptual understanding and professional practice (see Schön 1983; 1987; Kolb 1984; and Eraut 1994). It is from this body of work that such widely used terms as 'reflective practitioner' have emerged. Some of this work examines the ways in which professional knowledge is encoded in language (Gunnarsson *et al.* 1997), but apparently none has examined the styles of written language which have become associated with professional training. My starting point is that it is in the language practices, within an area of activity such as teachers' professional development, that the struggles over what constitutes important professional knowledge for teachers are played through. Nevertheless, the present research has drawn from this area of work as its theoretical framework has evolved. The project can be seen as a contribution to this area in so far as it examines the way in which professional knowledge constitutes, and is constituted in, specialized forms of language.

The other starting point for this research is that this is a form of 'practitioner research' for me. Most of my own professional practice over the past ten years has been located within the OU's MA in Education programme. In professional terms, I was trying to gain a deeper understanding of the issues surrounding academic writing for MA students in my own institution, in order to improve both the advice we give to students and the professional development we offer to tutors.

The Open University MA in education

At any one time there are about 4000 students in the OU's MA in Education programme in the UK, Ireland and continental western Europe. They are distance learners, working in comparative isolation with multimedia materials, and submitting written assignments to a tutor, whom they meet at fairly infrequent (optional) group tutorials. The programme is modular: students typically choose any three modules in order to complete their degrees. In 1997 there were 18 modules in the programme (see Table 11.1). Each module differs in the way it organizes its materials, and in the way students'

Table 11.1 Modules in the Open University's MA in Education programme, 1997

- E825 Language and literacy in social context
- E819 Curriculum, learning and assessment
- E820 Child development in social context
- E826 Gender issues in education: equality and difference
- E829 Developing inclusive curricula: equality and diversity in education
- E832 Primary education: the basic curriculum
- E833 Primary education: assessing and planning learning
- ES821 Science education
- E823 Technology education
- ME822 Researching mathematics classrooms
- E827 Adult learners: education and training
- E817 Education, training and employment
- E830 Mentoring
- E828 Educational management in action
- E834 Understanding school management
- E838 Effective leadership and management in education
- E824 Educational research methods
- E835 Educational research in action

progress is assessed. Some modules require students to carry out practical activities in schools; some place greater weight upon students' understanding and analysis of issues and concepts discussed in the course materials. Some require students to take a formal final examination, and all of them contain some element of research.

An analysis of specifications for written assignments

Most of this chapter reports on the results of one of the main strands in the research project – that being an analysis of the specifications for written assignments in the OU's MA in Education programme. This involved a careful analysis of each assignment booklet for the 18 modules in the programme in 1997. These assignment booklets are key documents, since they contain detailed specifications for each assignment a student is required to submit. The assignment specifications sometimes include general advice on writing assignments for the module, as well as guidance notes on each question which aim to help the students (and indeed the tutors) to understand what they assignment expects them to do. The specifications are standard for every student taking the course, no matter where in the world they live; the role of the tutor is therefore to interpret and mediate these requirements rather than to set questions themselves.

Inventory of types of writing across the programme

One element of my research involved compiling an 'inventory' of the types of writing required across the MA programme by analysing the way each assignment on each module was represented in the 18 assignment booklets. This required an analysis of over 100 specifications for written assignments across the programme.

The analysis revealed that, regardless of the three modules a student chooses to study, they will be expected to produce a very wide range of types of writing. Table 11.2 provides a list merely of the types of writing, or *genre categories*, required for written assignments across the 18 modules in the programme. These are very superficial analyses of the diversity of types of writing students are required to carry out within the programme. Nevertheless, from this it is clear that an individual student's programme of three modules could require them to produce as many as a dozen different types of writing. The meaning of these labels, like 'essay' or 'project report', varies from module to module, and even within individual modules, even when the same generic label is used. So it is only really by looking at individual assignment specifications that the meaning of these labels becomes clear. Nevertheless, with such an array of writing types across the programme – with some students only encountering certain genre categories once or

Table 11.2 Open University MA in education, 1997: genre categories for written assignments, by module

Module	*Types of writing required*					
E817 Education, training and employment	Essay	Project proposal	Project report	Exam		
E826 Gender issues in education	Essay	Essay plan	Essay	Critical literature review or pilot study	Project plan	Project report	Exam
E819 Curriculum, learning and assessment	Preliminary statement/rationale	Situational analysis	Curriculum development plan	Extended essay	Implementation plan	
E820 Child development	Essay	Critical book review	Small-scale study proposal	Small-scale study report	Essay	Exam
E825 Language and literacy	Essay	Text analysis	Essay	Project proposal	Essay	Project report
E829 Developing inclusive curricula	Project proposal	Project report	Project proposal	Project report	Project proposal	Project report
E827 Adult learners, education and training	Essay	Project proposal	Essay	Project report	Exam	
E830 Mentoring	Situational analysis	Case study	Case study	Project outline	Project report	
E828 Educational management in action	Project proposal	Project report	Project proposal	Project report	Project proposal	Project report
E834 Understanding school management	Essay	Essay	Report plan	Management report	Project proposal	Project report

Course						
E838 Effective leadership and management in education	Self-assessment of management development needs	Management activity plan	Report on strategic management	Reflective report on the management activity	Exam		
E832 Primary education: the basic curriculum	Essay	Personal perspective	Lesson plan/analysis	Lesson plan/analysis	Lesson observation/analysis	Project plan	Project report
E833 Primary education: assessing and planning learning	Personal position	Project report	Personal position	Project plan	Outline plan	Project report	
ES821 Science education	Description/analysis	Description/analysis	Report	Report	Description/analysis and critical appraisal	Exam	
E823 Technology education	Essay	Analysis	Analysis	Investigation	Evaluation		
ME822 Researching mathematics classrooms	Personal account and critical review	Description/analysis and critical review	Description/analysis and critical review	Description/analysis	Description/analysis	Essay	Project report
E824 Educational research methods	Essay	Critical evaluation of article	Essay				
E835 Educational research in action	Research topic outline	Essay	Assessment of article	First draft research proposal and pilot study plan	Final draft research proposal and report on pilot study	Exam	

twice during their studies – it is hardly surprising that some students find it difficult to build up a sense of confidence and progression in their ability to write academically as they move from one assignment to the next, and from one module to the next.

Text analysis of individual assignment specifications

Following the 'inventory' of the assignment specifications, a text analysis was carried out on the wording of each assignment question in the assignment booklets for the 18 modules in the programme, as well as any guidance notes produced by course teams designed to help students 'unpack' the question. After a preliminary analysis of these texts, four categories of text features were identified as significant:

1. Any explicit explanation of the conventions the student is expected to use.
2. Ways in which students' professional work as teachers is referred to, and ways in which students are advised to refer to their own professional work.
3. Ways in which the questions appear to 'position' students with respect to ideas in the course.
4. Uses of imperatives.

Explicit explanations of the conventions the student is expected to use
The analysis revealed that most advice on writing was concerned with structure (for example, suggestions on how to sequence elements of the text) and coverage (which readings should be drawn upon in answering the question) rather than on appropriate forms and uses of language for the piece of writing in question. With one or two exceptions no attempt was made to describe and account for the course team's notion of 'good writing' – let alone to problematize it. A small number of exceptions to this pattern were found. For example, the Child Development team attempted to define its expectations in the following ways:

> Assignments 01, 02 and 05 are conventional essay questions.

> Avoid being simply descriptive or prescriptive. This is an MA course, which demands critical analysis as well as a display of understanding of the course material. A string of summaries of relevant bits of the Study Guide and readings is not acceptable.

Although the meanings of the key terms in this passage ('descriptive', 'prescriptive', 'critical', 'analysis') are not defined or illustrated, this is one of the very few attempts made by a course team to make explicit the expectations students should meet.

On another issue, that of whether to use the 'first person' voice in assignments, the Child Development team explicitly favours a more detached writing style:

> Write impersonally: as far as possible avoid first person pronouns.

The Adult Learning team adopts a contrasting position:

> It is quite acceptable to write in the first person, but you should avoid personalized anecdotes, and will be penalized for rambling or unclear passages.

It should be emphasized that, while the contrast between these two pieces of advice may be noteworthy, they are the only two instances across the 18 modules where the question of 'voice' is explicitly considered at all.

Finally, with only one exception there was no acknowledgement of the differences between course teams in what they expect in this respect. The Educational Management team offers this advice to students about the important differences between the writing style expected for 'management reports' and the kinds of academic writing students may have been required to produce on other courses:

> It is important to understand that the E838 assignments are reports on management rather than academic essays. We have found from past experience that some students do not achieve as high a grade as they might have, had they appreciated the difference between these two types of writing. When writing an academic essay students are sometimes tempted to display their erudition by splicing together numerous quotations from academic authors and using a lot of academic jargon. This style prevents the writer from developing and communicating his or her own ideas in a clear and logical structure. It is not suited to the intended audience for a management report, and should be avoided.

It should be noted in passing that this advice could be accused of lampooning to some extent the expectations conventionally associated with academic essay writing. The sarcastic tone adopted when describing the way students 'are sometimes tempted to display their erudition' is not a description that would be universally recognized as one of 'best practice', even for academic essays. Moreover, there is an assumption that achieving clarity and logic is merely a matter of avoiding an over-dependence on quotations and the use of academic jargon, and that students will have been helped to understand what is expected of them by being told what is *not* expected of them. This point notwithstanding, the passage is significant for the purposes of this analysis, in the sense that it represents the only attempt in any of the 18 assignment booklets to recognize explicitly the fact that students may be approaching the course with a set of assumptions about academic writing that differs from the expectations for E838, based on their previous experience of study, and to point out some of the differences between management reports and academic essays.

Ways in which students' professional work as teachers is referred to, and
ways in which students are advised to refer to their own professional work
Of interest here was evidence of course teams' expectations of the ways in which students should and should not draw upon their own professional

experience when answering the question or completing the task assigned. This included any indications of how students should or should not identify the implications of their argument or analysis for their own professional work. Analysing instances of this feature was seen as one way of examining the way in which professional and academic traditions are played through in the requirements for writing. This feature of the language was examined in order to see how different course teams handled the tension between these two traditions.

Analysis of this feature of assignment questions revealed wide variations between modules (and to some extent within modules) in the way students are expected to represent their professional work when writing assignments. In some modules (notably 'Education, Training, and Employment', 'Child Development', 'Language and Literacy', and 'Gender Issues in Education') students are expected to keep to a minimum any discussion of professional circumstances, or of the professional development achieved as a result of study – though no advice is given on how to construct this linguistically. The examples of essay-style questions given in Table 11.3 provide an indication of the way students' professional work is referred to (if at all) in these modules. There is clearly no expectation underlying these assignments that students are expected to, or even able to, draw upon their professional experience as teachers in order to attempt, and succeed at, the writing task. Indeed, for most modules in this category there is an implication that students would be penalized if they include more than a passing reference to their professional work when constructing their assignments.

In other modules (notably 'Science Education', 'Researching Mathematics Classrooms', 'Mentoring', 'Primary Education' (both modules), and 'Effective Leadership and Management') students are expected to make visible the professional knowledge they have achieved through their study of the course – though here again no advice is given on how to construct this linguistically. 'Mentoring', for example, represents the relationship between the student's professional activity and the writing task in this way:

Project 4 is designed to help you look back in a structured manner over the experience of mentoring, and then to look forward to possible developments arising out of that experience.

In steps 1–4 you are asked to provide a critical review of the mentoring programme you have been involved in from the perspective of: the institution; the mentee; and your own professional development.

In step 5 you are asked to examine the concept of the 'mentoring school' and explore the potential for mentoring in other staff development processes within your institution.

You are required to locate your discussion within the wider educational debates on mentoring by referring to the research and literature in the field, such as are indicated in the Study Guide. In addition, you are encouraged to provide evidence from your own mentoring experience in support of your conclusions.

Table 11.3 Open University MA in Education: examples of 'essay-style' questions

---

From E817, Assignment 01, Question 1

Examine the view that since the economic crises of the 1970s, the political and economic agendas for education and training have been dominated by an 'economic instrumentalism' in which a prime objective has been to increase political control over educational practitioners and institutions. What would you say have been the main consequences of this policy for the development of vocational education and training?

From E826, Assignment 01, Question 3

How does this definition of 'hegemonic masculinity' help us to understand the way that subordinated masculinities and feminity are constructed?

From E820, Assignment 02, Question 1

Critically evaluate the contribution that Dunn's book, *The beginnings of social understanding*, has made to our understanding of child development and how to promote it.

From, E827, Assignment 03, Question 1

'A discourse of adult learning embraces leisure opportunities, education and training and does away with élitist distinctions between them.' Critically examine this contention and the consequences for the provision of learning opportunities for adults.

The eight remaining modules lie somewhere between these two poles on the professional–academic continuum. This aspect of the analysis clearly shows that, as students move from one module to another, they are required to negotiate possibly substantial shifts in the way they are expected to relate their studies to their professional work when writing assignments, and that these shifts are left almost entirely unacknowledged in the assignment booklets.

Ways in which the questions appear to 'position' students with respect to ideas in the course
Of interest here was the use of certain *discursive devices* (that is, specific features of discourse that contribute to its social function) which work within assignment specifications to position students with respect to ideas in the course. Some courses appeared implicitly to expect the student to position themselves fairly remotely from the issues in the course: the issues are 'out there', to be studied and understood, and the student's own personal or professional response to them is not strictly warrantable as an outcome. Other courses seemed implicitly to expect the student to position themselves at the very heart of the course: in such courses the student seemed to be expected to write themselves – and, in particular, their personal and professional development – into the assignment, almost as the 'main character'. Indeed, most courses implicitly contained some elements of both of these,

leaving students understandably uncertain about their personal position in relation to issues in the course. A further assumption was that assignments which demanded detachment were located in a more 'academic' tradition, and the assignments which demanded involvement were located in a more 'professional' tradition. Fairclough's (1989; 1995) system for describing and analysing discourse was used in order to identify key features which encoded these ideas, such as nominalization (that is, using noun forms rather than more active verb forms, denoting objectification and detachment), modality (that is, the degree of tentativeness or certainty expressed in a proposition), voice (active or passive) and agency (that is, how clearly the person being referred to is identified).

Here, too, there were wide variations between modules (and to some extent within modules) in the way students are expected to position themselves with respect to ideas in the course. Perhaps predictably, there was a close correspondence between the way modules divide in the 'academic–professional' distinction above, and the way they divide in the 'detachment–involvement' distinction here. The same modules identified in the preceding section, which expected students to keep to a minimum any discussion of professional development achieved as a result of study, showed significantly more usage of nominalizations, passive voice, indirect address to the student (that is, no explicit indication of agency) and (possibly surprisingly) tentative forms of modality ('perhaps', 'might'). Moreover, the modules identified in the preceding section, which expected students to make visible the professional knowledge they have achieved through their study of the course, used fewer nominalizations, more active voice, more explicit agency in the way the student is addressed ('you', 'your') and more assertive forms of modality ('you should'). (Please refer to the examples provided in the preceding section for illustrations of these points.) Although this result may suggest that the two categories of analysis could be conflated in future analyses, it is nevertheless noteworthy that there should be such a close correspondence between the way course teams refer to students' professional work and the way students are positioned, within specifications for written assignments, with respect to ideas in the course.

Uses of imperatives

Of interest here was the way instructions were expressed by course teams – these being indications of the way in which the assignment task is perceived. At issue here was not *whether* assignment booklets made use of imperative forms (they all did, in abundance), but the specific kinds of imperatives adopted. Table 11.4 gives a selection from the some 50 different imperative forms found in the 18 assignment booklets. These kinds of instructions will typically appear either within the main rubric of the assignment question, or within guidance notes accompanying the question. No pattern could be found in the way these imperatives were distributed across the modules, although the more overtly 'professional' modules showed a slight tendency to use a wider range of imperatives than the 'academic'

Table 11.4 A selection of imperatives taken from assignment specifications

Evaluate	Justify	Write a report
Critically evaluate	Construct a conceptual	Explain
Assess	framework	Consider
Analyse	Describe	Suggest
Critically appraise	Give a brief description	Comment on
Examine	Describe and analyse	Apply the model
Critically examine	Write a critical account of	Report what happens
Critically discuss	Provide a report	when you apply your
Reflect on	Make a plan	chosen model
Critically reflect upon	Outline	

modules. All modules were very similar, however, in their reluctance to define these imperatives. With only one or two exceptions, the course team's ideas about how to go about following such instructions is not made explicit, and yet these imperatives represent key indicators of the kind of writing task the student is expected to undertake. This remarkable range of instructions provides clear evidence of the taken-for-grantedness with which academic teams approach the task of preparing assignments, as well as the complexity of the 'code' which students need to crack in order to complete their assignments successfully. How, for example, should students understand the differences between 'critically evaluate', 'critically examine', 'critically discuss' and 'critically appraise' – and, indeed, between 'evaluate' and 'critically evaluate'? It is possible that, for some academic teams, the terms are virtually interchangeable, whereas a conscientious student might reasonably seek to distinguish the meanings of these different key terms.

Discussion

Space constraints do not permit a discussion here of the other strands of the research project, such as the interviews with students and tutors, and the analysis of students' written assignments and the written feedback received from their tutors. These will be reported in the future. Nevertheless, the following discussion, of issues arising from the foregoing analysis of the assignment booklets for the modules in the OU's MA programme, is informed to some extent by provisional findings from those other research strands.

These analyses of the assignment booklets raise a number of important questions, which extend well beyond the superficial issue of inadequate specificity in setting out the requirements for students' writing. The tensions identified by this analysis appear to reveal a deep confusion within the programme at the level of epistemology. There is clearly no consensus or consistency across the programme about the professional knowledge that teachers are expected to demonstrate by means of these highly stylized writing forms. The reluctance of course teams to make explicit the kinds of professional knowledge they aim to promote through written assignments suggests that these teams have either not given adequate consideration to this crucial issue, or have not deemed it important to make their aims visible to students. Many of the privileged genres of writing in the programme have for the most part been imported – possibly without conscious deliberation – from traditional academic disciplines such as sociology and psychology, and may therefore not be appropriate for promoting the professional knowledge that is (implicitly) warrantable within these courses.

These findings are illuminated by data from the interviews with students – most of whom placed paramount importance upon the practical and professional dimensions of their MA studies, rather than upon their ability to engage with academic debates or to handle theoretical concepts persuasively in their writing. In this sense, the predominance of impersonal and traditional academic writing genres within a number of modules accounts in part for their sense of uncertainty and frustration – especially since the relevance of such genres in relation to their professional aspirations is so rarely articulated within course materials.

The analysis also revealed enormous variation within and between modules, in the styles of writing required, in the kind of advice on writing offered, in the orientation towards the student's professional experience and expertise, and in the way students were positioned with respect to ideas in the course. These findings help to explain why, through the interview strand of the research, it became clear that the most successful students started from scratch, in their attempt to puzzle out the ground rules for academic writing, each time they moved to a new module. Less successful students tried to apply the approaches they developed in one module to subsequent modules. Students had little sense of cumulative 'progress' in their development as academic writers, except on a very general level of 'confidence' and 'practice'.

The findings from the analysis of tutors' written feedback on students' assignments also reinforced many of the issues emerging from the analysis of the assignment booklets. That analysis revealed how consistently tutors use their feedback to try to induct their students into a way of using language, which is considered by tutors not only to be unfamiliar to students but also to be an essential part of learning within their field of study. This process mirrors the function performed by specifications for written assignments, which appear to call for genres of academic writing imported from traditional academic disciplines such as sociology and psychology, rather than genres of writing which have been deliberately adopted, or developed, in order to support the forms of professional knowledge deemed by course teams, and indeed by students, as important.

All these findings, taken together, suggest that the writing assigned to teachers as part of their MA studies contributes significantly to the way the programme positions MA students as *novices*. This does not lie easily with the professional experience these students bring to the process of study, or with the professional purposes many of them have for studying. They are, almost without exception, experienced professionals, studying for largely professional reasons. They fully expect to be somewhat disabled when they start. They struggle to identify, and learn how to use, specialized language forms in order to succeed in what for many of them is a new field of activity. This in itself does not *surprise* them. I think what surprises them, though they may not articulate it this way, is that they sign up for the MA for professional reasons, and suddenly find that they are positioned as *novice academics* rather than as, say, *novice 'expert teachers'*. Much of the language used in the assignment booklets, and the feedback students receive from tutors on assignments, is framed in terms of inducting students into a specialized community of academic discourse. At best the subliminal message is: here is how to be a sociologist, or an applied critical linguist, or a psychologist, or a management theorist. The assumption is nearly, but not quite, that these students aspire to be professional academics like members of the course teams and like their own tutors, rather than *better informed or more effective professional schoolteachers*. Viewed in this way, the problem can be recast as one of competing conceptions of 'the novice', rather than one of competing orders of discourse – which are ultimately linguistic manifestations of this more fundamental tension.

Teachers have already gone through a process of induction into a new community of discourse once before in their lives: into the teaching profession. That is the professional culture with which they identify, and it is from the perspective of that culture that they have registered to study for an MA. They do not embark on their MA studies as the first step in a career change from professional teachers to professional academics, and yet many of the literacy practices in these programmes seem to be predicated on an assumption that they are doing just that.

In this sense, the academic–professional divide is inappropriate: both orders of discourse are *professional*. The issue, therefore, is one of two professional cultures clashing: the professional culture of schoolteaching and the (higher-status) professional culture of the academy. Whereas schoolteachers embark on their studies in order to enhance their effectiveness and/or status within the professional culture of schoolteaching, the discursive practices of the academy position them as novice academics. Part of the explanation for this must lie in the way that institutions of higher education use language to sustain and legitimate an epistemological hegemony – that is, an ideology which positions students of any type as relatively powerless (Bourdieu *et al.* 1994). The discourse and knowledge that schoolteachers bring to their studies, and indeed the discourse and knowledge that schoolteachers manage to construct for themselves as professionals as a result of their studies, are only sanctioned by the institution when they can be overtly realized in the language of the novice academic.

I would speculate that the literacy practices that have grown up around the study of education originated in contexts where people studying education at postgraduate level were negotiating a transition between one culture (schoolteaching) and another (academic research and scholarship). These traditions of academic practice have persisted, despite the fundamental changes that have taken place in the professional and personal circumstances within which most people work towards master's degrees in education. It also appears to be the case that many of the literacy practices comprising MA in Education courses have evolved from traditional academic disciplines, mainly in the social sciences, at undergraduate level. One possibility is that these practices have simply reproduced themselves within universities, thus missing the opportunity to consider a priori the kinds of knowledge which could and should be warrantable within such programmes, and to develop forms of writing which facilitate the acquisition of such knowledge. Indeed, it maybe that conventional academic genres of writing serve to constrain teachers' ability to construct professional knowledge for themselves.

Implications for theory

Although the analysis is still at an early stage, the project has already benefited from recent advances in theoretical understanding of academic literacy practices, introduced at the beginning of this chapter (and more fully in the Editors' Introduction to this volume), and at the same time contributed in a small way to the further elaboration of a more pluralistic and culturally sensitive perspective on the study of writing in higher education. The considerable range of genres of academic writing which confront MA students in the course of their studies, and the variety of ways students are expected (often implicitly) to represent their developing professional knowledge, demonstrate that this is a fruitful explanatory framework for research of this kind.

Implications for practice

At this stage of the research, two main implications for practice are suggested by the analysis. The first is the need for a more explicit and systematic approach for helping students to identify and to critique the kinds of expectations they are expected to fulfil in relation to written assignments. The analysis of specifications for written assignments in this chapter demonstrated the need for some overarching framework and language to help students to critique the kinds of writing expected of them within MA modules. An adaptation of Fairclough's (1989) approach to critical language study might provide students with the tools to interpret the assumptions underlying written assignments, and to gain a greater understanding of the subject positions such specifications create for them. Evidence from the interviews with students reinforced this finding: none of the students interviewed appeared to have a 'metalanguage' for discussing vital aspects of academic writing. Terms such as 'argument', 'critical' and 'analysis', which were often used in course materials and by their tutors in feedback, were still largely mysterious to them. This problem might be especially acute for those students who do not bring with them to their study of these courses the particular forms of 'cultural capital' (Bourdieu and Passeron 1977) which enable other students quickly to identify the discursive ground rules operating within their courses and to produce forms of writing which satisfy these ground rules. Nevertheless, it is an enterprise with which all students on such programmes could productively engage.

The second implication for practice is the need for a robust and self-critical debate among academic staff about the most appropriate forms of writing for helping teachers to develop professional knowledge within master's-level programmes in education. This debate should begin with a comprehensive examination of the kinds of professional knowledge which such programmes ought to foster, rather than with the forms of writing conventionally associated with the academic disciplines from which such programmes have evolved. We need to think more imaginatively, in order to offer genres of academic writing to MA students which provide real support for professional learning, and to problematize the assumptions about academic writing which underlie our advice to students and our work with fellow tutors.

Acknowledgements

I am grateful to Val McGregor, Sandy Sieminski and Margaret Bird, School of Education staff tutors in the Open University's London Regional Office, for their co-operation and assistance with the arrangements for interviewing tutors and students. I am also indebted to the following people who have provided valuable advice at various stages of the project: Neil Mercer, Janet Maybin, Charles Bazerman, Mary Lea, Barbara Mayor, Fiona Leach, Harry Torrance, Ros Ivanič and Simon Pardoe.

References

ANC (1994) *Policy Framework for Education and Training.* Johannesburg: ANC.

Baker, D., Fox, C. and Clay, J. (eds) (1995) *Challenging Ways of Knowing in Maths, Science and English.* Lewes: Falmer Press.

Ball, C., Dice, L. and Bartholomae, D. (1990) Developing discourse practices in adolescence and adulthood, in R. Beach and S. Hynds (eds) *Advances in Discourse Processes* Vol. XXXIX. Norwood, NJ: Ablex.

Barnes, D., Britton, J. and Torbe, M. (1990) *Language, the Learner and the School,* 3rd edition. Harmondsworth: Penguin.

Bartholomae, D. (1985) Inventing the university, in M. Rose (ed.) *When a Writer Can't Write: Studies in Writer's Block and Other Composing-Process Problems.* New York: Guilford Press.

Barton, D. (1994) *Literacy: An Introduction to the Ecology of Written Language.* London: Blackwell.

Baynham, M. (1995a) *Literacy Practices.* London: Longman.

Baynham, M. (1995b) Narrative in argument, argument in narrative, in P.J.M. Costello and S. Mitchell (eds) *Competing and Consensual Voices: The Theory and Practice of Argument.* Clevedon: Multilingual Matters.

Baynham, M., Beck, D., Gordon, K. and San Miguel, C. (1995) Constructing a discourse position: quoting, referring and attribution in academic discourse, in K. Chanock (ed.) *Integrating the Teaching of Writing in the Disciplines.* Melbourne: LaTrobe University.

Bazerman, C. (1981) What written knowledge does: Three examples of academic discourse. *Philosophy of the Social Sciences,* 11: 367–87.

Bazerman, C. (1988) *Shaping Written Knowledge: The Genre and Activity of the Experimental Article in Science.* Madison: University of Wisconsin Press.

Beecher, T. (1989) *Academic Tribes and Territories: Intellectual Enquiry and the Cultures of Disciplines.* Buckingham: Open University Press/SRHE.

Berkenkotter, C. and Huckin, T. (1995) *Genre Knowledge in Disciplinary Communication.* New York: Erlbaum.

Bernstein, B. (1990) *The Structuring of Pedagogic Discourse.* London: Routledge.

Bernstein, B. (1996) *Pedagogy, Symbolic Control and Identity: Theory, Research, Critique.* London: Taylor & Francis.

Biber, D. (1988) *Variation across Speech and Writing.* Cambridge: Cambridge University Press.

Bines, H. and Watson, D. (1992) *Developing Professional Education.* Buckingham: Open University Press/SRHE.

Bisset, R. and Tomlinson, P. (1988) Monitoring and auditing of impacts, in P. Wathern (ed.) *Environmental Impact Assessment: Theory and Practice.* London: Routledge.

Boud, D. (1995) *Enhancing Learning through Self Assessment.* London: Kogan Page.

Bourdieu, P. and Passeron, J.C. (1977) *Reproduction in Education, Society and Culture.* London: Sage.

Bourdieu, P., Passeron, J.C. and Saint Martin, M. (1994) *Academic Discourse: Linguistic Misunderstanding and Professorial Power.* Cambridge: Polity Press.

Britton, J. (1970) *Language and Learning.* London: Allen Lane.

Brown, A. and Dowling, P. (1998) *Doing Research/Reading Research: A Mode of Interrogation for Education.* London: Falmer Press.

Capel, S., Leask, M. and Turner, T. (1995) *Learning to Teach in the Secondary School.* London: Routledge.

Carson, T.R. (1995) Reflective practice and a reconceptualization of teacher education, in M.F. Wideen and P.P. Grimmett (eds) *Changing Times in Teacher Education: Restructuring or Reconceptualization?* London: Falmer Press.

Chiserie-Strater, E. (1991) *Academic Literacies: The Public and Private Discourse of University Students.* Portsmouth, NH: Boynton/Cook.

Clark, R. (1992) Principles and practice of C.L.A. in the classroom, in N. Fairclough (ed.) *Critical Language Awareness.* London: Longman.

Clark, R. (1993) Developing practices of resistance: Critical reading for politics students, in D. Graddol (ed.) *Language and Culture,* Proceedings of the BAAL Annual Meeting, September 1992. Clevedon: Multilingual Matters.

Clark, R. and Ivanič, R. (1991) Consciousness-raising about the writing process, in P. Garrett and C. James (eds) *Language Awareness in the Classroom.* London: Longman.

Clark, R. and Ivanič, R. (1997) *The Politics of Writing.* London: Routledge.

Clark, R., Cottey, A., Constantinou, C. and Yeo, O.C. (1990) Rights and obligations in student writing, in R. Clark, N. Fairclough, R. Ivanič, N. Mcleod, J. Thomas and P. Meara (eds) *Language and Power: Selected Proceedings of the BAAL Annual Meeting, September 1989.* London: Centre for Information on Language Teaching and Research.

Clifford, J. and Marcus, G. (eds) (1986) *Writing Culture: The Poetics and Politics of Ethnography.* Berkeley: University of California Press.

Coates, J. (1987) Epistemic modality and spoken discourse. *Transactions of the Philological Society,* 1987, 110–31.

Cohen, A. and Cavalcanti, M. (1990) Feedback on compositions: teacher and student verbal reports, in B. Kroll (ed.) *Second Language Writing: Research Insights for the Classroom.* Cambridge: Cambridge University Press.

Cohen, M. (1993) Listening to students' voices: what university students tell us about how they can learn. Paper presented to Annual Meeting of the American Educational Research Association, Atlanta, GA.

Cooper, M. and Selfe, C. (1990) Computer conferences and learning: Authority, resistance and internally persuasive discourse, *College English,* 52: 847–69.

Dearing, Sir Ron (1997) *Report of the National Committee of Inquiry in Higher Education: Higher Education in the Learning Society.* London: HMSO.

Department of Education (1995) *White Paper on Education and Training.* Cape Town: Government Printers.

Department of the Environment (1989) *Environmental Assessment: A Guide to the Procedures.* London: HMSO.

Edwards, D. and Mercer, N. (1987) *Common Knowledge: The Development of Understanding in the Classroom.* London: Methuen/Routledge.

Elbow, P. (1981) *Writing with Power.* New York and Oxford: Oxford University Press.

Eraut, M. (1994) *Developing Professional Knowledge and Competence.* London: Falmer Press.

Fairclough, N. (1989) *Language and Power.* Harlow: Longman.

Fairclough, N. (ed.) (1992a) *Critical Language Awareness.* London: Longman.

Fairclough, N. (1992b) *Discourse and Social Change.* Cambridge: Polity Press.

Fairclough, N. (1995) *Critical Discourse Analysis: The Critical Study of Language.* Harlow: Longman.

Flower, L. (1994) *The Construction of Negotiated Meaning: A Social Cognitive Theory of Writing.* Carbondale and Edwardsville: Southern Illinois University Press.

Foley, G. (ed.) (1995) *Understanding Adult Education and Training.* Sydney: Allen & Unwin.

Foucault, M. (1972) *The Archaeology of Knowledge* (trans. A. Sheridan Smith). London: Tavistock.

Freedman, A. (1980) During not after: an untraditional approach to the teaching of writing. *English in Education,* 14(1): 2–9.

Freedman, A., Adam, C. and Smart, G. (1994) Wearing suits to class: Simulating genres and simulations as genre. *Written Communication,* 11(2): 193–226.

Freedman, A. and Medway, P. (eds) (1994) *Learning and Teaching Genre.* Portsmouth, NH: Heinemann/Boynton Cook.

Fullan, M. (1991) *The New Meaning of Educational Change.* London: Cassell Educational.

Gardener, S. (1985) *Conversations with Strangers.* London: Adult Literacy and Basic Skills Unit Write First Time.

Gee, J.P. (1990) *Social Linguistics and Literacies: Ideology in Discourses.* London: Falmer Press.

Gee, J.P. (1996) *Social Linguistics and Literacies: Ideology in Discourses,* 2nd edition. London: Taylor & Francis.

Geertz, C. (1975) *The Interpretation of Cultures: Selected Essays.* London: Hutchinson.

Geertz, C. (1976) Toward an ethnography of the disciplines. Mimeo: Princeton Institute for Advanced Study.

Gibbs, G. (1994) *Improving Student Learning: Theory and Practice.* Oxford: Oxford Centre for Staff Development.

Giesler, C. (1994) *Academic Literacy and the Nature of Expertise: Reading, Writing and Knowing in Academic Philosophy.* Hillsdale, NJ: Erlbaum.

Gilbert, G.N. and Mulkay, M. (1984) *Opening Pandora's Box: A Sociological Analysis of Scientists' Discourse.* Cambridge: Cambridge University Press.

Goggin, M.D. (1995) Situating the teaching and learning of argumentation within historical contexts, in P. Costello and S. Mitchell (eds) *Competing and Consensual Voices: The Theory and Practice of Argument.* Clevedon: Multilingual Matters.

Goodman, S. and Graddol, D. (1996) *Redesigning English: New Texts, New Identities.* London: Open University/Routledge.

Gordon, K., Baynham, M., Lee, A. and San Miguel, C. (1996) Academic writing and disciplinary politics: What every student needs to know. Paper presented at Knowledge and Discourse conference, University of Hong Kong, 18–21 June.

Graham, R.J. (1991) *Reading and Writing the Self: Autobiography in Education and the Curriculum.* New York: Teachers College Press.

Gray, G. and Pratt, R. (1989) *Issues in Australian Nursing.* Melbourne: Churchill Livingstone.

Gray, G. and Pratt, R. (eds) (1995) *Scholarship in the Discipline of Nursing.* Melbourne: Churchill Livingstone.

Green, J. and Bloome, D. (1997) Ethnography and ethnographers of and in education: a situated perspective, in J. Flood, S. Brice Heath and D. Lapp (eds) *Handbook of Research on Teaching Literacy through the Communicative and Visual Arts*. New York: Simon & Schuster/Macmillan.

Greenwood, J. (1993) Reflective practice: A critique of the work of Argyris and Schön. *Journal of Advanced Nursing*, 18: 1183–7.

Gumperz, J.J. (1982) *Discourse Strategies*. Cambridge: Cambridge University Press.

Gunnarsson, B.-L., Linell, P. and Nordberg, B. (eds) (1997) *The Construction of Professional Discourse*. Harlow: Longman.

Halliday, M. and Martin, J. (1993) *Writing Science*. London: Falmer Press.

Harré, R. (1983) *Personal Being*. Oxford: Basil Blackwell.

Heath, S.B. (1983) *Ways with Words*. Cambridge: Cambridge University Press.

Hoadley-Maidment, E. and Mercer, N. (1996) English in higher education, in N. Mercer and J. Swann (eds) *Learning English: Development and Diversity*. London: Routledge/Open University.

Hounsell, D. (1988) Towards an anatomy of academic discourse: Meaning and context in the undergraduate essay, in R. Säljö (ed.) *The Written World. Studies in Literate Thought and Action*. Berlin: Springer-Verlag.

Hull, G. (ed.) (1997) *Changing Work, Changing Workers: Critical Perspectives on Language, Literacy, and Skills*. Albany: State University of New York Press.

Hull, G. and Rose, M. (1989) Rethinking remediation: toward a social-cognitive understanding of problematic reading and writing. *Written Communication*, 6(2): 139–54.

Hymes, D. (1994) Towards ethnographies of communication, in J. Maybin (ed.) *Language and Literacy in Social Practice*. Clevedon: Multilingual Matters/Open University.

Ivanič, R. (1996) Linguistics and the logic of non-standard punctuation, in N. Hall and A. Robinson (eds) *Learning About Punctuation*. Clevedon: Multilingual Matters.

Ivanič, R. (1998) *Writing and Identity: The Discoursal Construction of Identity in Academic writing*. Amsterdam: John Benjamins.

Ivanič, R. and Simpson, J. (1992) Who's who in academic writing? in N. Fairclough (ed.) *Critical Language Awareness*. London: Longman.

James, D. (1995) Mature studentship in higher education: Beyond a 'species' approach. *British Journal of Sociology of Education*, 16(4): 451–66.

Jones, C. (1998) The unreliable transcript, contingent technology and informal practice in asynchronous learning networks, in S. Banks, C. Graebner and D. McConnell (eds) *Networked Lifelong Learning: Innovative Approaches to Education and Training through the Internet*. Sheffield: Centre for the Study of Networked Learning/Division of Adult Continuing Education, University of Sheffield.

Jones, C., Street, B. and Turner, M. (in press) *Student Writing in the University: Cultural and Epistemological Issues*. Amsterdam: John Benjamins.

Joseph, K. (1983) Speech on teacher training at Durham University. *Durham and Newcastle Research Review*, 10(50): 38–9.

Kasworm, C. (1990) Transformative contexts in adult higher education. Revision of a paper presented at the Second International Congress for Research on Activity Theory, Lahti, Finland, 21–25 May.

Kaufer, D.S. and Geisler, C. (1989) Novelty in academic writing. *Written Communication*, 6(3): 286–311.

Klein, J.T. (1993) Blurring, cracking and crossing: Permeation and the fracturing of discipline, in E. Messer-Davidow, D.R. Shumway and D.J. Sylvan (eds) *Knowledges: Historical and Critical Studies in Disciplinarity*. Charlottesville: University Press of Virginia.

Knox, M. (now Lea, M.) (1992) 'I thought I could write until I came here'. Competing discourses: an examination of student writing in the context of academic discourse as ideology. Unpublished MA dissertation, Department of Cognitive Sciences, University of Sussex.

Kolb, D. (1984) *Experiential Learning as a Source of Learning and Development.* Englewood Cliffs, NJ: Prentice Hall.

Lankshear, C. (1997) *Changing Literacies.* Buckingham: Open University Press.

Latour, B. (1987) *Science in Action: How to Follow Scientists and Engineers Through Society.* Cambridge, MA: Harvard University Press.

Latour, B. (1993) *We Have Never Been Modern.* London: Harvester Wheatsheaf.

Lea, M. (1994) I thought I could write till I came here: student writing in higher education, in G. Gibbs (ed.) *Improving Student Learning: Theory and Practice.* Oxford: Oxford Centre for Staff Development.

Lea, M. (1998) Academic literacies and learning in higher education: constructing knowledge through texts and experience. *Studies in the Education of Adults,* 30(2): 156–71.

Lea, M.R. and Street, B.V. (1997a) Models of student writing in higher education. Paper presented to Higher Education Funding Council for England Social Anthropology Teaching and Learning Network workshop, University of Sussex, June.

Lea, M.R. and Street, B.V. (1997b) *Perspectives on Academic Literacies: An Institutional Approach.* Swindon: Economic and Social Research Council.

Lea, M.R. and Street, B.V. (1998) Student writing in higher education: An academic literacies approach. *Studies in Higher Education,* 23(2): 157–72.

Lee, A. (1997) Working together? Academic literacies, co-production and professional partnerships. *Literacy and Numeracy Studies,* 7(2): 65–82.

Lee, A., Baynham, M., Beck, D., Gordon, K. and San Miguel, C. (1995) Researching discipline specific academic literacy practices: Some methodological issues, in A.C. Lynn Zelmer (ed.) *Higher Education: Blending Tradition and Technology. Research and Development in Higher Education,* 18: 464–82.

Leki, I. (1990) Coaching from the margins: issues in written response, in B. Kroll (ed.) *Second Language Writing: Research Insights for the Classroom.* Cambridge: Cambridge University Press.

Levine, J. (1990) *Bilingual Learners and the Mainstream Curriculum.* London: Falmer Press.

Lindstrom, L. (1993) Context contests: debatable truth statements on Tanna (Vanuatu), in A. Duranti and C. Goodwin (eds) *Rethinking Context: Language as an Interactive Phenomenon.* Cambridge: Cambridge University Press.

Marton, F., Housell, D. and Entwistle, N. (eds) (1997) *The Experience of Learning.* Edinburgh: Scottish Academic Press.

Mason, R. (ed.) (1993) *Computer Conferencing: The Last Word . . . .* Victoria, BC: Beach Holme.

Mason, R. and Kaye, A. (1989) *Mindweave: Communication, Computers and Distance Education.* Oxford: Pergamon Press.

McMillan, J. (1997) Boundaries, border crossings and context(s): learning as 'negotiating meaning'. Paper presented at the 27th Annual Standing Conference on University Teaching and Research in the Education of Adults (SCUTREA), University of London, 1–3 July.

McMillan, J. (1998) Adult learners, access and higher education: learning as meaning-making and negotiation in context. Unpublished M. Phil. dissertation, University of the Western Cape.

Mercer, N. (1995) *The Guided Construction of Knowledge: Talk amongst Teachers and Learners.* Clevedon: Multilingual Matters.

Messer-Davidow, E., Shumway, D.R. and Sylvan, D.J. (eds) (1993) *Knowledges: Historical and Critical Studies in Disciplinarity.* Charlottesville: University Press of Virginia.

Mitchell, C. (1984) Case studies, in R. Ellen (ed.) *Ethnographic Research: A Guide to General Conduct.* London: Academic Press.

Mitchell, J.M. (1998) Report on a social anthropology staff development workshop. Mimeo: University of Sussex.

Mitchell, S. (1995) Conflict and conformity: the place of argument in learning a discourse, in P.J. Costello and S. Mitchell (eds) *Competing and Consensual Voices: The Theory and Practice of Argument.* Clevedon: Multilingual Matters.

Mitchell, S. (1996a) *Improving the Quality of Argument in Higher Education: Interim Report.* London: Middlesex University, School of Education.

Mitchell, S. (1996b) Institutions, individuals and talk: the construction of identity in fine art. *Journal of Art and Design Education,* 15(2): 143–54.

Morgan, A. (1993) *Improving Your Students' Learning: Reflections on the Experience of Study.* London: Kogan Page.

Myers, G. (1990) *Writing Biology.* Madison: University of Wisconsin Press.

Northedge, A. (1992) *Teaching Access: A Tutor's Handbook for Living in a Changing Society* (provisional edition). Milton Keynes: Open University.

O'Connell, D. (1994) *Implementing Computer Supported Cooperative Learning.* London: Kogan Page.

Olson, D.R. (1977) From utterance to text: the bias of language in speech and writing, *Harvard Educational Review,* 47(3): 257–81.

Open University (1997) *Professional Development in Education 1997–98.* Milton Keynes: Open University.

Pardoe, S. (1993) *Learning to Write in a New Educational Setting: A Focus on the Writer's Purpose,* Working Paper no. 58. Lancaster: Centre for Language in Social Life, Department of Linguistics and MEL, Lancaster University.

Pardoe, S. (1994) Writing in another culture: The value of students' KAL in writing pedagogy, in D. Graddol and J. Swann (eds) *Evaluating Language.* Clevedon: British Association for Applied Linguistics/Multilingual Matters.

Pardoe, S. (1997) Writing professional science: genre, recontextualization and empiricism in the learning of professional and scientific writing within an MSc course in Environmental Impact Assessment. Ph.D. thesis, Lancaster University.

Pardoe, S. (1999) Respect and the pursuit of 'symmetry' in researching literacy and student writing, in D. Barton, M. Hamilton and R. Ivanič (eds) *Situated Literacies.* London: Routledge.

Radecki, P.M. and Swales, J.M. (1988) ESL student reaction to written comments on their written work, *System,* 16(3): 355–65.

Reiff, J. and Kirscht, J. (1992) Inquiry as human process: interviews with researchers across the disciplines, *Journal of Advanced Composition,* 12: 359–72.

Rimmershaw, R. (1993) Students' changing conceptions of academic writing, in G. Eigler and T. Jechle (eds) *Text Production: Current Trends in European Research.* Freiburg: Hochschulverlag.

Rose, M. (ed.) (1985) *When a Writer Can't Write: Studies in Writer's Block and Other Composing-Process Problems.* New York: Guilford Press.

Rose, M. (ed.) (1989) *Lives on the Boundary: A Moving Account of the Struggles and Achievements of American's Educational Underclass.* New York: Free Press.

Ross, M., Radnor, R., Mitchell, S. and Bierton, C. (1993) *Assessing Achievement in the Arts.* Buckingham: Open University Press.

Ruscio, K.P. (1987) Many sectors, many professions, in B.R. Clark (ed.) *The Academic Profession: National, Disciplinary and Institutional Settings*. Berkeley: University of California Press.

Schön, D. (1983) *The Reflective Practitioner: How Professionals Think in Action*. New York: Basic Books.

Schön, D. (1987) *Educating the Reflective Practitioner: Toward a New Design for Teaching and Learning in the Professions*. San Francisco: Jossey-Bass.

Scollon, R. (1995) Plagiarism and ideology: identity in intercultural discourse. *Language in Society*, 24: 1–28.

Shaunessy, M.P. (1977) *Errors and Expectations: A Guide for the Basic Teacher of Writing*. New York: Oxford University Press.

Stierer, B. (1997) Mastering education: a preliminary analysis of academic literacy practices within master-level courses in education. Milton Keynes: Centre for Language and Communications, School of Education, Open University.

Street, B. (1984) *Literacy in Theory and Practice*. Cambridge: Cambridge University Press.

Street, B. (ed.) (1993) *Cross-cultural Approaches to Literacy*. Cambridge: Cambridge University Press.

Street, B. (1995) Academic literacies, in D. Baker, C. Fox and J. Clay (eds) *Challenging Ways of Knowing in Maths, Science and English*. Lewes: Falmer Press.

Swales, J. (1990) *Genre Analysis: English in Academic and Research Settings*. Cambridge: Cambridge University Press.

Taylor, G., Ballard, B., Beasley, V. *et al.* (1988) *Literacy By Degrees*. Milton Keynes and Philadelphia: Society for Research in Higher Education/Open University Press.

Thesen, L. (1994) Voices in discourse: re-thinking shared meaning in academic writing. Unpublished MPhil dissertation, University of Cape Town.

Toulmin, S. (1958) *The Uses of Argument*. Cambridge: Cambridge University Press.

Toulmin, S., Rieke, R. and Janik, A. (1984) *An Introduction to Reasoning* (2nd Edn). New York: Macmillan.

Turner, K. (1993) You do not seem to have understood the question. Unpublished MA dissertation, Department of Educational Research, Lancaster University.

Usher, R. (1993) Experiential learning or learning from experience: does it make a difference?, in D. Boud, R. Cohen and D. Walker (eds) *Using Experience for Learning*. Buckingham: Open University Press.

Webb, C. (1992) The use of the first person in academic writing: objectivity, language and gatekeeping. *Journal of Advanced Nursing*, 17: 747–52.

Weil, S. (1986) Non-traditional learners within traditional higher education: discovery and disappointment, in D. Wildermeersch and T. Jansen (eds) *Adult Education, Experiential Learning and Social Change: The Postmodern Challenge*. Driebergen, South Africa: VTA.

Wilkin, M. (1996) *Initial Teacher Training: The Dialogue of Ideology and Culture*. London: Falmer Press.

Yates, S. (1996) Oral and written aspects of computer conferencing, in S. Herring (ed.) *Computer-Mediated Communication: Linguistic, Social and Cross-Cultural Perspectives*. Amsterdam: John Benjamins.

Zak, F. (1990) Exclusively positive responses to student writing. *Journal of Basic Writing*, 9(2): 40–53.

Zamel, V. (1985) Responding to student writing. *TESOL Quarterly*, 19(1): 79–101.

Ziv, N.D. (1984) The effects of teacher comments on the writing of four college freshmen, in R. Beach and L. Bridwell (eds) *New Directions in Composition Research*. New York: Guilford Press.

Index

academic
  conventions, 28, 62, 90
  disciplines, 1, 3, 4, 6, 7, 18, 22–3, 25,
    38, 45, 97, 165, 166, 167, 181,
    192, 194
  discourses, 34, 74, 117, 118, 166,
    167, 169, 174–6, 180, 193
  knowledge, 37, 40, 43, 69, 77–80,
    82, 83, 153, 154, 177
  literacies, 7, 18, 34, 47, 98, 165–78,
    179–89
  practices, 35, 64, 103, 152, 194
  socialization, 7, 34, 173
access, 151–2, 161
  courses, 41
  epistemological, 149
  institutional, 35, 149, 150
adult, 149, 150, 169, 175
  education, 18, 20, 21, 149–64, 169
agency, 112–24, 160, 190
argument, 29, 39, 43–4, 51–4, 59, 62,
    86, 94, 96, 99–102, 114, 116, 120,
    127, 144, 159, 162–3, 180, 188,
    194
assessment, 2–4, 8, 13, 39, 44, 45, 49,
    61, 64, 69, 82–4, 98, 105, 110,
    114, 116, 131, 133, 150–2, 154,
    160–1, 176, 180
assignment, 23–4, 37–9, 42–3, 45, 56,
    64, 70–1, 76, 81–3, 105, 114–17,
    119, 130, 151, 155, 157, 160, 172,
    176, 249ff
authority, 25, 27, 37, 42–5, 62, 73, 75,
    77, 83, 84, 94, 105, 120, 158, 181

Ball, 17, 20, 30, 31
Bartholomae, 17, 20, 30, 31
Bazerman, 19, 40, 99, 115, 117, 120,
    123
Berkenkotter, 40, 76
Bernstein, 21, 116, 122
Bines, 165, 174, 178
Bourdieu, 193, 195

case study, 21, 29, 30, 36, 150, 155,
    174, 179
Clark, 50, 63, 65, 153
Coates, 78–80
comments, 47–65, 134, 137
  examiner, 114
  marker, 26
  tutor, 43–4, 140, 141
competence, 2, 79, 45, 47, 115, 117,
    119, 121, 123, 150, 165, 169, 166,
    172, 174, 177, 180
  communicative, 64
  linguistic, 37
  professional, 180
competencies, 116, 151
Cooper, 75, 76
course switching, 37, 41, 45

Dearing Committee, 2, 46
deficit, 3, 34–5
  model, 32
dialogue, 48, 50, 55, 57, 61, 93, 100,
    169, 170–1, 175
diaries, 120, 171
  reflective, 97–110, 170, 175–6

Dice, 17, 20, 30, 31
disciplinary politics, 18ff
discourse, 17, 30–1, 34, 35, 80, 87, 90,
    103, 112, 115, 117, 120–1, 124,
    152–3, 157, 159, 161, 168–9, 170,
    174, 176, 180, 188
  academic, 9, 34, 74, 117, 118, 116,
    167, 169, 174–6, 186, 193
  analysis, 33, 35, 190
  communities, 7, 18, 74, 161, 166,
    193
  institutional, 2
  internally persuasive, 75–6
  orders of, 180, 193
  professional, 9, 178, 180, 193
distance learning, 69, 71, 165, 168,
    171, 173–7, 182

epistemology, 7, 33, 35, 37, 39, 80, 85,
    191
epistemological, 33, 38, 43, 89, 94, 98,
    103, 110, 149, 193
Eraut, 165, 170, 178, 181
essay, 40, 63, 86–8, 91–6, 99–102, 105,
    107, 114, 126, 127, 167, 169, 174,
    176, 187
  argumentative, 48
  expository, 25
  genre, 82
  text, 39
  traditional, 4, 42, 97
ethnographic, 36, 64, 100, 155
ethnography of communication, 73

Fairclough, 38, 151, 190, 194
Feedback, 3, 36, 38, 40–4, 48, 61,
    62–4, 70, 98, 170, 175, 177, 179,
    191–2
Flower, 149, 153
Foucault, 168
Freedman, 19, 50

Gee, 2, 151, 87, 90, 152
Geisler, 89, 90
genre, 34, 35, 40, 43–5, 69, 74–6, 83,
    85, 100, 102, 106, 130, 144, 167,
    176, 183, 192, 194
  academic, 76–7, 99, 176
  analysis, 19
  new, 82

Harrè, 89, 90
Huckin, 40, 76
Hymes, 73, 74

identity, 11–13, 33, 35, 45, 47, 72, 77,
    87, 89, 90, 95, 96, 97, 102, 104,
    109, 112–24, 154, 158, 161, 181
ideology, 60, 63, 193
ideological, 35, 43, 63
interdisciplinary, 3, 6, 38, 97, 98,
    103–4, 107, 108
Ivanič, 31, 35, 50, 63, 64, 102, 153, 181

Kasworm, 155–6, 159
Kaufer, 89, 90
Klein, 17, 30
knowledge, 3–4, 7, 17–18, 32, 37–8,
    45, 51, 61, 69, 72, 77, 82, 89, 95,
    99, 109, 114, 118–19, 125, 128,
    132, 137, 153, 168, 181, 193
  academic, 38, 39, 40, 43, 79, 153
  course based, 41
  disciplinary, 19, 39, 43, 99, 141
  personal, 42, 102
  practical, 21, 25
  propositional, 85

Lankshear, 2
Lea, 35, 153, 155, 161
learning journals, 137–57
learning support, 2, 36–7, 45
lifelong learning, 2, 8

meaning making, 61, 99, 114, 119,
    121, 153, 154, 159, 160
Mercer, 144, 168
Mitchell, 89, 174–5
modality, 43, 77–82, 190
modular
  programme, 3, 38, 44
modularity, 7, 45
multimodal texts, 71–2, 85

narrative, 41, 100, 108, 120, 174
new technology, 4, 69–85

personal, 79, 120, 121, 165–78, 189
  experience, 102, 104, 107, 108
  identity, 35, 87, 89, 96
  knowledge, 42

pronoun, 51, 58, 109, 186–7
'the', 7, 97–111
viewpoint, 42, 56, 64
power, 34–5, 42–3, 45, 60, 61, 62, 73,
75–6, 84, 102, 132
relations, 7, 33
practice based
approach, 19
disciplines, 20
models, 165
practices, 3, 33, 47, 63, 93, 128, 144,
161
academic literacy, 4, 32, 70, 84, 152,
153, 161, 194
assessment, 84
communicative, 35
disciplinary, 18, 127
discursive, 19, 193
institutional, 33–5, 45
linguistic, 34–5
professional, 129–32, 143–4
reading, 33
social, 20, 34
professional, 32, 118, 126, 156,
165–78, 179–95, 125–45
courses, 8–11
development, 179, 180
training, 181
project, 116, 123, 166, 167, 172–4,
176, 179, 183

reflective
journal, 18, 19, 97–110
learners, 77
practice, 112

practitioner, 17, 113, 124, 150, 151,
160, 165–78, 181
reflexivity, 84, 100–5, 107
report writing, 39–40, 42, 86, 130, 132,
135, 140, 165, 167, 169, 175–6,
183, 187
Rimmershaw, 57, 65

Schön, 150, 169, 175, 181
self, 102, 103, 105, 108–9, 118–20,
123, 149
skills based
approach, 19, 46
model, 32
social practice, 2–3, 6, 20, 33–5, 109,
181
Stierer, 35
Street, 2, 33, 35
study skills, 2, 19, 34–5, 40, 45, 85, 128
subjectivity, 106, 113–15, 124, 152
Swales, 19, 126, 166

text based
approach, 19
theory, 112, 114, 121
and practice, 27, 31, 113ff, 170ff
transferable skills, 34, 39, 41, 121, 123

voice, 25, 31, 87, 101, 106, 108–10,
136, 144, 152, 161, 186, 190
academic, 28
disciplinary, 30–1
experiential, 28, 31

Watson, 165, 174, 178

The Society for Research into Higher Education

The Society for Research into Higher Education (SRHE) exists to stimulate and coordinate research into all aspects of higher education. It aims to improve the quality of higher education through the encouragement of debate and publication on issues of policy, on the organization and management of higher education institutions, and on the curriculum, teaching and learning methods.

The Society is entirely independent and receives no subsidies, although individual events often receive sponsorship from business or industry. The society is financed through corporate and individual subscriptions and has members from many parts of the world.

Under the imprint *SRHE & Open University Press*, the Society is a specialist publisher of research, having over 80 titles in print. In addition to *SRHE News*, the society's newsletter, the society publishes three journals: *Studies in Higher Education* (three issues a year), *Higher Education Quarterly* and *Research into Higher Education Abstracts* (three issues a year).

The society runs frequent conferences, consultations, seminars and other events. The annual conference in December is organized at and with a higher education institution. There are a growing number of networks which focus on particular areas of interest, including:

Access	Learning Environment
Assessment	Legal Education
Consultants	Managing Innovation
Curriculum Development	New Technology for Learning
Eastern European	Postgraduate Issues
Educational Development Research	Quantitative Studies
FE/HE	Student Development
Funding	Vocational Qualifications
Graduate Employment	

Benefits to members

Individual

- The opportunity to participate in the Society's networks

- Reduced rates for the annual conferences
- Free copies of *Research into Higher Education Abstracts*
- Reduced rates for *Studies in Higher Education*
- Reduced rates for *Higher Education Quarterly*
- Free copy of *Register of Members' Research Interests* – includes valuable reference material on research being pursued by the Society's members
- Free copy of occasional in-house publications, e.g. *The Thirtieth Anniversary Seminars Presented by the Vice-Presidents*
- Free copies of *SRHE News* which informs members of the Society's activities and provides a calendar of events, with additional material provided in regular mailings
- A 35 per cent discount on all SRHE/Open University Press books
- Access to HESA statistics for student members
- The opportunity for you to apply for the annual research grants
- Inclusion of your research in the *Register of Members' Research Interests*

Corporate

- Reduced rates for the annual conferences
- The opportunity for members of the Institution to attend SRHE's network events at reduced rates
- Free copies of *Research into Higher Education Abstracts*
- Free copies of *Studies in Higher Education*
- Free copies of *Register of Members' Research Interests* – includes valuable reference material on research being pursued by the Society's members
- Free copy of occasional in-house publications
- Free copies of *SRHE News*
- A 35 per cent discount on all SRHE/Open University Press books
- Access to HESA statistics for research for students of the Institution
- The opportunity for members of the Institution to submit applications for the Society's research grants
- The opportunity to work with the Society and co-host conferences
- The opportunity to include in the *Register of Members' Research Interests* your Institution's research into aspects of higher education

Membership details: SRHE, 3 Devonshire Street, London
W1N 2BA, UK. Tel: 0171 637 2766. Fax: 0171 637 2781.
email: srhe@mailbox.ulcc.ac.uk
world wide web: http://www.srhe.ac.uk./srhe/
Catalogue: SRHE & Open University Press, Celtic Court,
22 Ballmoor, Buckingham MK18 1XW. Tel: 01280 823388.
Fax: 01280 823233. email: enquiries@openup.co.uk

WRITING AT UNIVERSITY
A GUIDE FOR STUDENTS

Phyllis Creme and Mary R. Lea

- As a student, what do you need to do to tackle writing assignments at university?
- How can you write more confidently and effectively?
- How can you address the variety of written assignments that you encounter in your studies?

Writing at University will make you more aware of the complexity of the writing process. It provides useful strategies and approaches that will allow you to gain more control over your own academic writing. You are encouraged to build upon your existing abilities as a writer and to develop your writing in academic settings through applying a series of practical tasks to your own work. The complete process of writing assignments is considered, including attention to disciplinary diversity, the relationship between reading and writing, the use of the personal, and textual cohesion.

This book is an essential tool to help you develop an awareness and understanding of what it means to be a successful student writer in higher education today.

It will also be invaluable to academic staff who want to support students in their writing.

Contents

You and university writing – First thoughts on writing assignments – Writing for different courses – Beginning with the title – Reading as part of writing – Organizing and shaping your writing – Writing your knowledge in an academic way – Putting it together – Completing the assignment and preparing for next time – References – Index.

160pp   0 335 19642 X (Paperback)   0 335 19643 8 (Hardback)

TEACHING FOR QUALITY LEARNING AT UNIVERSITY

John Biggs

... full of downright good advice for every academic who wants to do something practical to improve his or her students' learning ... there are very few writers on the subject of university teaching who can engage a reader so personally, express things so clearly, relate research findings so eloquently to personal experience.

Paul Ramsden

John Biggs tackles how academics can improve their teaching in today's circumstances of large classes and diverse student populations. His approach is practical but not prescriptive. Teachers need to make decisions on teaching and assessment methods to suit their own circumstances. In order to do that they need a conceptual framework to inform their decision-making. Such a framework is clearly described and exemplified by this book. University teachers can readily adapt the ideas here to their own subjects and teaching conditions. Particular foci in *Teaching for Quality Learning at University* include:

- making the large lecture a more exciting and productive learning experience;
- using assessment methods that reveal the complexity and relevance of student learning and that are manageable in large classes;
- teaching international students;
- helping teachers to reflect on and improve their own practice.

This is an accessible, jargon-free guide for all university teachers interested in enhancing their teaching and their students' learning.

Contents

Changing university teaching – Constructing learning by aligning teaching: constructive alignment – Formulating and clarifying curriculum objectives – Setting the stage for effective teaching – Good teaching: principles and practice – Enriching large-class teaching – Teaching international students – Assessing for learning quality: I. Principles – Assessing for learning quality: II. Practice – Some examples of aligned teaching – On implementation – References – Index – The Society for Research into Higher Education.

272pp   0 335 20171 7 (Paperback)   0 335 20172 5 (Hardback)

ON BECOMING AN INNOVATIVE UNIVERSITY TEACHER
REFLECTION IN ACTION

John Cowan

This is one of the most interesting texts I have read for many years . . . It is authoritative and clearly written. It provides a rich set of examples of teaching, and a reflective discourse.

Professor George Brown

. . . succeeds in inspiring the reader by making the process of reflective learning interesting and thought provoking . . . has a narrative drive which makes it a book too good to put down.

Dr Mary Thorpe

What comes through very strongly and is an admirable feature is so much of the author's own personal experience, what it felt like to take risks and how his own practice developed as a result of taking risks, exploring uncharted territory . . . The book has the potential to become the reflective practitioner's 'bible'.

Dr Lorraine Stefani

This unusual, accessible and significant book begins each chapter by posing a question with which college and university teachers can be expected to identify; and then goes on to answer the question by presenting a series of examples; finally, each chapter closes with 'second thoughts', presenting a viewpoint somewhat distinct from that taken by John Cowan. This book will assist university teachers to plan and run innovative activities to enable their students to engage in effective reflective learning; it will help them adapt other teachers' work for use with their own students; and will give them a rationale for the place of reflective teaching and learning in higher education.

Contents

Introduction – What is meant in education by 'reflecting' – What does reflection have to offer in education? – Is there a methodology you can and should follow? – What can you do to encourage students to reflect? – What is involved for students in analytical reflection? – What is involved in evaluative reflection? – How can you adapt ideas from my teaching, for yours? – How should you get started? – How can such innovations be evaluated? – Where should you read about other work in this field? – A postscript: final reflections – References – Index – The Society for Research into Higher Education.

192pp   0 335 19993 3 (Paperback)   0 335 19994 1 (Hardback)